Boy George was brought up as one of six children of Irish parents in south-east London. In the 1980s, he rose to international fame as the lead singer, songwriter and driving force behind Culture Club, selling over 55 million records worldwide. After the collapse of the band, he became one of the leading figures in the dance music revolution, DJing around the world and setting up the independent record label, More Protein. He was also the co-writer and occasional star of the hit West End, Broadway and touring show *Taboo*, which tells the story of the eighties club scene and garnered a clutch of Olivier and Tony awards.

Boy George continues to make music as a solo artist and is a photographer of note. He is also the design vision behind the fashion label B-RUDE. Boy George currently lives in New York City.

Paul Gorman is a London-based writer. His books include: *The Look: Adventures In Pop & Rock Fashion;* the definitive history of the music press *In Their Own Write;* Goldie's autobiography *Nine Lives;* the story of Dexy's Midnight Runners: *Let's make This Precious* and Dinah O'Dowd's *Cry Salty Tears.*

straight

Boy George

with Paul Gorman

arrow books

Published in the United Kingdom by Arrow Books in 2007

16

First published in the United Kingdom in 2005 by Century

Arrow Books
The Random House Group Limited
20 Vauxhall Bridge Road, London, SW1V 2SA

Addresses for companies within The Random House Group Limited
can be found at www.randomhouse.co.uk/offices.htm

The Random House Group Limited Reg. No. 954009

A CIP catalogue record for this book
is available from the British Library

ISBN 9780099464938

Penguin Random House is committed to a sustainable future for
our business, our readers and our planet. This book is made from
Forest Stewardship Council® certified paper.

Printed and bound in Great Britain by Clays Ltd, Elcograf S.p.A.

This book is dedicated to my dad Jerry O'Dowd,
the most formidable force in my life.

Contents

Acknowledgements

I'd like to thank (or spank) some of the following creatures who make my life more interesting, complicated and colourful.

Most importantly my mum Dinah and my sister Siobhan, brothers Richard, Kevin, Gerald, David and all their loved ones. My friend and co-writer Paul Gorman, who has a great sense of humour and a Jamaican-cum-Spanish sense of panic; Simon Trewin, the publishers, especially Hannah Black for putting up with delays and changes; my manager Tony Gordon; Paul Farrell & Annie (get your gun); my demented friends Philip Sallon, Amanda Ghost & Gregor; Paul Starr, Bonnie Lippel, Dave, Laura, Tracey & Nick; Dragana & Simon; Tony Denton & Bennie; Andria Law & Johnston; Eileen Schembri & Ritchie; Dean, Mike Nicholls & Graham; Christine Bateman, Johnny Slut, Eva, Vassos & Vivienne; John Themis, Kevan & Matt Frost; Kinky Roland, Euan Morton, Declan & Luke (Linda) Evans, Gailey Sue and the entire *Taboo* cast; Allessandro and the US *Taboo* cast and crew, Lori Seid & Jen Lebeau and you Rosie, (thanks for showing me Broadway) and Kelly too; Dusty O, Melanie Waxman, Aimee, Drew, Mackie, Richie, Traver, Amanda LePore, Alex, Ryan, Antony, Tasty Tim, Bel & Dave at More Protein; Jeni Innocent, Paul and my beautiful god-daughter Hollie, little Michael, Kelly O'Dowd & Gwen; Molly, Milly, Aaron, Zak, Joseph, Jan, Lisa, Aunty Theresa, Uncle Barry and family; Phyllis Valentine and family; my late Uncle Frank and all his loved ones and all the Irish posse. All the boys in my life who keep the quest for intimacy a never-ending complication and last but never least, Jon, Roy, Mikey and all their clans.

Paul Gorman would like to thank for assistance, patience, love and inspiration in the creation of this book: Antony, Stanley Banks, Consuela Christine Bateman, Hannah Black, Taylor

Brittenham, Dragana and Simon Brown, Michael Cavadias, Lindsay Davies, Mackie Dugan, Drew Elliot, Paul Farrell, Kevan Frost, Claire Gill, Tony Gordon, Steve Hulme, El Rey Robert Lopez, Gary Lux, Judge Jules, Paul Masterson, Petè McGlinchey, Baroness von Fistenberg, Miss Guy, none-more-punk Mike Nicholls, Sharon O'Neill, Jo Pestell, Aimee Phillips, Mark Powell, Richie Rich, Kevin Rowland, Chris Sullivan, Eileen Schembri, Richie Stevens, John Themis, Simon Trewin, Vicky, Leo Whiteley.

Never last nor least: the butler Buckley aka Gina – generosity, love and laughter without boundaries.

The Straight CD

These songs are very personal, romantic, cynical, caustic even, and reflective of stories told in *Straight*. They are a gift from me to you and any reference to living entities is just as well.

1. 'Kookie Jar', written by George O'Dowd/Kevan Frost (Cometmarket Ltd/Notting Hill Music (UK) Ltd/Screen Music Services).

2. 'Panic', written by George O'Dowd/Kevan Frost (Cometmarket Ltd/Notting Hill Music (UK) Ltd/Screen Music Services).

3. 'Only Child', written by George O'Dowd/Kevan Frost (Cometmarket Ltd/Notting Hill Music (UK) Ltd/Screen Music Services).

4. 'Julian', written by George O'Dowd/Kevan Frost (Cometmarket Ltd/Notting Hill Music (UK) Ltd/Screen Music Services).

5. 'Song For A Boy', written by George O'Dowd/Richie Stevens (Cometmarket Ltd/Notting Hill Music (UK) Ltd/Hornall Brothers).

Permissions

sion of EMI/Virgin Music Ltd; 'Elektro Hetero' words and music George O'Dowd/Roland Faber reproduced by permission of Cometmarket Ltd/Notting Hill Music (UK) Ltd/Copyright Control; 'Genocide Peroxide' words and music by George O'Dowd/John Themis © 1995 reproduced by permission of EMI Virgin Music Ltd/Perfect Songs; 'Here Come The Girls' words and music by George O'Dowd/Becca Grover/Cheska Grover/Roland Faber reproduced by permission of Cometmarket Ltd/Notting Hill Music (UK) Ltd/Copyright Control; 'Ich Bin Kunst' words and music by George O'Dowd/Kevan Frost, reproduced by permission of Cometmarket Ltd/Notting Hill Music (UK) Ltd/Music Copyright Solutions; 'Il Adore' words and music by George O'Dowd/John Themis © 1995 reproduced by permission of EMI Virgin Music Ltd/Perfect Songs; 'Julian' words and music by George O'Dowd/Kevan Frost reproduced by permission of Cometmarket Ltd/Notting Hill Music (UK) Ltd/Music Copyright Solutions; 'Ode To Attention Seekers' words and music by George O'Dowd/John Themis, reproduced by permission of Cometmarket Ltd/Notting Hill Music (UK) Ltd/Chrysalis; 'Panic' words and music by George O'Dowd/Kevan Frost reproduced by permission of Cometmarket Ltd/Notting Hill Music (UK) Ltd/Music Copyright Solutions; 'Poverty' words and music by George O'Dowd/Paul Masterson/Julius O'Riordan, reproduced by permission of Cometmarket Ltd/Notting Hill Music (UK) Ltd/Chrysalis/Peermusic; 'Sanitised' words and music by George O'Dowd/Roland Faber, reproduced by permission of Cometmarket Ltd/Notting Hill Music (UK) Ltd/Copyright Control; 'Satan's Butterfly Ball' words and music by George O'Dowd/John Themis © 1995 reproduced by permission of EMI Virgin Music Ltd/Perfect Songs; 'Stranger In This World' words and music by George O'Dowd/John Themis/Richie Stevens reproduced by permission of Cometmarket Ltd/Notting Hill Music (UK) Ltd/Chrysalis/Hornall Bros; 'The Original Sin' © 1980 words and music by Kirk Brandon used by permission of Metropolis Music BV/Warner/Chappell Music Ltd; 'These Are The Things That Dreams Are Made Of' words and music by Philip Oakey/Philip Adrian Wright © 1981 reproduced by permis-

Boy George

By Paul Gorman

George isn't good in the mornings.

He strides out of his room, straight back, arms paddling by his side, in black. He catches your eye. You say: 'Morning.' He might grunt. He might say, mock-querulously, shortly and sharply: 'Hello,' pursing his lips as he does.

He may describe the dream from which he has just awoken, there and then. More likely he will march past, and look you up and down as he does, raising an eyebrow. 'Ridiculous,' he will utter, apropos of nothing.

If you ask: 'How are you?' George may say: 'Utterly rancid.' Or he may keep quiet, patrolling the loft, stopping at the kitchen sink, where he washes off the residue of last night's maquillage (with Fairy Liquid no less), then his own bathroom and dressing room and finally the computer.

Your question: 'Like another coffee?' will be answered with a tart 'Ta.' Then don't speak to him for a while. Twenty minutes, maybe even more. Read the *Times* or the *Voice*, but don't bother pointing out what Michael Mustgo has to say. Tell him later because George is pecking at his laptop in his office space, blue eyes widening awake at the news from home and abroad.

He may sometimes emit a sharp bark: 'Ha!', 'Fuck!', or

'Ohforgodsake!' Rarely will you be informed right then what these exclamations relate to.

Usually this is saved for later, as you sit with tea and make breakfast.

He fills you in and interrupts himself, asking rhetorically, 'Is SHE up yet?' Then he hammers on Christine's bedroom door: 'CHRISTINE?! Get the fuck up!'

Glancing at the glitter-sprinkled clock he will lie, often by as much as an hour. 'It's fucking one o'clock! GET UP!!'

George is industrious.

Never has a day gone by in his company when a project hasn't been attended to: a new silkscreen, a line of t-shirt designs, a lyric written to a tune sent across by Amanda or Richie, a vocal recorded, a backing track mixed, a chapter of the book tweaked, a photography session booked, a DJ set compiled . . .

George is a good cook - apart from rice. He hasn't the patience, you see.

But he knows his vegetables, and he moves quickly, just as he eats, snipping and snapping and cutting and chopping. While you eat you talk about the food, where it comes from and what it does for you. Then you have more tea and light fags and talk about this gossip or that record or Nine Ki or new movies or Asperger's Syndrome or boys (or a boy in particular) or a dream or Bowie or tonight's party or fashion or last night's meal or growing up in a family of eight lunatics in the 60s and 70s or this weekend's adventure or last weekend's disaster.

George is good at shopping.

Whether among the tradesmen and builders and art students at Industrial Plastics on Canal, or darting between the preppy couples and Soho bohos at Dean & DeLuca and The Gourmet Garden, there's George, ploughing ahead, gathering up paint mixers and brushes or the crunchiest kale, the tastiest tofu.

He lopes the sidewalks in the same fashion, ahead of everyone, his stroll discernible in the Lower East Side crowds even in shades, hoodie and trackies. If you keep up with him not much is said; a twitch at a shirtless road-digger, a wince at an overstuffed gargoyle.

George gets fractious around early evening.

Something to do with his energy levels, I think. Maybe he's heard enough of Christine, or had enough of my company, but he sometimes becomes snippy and snappy and can be downright rude.

Then he might have a lie down or, more likely, return to his laptop and stab at the keys, on a variety of missions; Photoshopping the rude pictures he takes of barely dressed boys, spurting out email responses to Kinky and Kevan and Paul and Mike, draining some of those creative juices.

George says he hates phones, though he is often on them.

His UK mobile will ring and ring until you shout: 'Shall I get it?'

'Yeah - find out who it is.'

George is good fun.

He usually refuses a shandy first off, implying that I drink too much beer and stating openly: 'You're not giving that old drunk any more are you? She's pissed already.' Even though she is still nursing her first glass, Christine giggles and continues her sewing and stitching and gluing unperturbed.

Later he will ask: 'Any more of that shandy? Or have you drunk it all?' and by that time the music may have hit the right note. One evening we had punk aerobics to The Ramones: stretches and knee bends and pogo twists to 'The KKK Took My Baby Away' and 'Rock 'n' Roll High School'.

Otherwise there were mournful singalongs to 'Diamonds and Rust' and 'God Give Me Strength'.

Another time we pretended to be monged-up, cross-eyed clubbers to 'The Twin', and one memorable night we jumped and weaved to '4 My People and I Am The Fly', helping me forget the fact that somebody I knew had suddenly died in London and I couldn't do anything about the pain this had inflicted upon his widow and her best friend, my brother.

George can be a right cow, throwing tantrums and once a coffee cup, but never tiaras.

George is unreasonable.

So am I, in my insistent way. And so is Christine in her demonstrative manner. And so are all of us who have been around him but will never fully comprehend the experience of actually being George.

George is soft.

I remember his weeping when he first heard the finished version of his aching duet with Antony, 'You Are My Sister', thinking of Siobhan so far away.

George is tough.

He has to be. There are a lot of arseholes out there, the ones who have and always will run to him, mooing: 'Boy Ge-orge! Boy Ge-orge!! I LOVE the 80s!!!' snapping their phone cameras two inches from his face.

When he says: 'Actually could you leave me alone? I'm with my friends at the moment,' they turn. And how.

'Fuck you asshole!' they scream, crimson-faced at his temerity. 'Fat loser!! F U-Uck Yo-OU!!!'

George can crack jokes like they are going out of (and into) fashion, a never-ending stream which you can try and counter before giving up. All those thousands of hours whiled away on the road, I expect.

George can dance.

Once, at a Fashion Week party there were just the handful of us Brits making the moves; Christos and Chris and Christine and George and I.

We disco-cavorted London-style, unconcerned, while the rest of the party were either too off it or too self-consciously hip; Kate Moss was there, after all, and what would she think if they fluffed a step in front of her?

A couple of skinny-tied, side-parted members of Franz Ferdinand looked on, uncomfortable. Then a silly American woman made the inevitable approach to George: 'Gahhd! I didn't know you could dance!!'

Rude cow. What did she expect?

George can sing Irish rebel songs like any armchair Paddy, you know.

George can tell stories about meeting Margaret Thatcher and

Princess Diana, just as he can quote lyrics from a Fatal Microbes single.

George is good.

He's George, isn't he?.

Paul Gorman
London 2004

Boy Paul

By Boy George

Paul Gorman is one of those people I've known forever and yet never really spoken to. We were forced together one afternoon at my gothic pile in Hampstead after it was decided that he should assist me in writing this book.

After a delicious macrobiotic meal cooked by my friend Dragana Brown, Paul was given a Nine Ki assessment by Drags. She and her partner Simon Brown advise me how to move my energy around the globe and I am godparent to their son Michael, who, unlike most kids, eats broccoli and tofu joyfully.

Luckily, the omens were spot-on for a good partnership and Paul and I started the arduous task of putting this book together.

I don't believe in 'metrosexuals' (or heterosexuals for that matter) but, if I were forced to label Paul, I would say he was veering, flirting in the 'metro' vicinity. For example, he can discuss queer sex and the possibility that we are all a bit of everything without clenching his buttocks or curling an often-painted toenail.

He can cook rice.

What he does to kale is quite frankly a crime against nutrition.

Like myself he has an 'Irish heart and English blood' so charm is just part of the make-up. Oh yeah, I think he has worn eyeliner!

He loves fashion but more than that he loves music and he's

a bit of a tart when it comes to the ladies and will readily comment on a passing female's dress sense or choice of shoes.

Paul is detail-obsessed and once we had a debate for an hour over a word that was so commonplace I now forget what it was.

It might have been 'why?'.

Paul is never boring and he can tell stories better than an old Irish biddy and he's a great houseguest. Christine loves having him (yes!) here in New York because he is a proper gentleman and Christine often has days when she regresses back to a former life when she had as many servants as sequins.

Paul will always get the milk.

The smokes.

The Coronas.

Once he even went to Duane Reed to purchase a selection of sewing needles.

If Paul were queer he'd probably be husband material but when he goes into Christine's room he isn't always having his toenails painted!

Paul is a heterosexual, but not one of those dumb ones who can't say an obviously good-looking chap is cute.

Paul is proudly emotional, interesting, opinionated, a great writer, rice boiler, bunny boiler (I hear) but beyond all that he is one of the coolest blokes I've had the pleasure to meet in years.

Boy George
New York 2004

Introduction

Born Gobby

There I was, propping up a speaker, drink in hand, eyes sparkling under the weight of glitter that ran Zorro-like across my face. I had just finished a performance as Leigh Bowery in *Taboo* at the Venue in London and decided to go for a drink, which turned into a club crawl. The banging tribal house was bone-rattling at DTPM nightclub and I had drunk a fair bit before being approached by a young guy who seemed to be trying to tell me something important.

'It's really loud in here,' I mumbled as he waved his arms wildly and mouthed: 'Are you Boy George?'

In such situations I am usually thinking: 'Obviously or you wouldn't be speaking to me,' but on this occasion I snarled: 'No, I'm Gloria Fucking Swanson.'

After more arm-waving and lip-moving I beckoned him closer and heard him softly say: 'I'm deaf.' Without thinking I pointed to my face and shouted: 'You're not fucking blind are you?'

For a second I felt terrible until I saw the smirk on his face, which exploded into laughter.

'Good one!' he said as he returned to the dance-floor and I chuckled to myself.

As I rode home in the back of one of those illegal mini cabs I was still laughing when the Indian cabbie decided to pipe up and tell me: 'I wasn't sure at first if it was you. You know, you have put on a lot of weight!'

The urge to tell him he was no oil painting was almost irresistible. Instead I snapped coldly: 'Just take me to Hampstead.'

Some days I feel as though my only purpose is to negotiate my way through people's assumptions and preconceptions about how I should look and behave.

At the height of my fame I was much more worried about people's opinions. I'm not pretending I don't care, but I certainly care less. I don't believe any famous person who says they don't read reviews or aren't affected by rudeness or negativity. Almost everything we do relies on the approval of others.

As a teenager I equated fame with being popular, being loved, having some kind of purpose. As the middle child in a pack of six children I was left to my own devices. Because I didn't join in with those 'normal' boys' pursuits – playing football or climbing trees – I was left to dream and drift. From the age of twelve to seventeen my main fantasy was to befriend David Bowie and hang out with him at Haddon Hall in Beckenham. I thought: 'He'd really understand me. We'd have so much in common.'

Some days I'd bunk off school and get a Red Bus Rover into London's West End and visit places like Chelsea Girl, where I'd see people with coloured streaks in their hair and glam clothing. I'd think it would be so great to befriend them, but could never bridge the gap between their cool and my terror.

How strange that panic was still in place twenty-odd years later when I sat with my hero in a New York restaurant. I faked cool but every corpuscle in my body was screaming: 'Ohmigod, it's Ziggy Stardust!!'

I guess however famous you are there's always somebody more famous. I think the same applies to most things in life: beauty, wealth, talent, charm, wit, eyeliner.

As a kid I was always described as highly strung, theatrical or needy. What else could I do but become famous?

I can honestly say I was never drawn to the power aspects of fame such as money, yachts and houses in the south of France.

Having met lots of other famous people in my life – some I

respect, some I don't – I have learnt that fame sits comfortably on some shoulders. There are days when I hate being famous. This may sound like heresy, since we live in a society obsessed by the subject.

For most people, encounters with the famous are fleeting and insincere. After all, what do you say to somebody you've never met who is convinced they know everything about you?

The rule is, when someone asks: 'Can I just tell you something?' it is usually wise to say: 'No' or run because they are invariably about to tell you their entire life story.

Whether you're famous or not, there are only so many life stories you can handle in one evening.

One night I was trying to move through the crowd at New York's smallest and sleaziest gay bar, the Cock, and some admirer demanded a hug. 'Sorry, no,' was my reaction but he was having none of it and hemmed me into a corner, insisting: 'I buy your records, I'm a fan.' I told him: 'There are loads of people I'd love to hug but life's not that simple. I buy Dolly Parton's records but I'd never approach her and demand a French kiss.' Some people have this crazy idea that they can force a conversation with you just because they know the chorus to 'Karma Chameleon'. The worst types are those who just stare at you all night thinking that such behaviour is going to result in a lasting friendship.

Perhaps people imagine that I never have to deal with rejection myself. Trust me, there are many gorgeous boys I encounter who give me the cold shoulder. On top of this you constantly have to dodge the barbed comments of those who think they are cooler than you, or those who think you think you are cooler than them. Comments like: 'Who does he think he is?!' are flung at you for simply entering a room. If there are unspoken guidelines you are meant to follow they simply require you to be fake at all times. I am not prepared to live with that.

On a practical level I have to be snippy and unfriendly to get from A to B. You can't be all things to all people. Just popping out to buy a pint of milk can result in the devastation of somebody's heartfelt connection with you. These days I tend to handle such encounters based on how I'm feeling at the time. For years

I would beat myself up about having been unfriendly. Now I know it's a necessary survival mechanism.

Because I choose not to hide behind bodyguards or velvet ropes, I'm left with the job of telling people to get out of my face.

I have in my own way dismantled certain aspects of my fame, but I know I'm never going to escape it completely. I also know I'm being a bit of a hypocrite here, because I hate it when I hear others whingeing about being famous. I think to myself: 'Oh just get on with it,' which is exactly what I try to do in my own ham-fisted way.

Living in New York, where fame is put on a higher pedestal and where people have greater expectations, has driven this home.

I'm pretty fearless once I've got my glad rags and make-up on; it's like armour. People treat me differently when the sow's ear is turned into a silk purse. Fame is a figment of other people's imaginations. They have ideas about how a star should or might act, and forget you are just another human being who farts and belches and feels pain.

In the eighties I went through a lunatic stage, and I accept that lunacy is always looming. Sometimes, when the spotlight was directly on me, the only way to be heard was to throw a fit. At the height of it all, I lost control of my life. I became a commodity and I feel that a lot of my worst behaviour was a vain attempt to regain some control.

In order to justify their roles, the people surrounding somebody in my position can use every trick in the book to manipulate you into doing stuff you don't necessarily want to do. It's assumed that every artist is so fragile and self-obsessed that they can't handle the truth. On so many occasions I would be provided with half the facts; a glamorous two-hour flight would turn into an uncomfortable nine-hour journey, culminating in a helicopter ride sitting on plastic garden furniture for a gig in the bowels of Bulgaria.

Eventually I realised that by exploding I was only confirming the view that I should be treated with kid gloves. Learning to just say 'no' was a life-saver. Once, in Brazil, my manager Tony excitedly announced that Culture Club had been offered a one-day shoot for a choc-ice commercial: 'It's sixty grand for a day's work and no one will ever see it back home!' I sat him down and slowly broke down the figures. Then I said: 'So, for twenty thousand dollars I'm going to look like an idiot? I don't think so!'

The most comical offer came from Burger King only a couple of years ago. The fast-food chain wanted to use 'Karma Chameleon' for an ad campaign. The rest of the band were hoping that, as a confirmed vegetarian of nineteen years' standing, I'd put my morals on ice. I felt guilty that the others would miss out on a huge pay-out but I refused to sign off on the deal. It's not that I enjoy turning down silly money but I wouldn't sell my soul to Burger King if I was homeless.

More recently I was offered the most money anybody has ever been promised to appear on *I'm A Celebrity...Get Me Out Of Here!*. My agent Tony Denton urged me to take the meeting. I said: 'How would you fancy appearing on television in the jungle looking like a sweaty pig jumping into vats of creepy-crawlies?'

He said: 'I wouldn't do it.'

To which I replied: 'There you go.'

Like me, Tony knows that heat is the enemy of drag.

Whenever I see anybody on those type of programmes it smacks of desperation. I'm far too vain.

Last year I also declined an MBE. My mum was furious and said: 'I could have gone to Buckingham Palace! You're so spiteful. I could have hung that in my front window. If it wasn't for me you wouldn't have been born.'

I told her: 'Well, too bad you didn't give birth to Cliff Richard.'

I portray myself as an open book – and I am essentially open – but there is so much I mask with make-up and wit. The make-up is a mask of sorts, but one that draws attention. It hides George O'Dowd and gives Boy George, or the public perception of that character, the centre stage.

Of course, I don't think they are two separate entities. George O'Dowd and Boy George are one and the same. George in make-up is a little spikier and perhaps more defensive, yet fearlessly confident. Make-up on a man tends to make people (other men mostly) nervous, especially if it is connected to a strong sexual energy. However much the media and my detractors try to render me sexless and doll-like, I unnerve people because I contradict their perceptions of masculinity and what it means to be queer.

I've never really been ashamed or uncomfortable with my sexual preference. I may have taken my time to announce it to the universe but I came out to my parents at the age of fifteen. I learned at a young age that shouting about it can make you unpopular. From five years old I was dodging abuse about my sexuality. I was outed long before it was fashionable.

Don Letts, the dreadlocked punk film-maker, called me a 'user-friendly homosexual', but you could just as easily call him a user-friendly Rastafarian. I would never think to suggest he was letting other black men down by working in a mostly white rock medium and therefore not being 'black' enough.

I wonder how different things would have been if, instead of saying: 'I prefer a cup of tea to sex,' I had told Russell Harty: 'Can't answer that right now, I've got a cock in my mouth.' Look what good old honest vulgarity did for comedian Julian Clary's career. His famous comment 'Sorry I'm late, I was out the back fisting Norman Lamont' should have resulted in a knighthood but it killed his TV career for a long time. As an openly gay artist you are constantly trying to be true to yourself and not frighten the horses. I didn't create a palatable gay persona, I was just born gobby.

Other gay artists such as Jimmy Somerville called me a 'pantomime dame' but when did Danny La Rue or even Somerville himself ride the London Underground dressed as a nun? Somerville was brave in many respects, but my sexuality, or the desire to have sex with my own kind, has never been the guiding factor of my life.

I am not the sort of gay man who centres his world around fucking. If it happens, great, but I don't hang around in bushes or gay bars with my tongue out. Somerville's gripe with me was that I wasn't the right type of queer. Well, sorry, I've always preferred soft sheets to cold tiles. And I look lousy in a vest. Amusingly, it was George Michael who turned out to be the gay cliché. All through the eighties I kept saying: 'The hair, dear, the hair!' Perhaps history has vindicated me.

A lot of people think if you're not on the telly every day, you're sitting around watching reruns of old interviews and wallowing in past glories. I no longer desire the type of success I enjoyed in the eighties, but I do lots of different things and work very hard. I never measure my worth by how many records I sell.

Well, what would be the point?

It's easy to get caught up in all that and I admit I have at times wept uncontrollably if a record has flopped. But, when you look at what succeeds these days, it's not worth fretting about. I've always made a decent living. I've kept my house in Hampstead and I live very comfortably. I had to laugh when artist Tracey Emin walked into my home and said: 'I'm glad to see it didn't all go up your nose.'

In a club not so long ago somebody approached me and said: 'Boy George PLC is doing very well at the moment. You never really go away, do you?' I felt so insulted. I'm not some sort of corporate conglomerate like Madonna, or McDonna as I like to call her.

I have accepted that not everyone likes me and maybe I have exhausted far too much time trying to make them. I receive a lot of love in my daily life, people say sweet things to me, but it's always the cruelty that sticks. I also receive equal amounts of support and animosity from fellow homosexuals. Only recently I received an email from a stranger: 'Stop trying to reinvent yourself. You're a has-been and I know why you paint your neck black.'

'So do I,' was my response, 'for fierce jawline drama and effect.'

I'm not much of a planner. There is no grand, glorious scheme. I just work and work and work, and whatever happens, happens, as you'll see from this book, which tells the story of my adventures from my colourful trips to India in the early nineties to the opening and closure of my musical *Taboo* on Broadway. The extremities of my life never cease to amuse me.

For me, the opening night on Broadway was weird. By then I'd been living back in New York for a couple of months – the first concentrated period I had spent there since my drug-addled days with a variety of misfits in tow. It was a strange experience being newsworthy in America again. After all, Culture Club were absolutely massive there in the mid-eighties, and the whirlwind that we reaped meant that we could successfully tour the US again when we reformed in the nineties, though that wasn't without its dramas, as you will also see.

One of the greatest aspects of *Taboo* is that it has provided the opportunity to show that I'm not just a quip in a hat but a quality songwriter. It has also given me the opportunity to move away from the pop medium, which at best is uncharitable and has a very short memory. More than one reviewer said that the score for the show was the best on Broadway for twenty years. New York's notoriously tough critics were scathing about every other aspect of *Taboo*, but no one slated the music.

One night, backstage during the New York run of *Taboo*, I watched Euan Morton – the young actor who was playing me – hold back tears because of some nasty comment in the press. I told him it was OK to acknowledge the hurt, because it never gets any easier.

Seconds later, Euan's smiling face, crowned by a huge white plumed headdress, appeared at my dressing-room door. He let out a disgusting belch, then, as he marched towards the stage, he matched the belch with an even louder fart and disappeared out of sight, laughing insanely.

I watched him from the side of the stage singing like an angel and I felt so sentimental and embarrassingly proud. It's been years since I heard a voice so flawless and full of feeling.

It had been a particularly trying week for all of us. Panic was setting in as we tried to prepare the show for the big opening night and our producer Rosie O'Donnell often lacked subtlety when trying to make a point. Among her most memorable outbursts was the one which went: 'With all due respect, I don't give a flying fuck what anyone thinks.'

Then there was the occasion when one of our lead actors, Raul Esparza, stormed out of the theatre after a spectacular blow-out with Rosie. I was proud of him for taking a stand, even though his exit was rendered pure comedy by the medieval breeches he was wearing. Rosie was unapologetic and said: 'If he's not back by seven-thirty we hire another actor.' The show's writer Charles Busch found Raul and persuaded him to return. I had faith in Raul's professionalism and he didn't let me down.

At times it felt like we were all losing sight of something magical but that's the nature and the beauty of the beast. The New York critics were baying for our blood weeks before *Taboo* opened for preview and the future prospects for the show seemed like a foregone conclusion.

I didn't sit down one night with a notepad and think: 'Right: tomorrow I'm out to conquer America again.' I have no desire to carve out the sort of career I had in the eighties. I'm more than happy being a marginalised artist, as long as I can work, pay the bills and be creative.

I would be lying if I said I didn't want my work to be successful. I really would like to sell more records. It would be great to be played on the radio without constantly being referred to in the past context. 'I used to love you in the eighties' starts to grate after you've heard it 25 million times.

Since publishing my first book, *Take It Like a Man*, there hasn't been a day when someone hasn't approached me and told me how much they'd enjoyed reading it, to which I've always answered: 'Trust me, it was easier than living it.'

With the previous book my agenda, perhaps naively, was to address the acres of incorrect column inches and whispers directed at, and often attributed to, me. Since *Take It Like a Man*, I've continued to do so, and with this book maybe I just want to be the new Shirley MacLaine, although my intentions are not always entirely spiritual.

At the height of Culture Club, I was a pretty innocent chap, albeit with a rapid-fire tongue. I was often miffed by people's reaction to me, such as protestors parading outside American stadiums with placards proclaiming: 'Boy George is the Devil.' Around that time I was banned, or at least told I wasn't welcome, in the state of Utah. I even heard they'd burned my records. Very disco.

Many years later I actually played a solo gig in Salt Lake City and was invited on to Mormon radio shows where I spoke openly and calmly about my sexuality and what I felt were continuing ignorant and unnecessary attitudes towards personal freedom. It coincided with the paperback release of *Take It Like a Man*, which had a cover depicting me as the Devil. We were selling T-shirts with that image on the tour. I remember telling my merchandiser Bob: 'We ain't gonna sell anything here.' But such was the demand for those T-shirts in Salt Lake City we had to reprint for the rest of the tour.

When I took to the stage I said: 'At the height of my fame, you banned me from this place. And you know what? Back then, I was a bit like Marie Osmond with bigger eyelashes. Now I'm more of a threat than ever because I've worked some shit out.'

Writing, whether songs, poetry or books, can be a wonderful way of making sense of life and also of evoking fabulous memories and sometimes even the most turgid situations which, as human beings, we have a way of conveniently disowning.

Writing this book has allowed me to reflect on all of my experiences, from the last fifteen years and beyond; not least my colourfully chaotic childhood in Eltham where, in the O'Dowd household, a change of wallpaper was often made possible by a flying plate of Sunday roast.

In all, there were eight of us at 29 Joan Crescent, headed by my tanklike warrior of a mother Dinah and my equally tanklike warrior of a father Jeremiah – though he never really knew who he was at war with.

Dad could be whistling happily at the car wheel one minute, and then explode with rage because another driver had cut him up. Suddenly he'd be brandishing the baseball bat he kept in the car and threatening to smash someone's skull in. We'd be sat hanging our heads in shame as yet another violent interlude played itself out.

Growing up, I was deeply affected by my father's violent outbursts and could never understand his ability to switch moods on a ha'penny. A tyrannical tirade followed immediately by an arm around the shoulder – 'I didn't mean it, son' – can leave a child deeply traumatised.

It's always difficult for me to talk about my father in this way, because I'd hate to suggest that he was a bad parent. If he was only a bad person it would be so much easier, but there were many ways in which he supported me, not least when I came out. But the damage caused by his emotional unavailability left its mark.

My family home included my brothers – descending from Richard and Kevin to Gerald and David, with me in the middle – and last, but never least, my take-no-prisoners saint of a sister Siobhan.

Number 29 Joan Crescent could never really be described as a musical household. Richard was the one guilty of introducing the likes of Status Quo, David Bowie and Alice Cooper to the O'Dowd record collection, which at the time consisted mainly of jazz – Sinatra, Johnny Ray, and occasional gems like Pearl Bailey and Dinah Washington which Dad picked up when he was clearing houses. There were also the obligatory albums of Irish rebel songs and to this day I know pretty much all of them, though they are not the kind of ditties you can get away with singing openly in public.

In this book I also write about the notoriety of being a club-land freak in the late seventies and early eighties, the ups and downs of pop success with Culture Club, being a superstar DJ (whatever that means), performing in my own right as a singer-songwriter and in a variety of other guises. I talk about spirituality and sexuality, my lovers, soulmates and enemies, and the weird and wonderful cast of characters who populate my life.

I know that I am good at my craft but also realise I have done much to distract people from what it is I actually do. My passion is music. I don't enjoy the process of trying to sell it to others but creating it and then having it touch strangers is very rewarding. I have been, and continue to be, very lucky. I get paid for doing the things I love and I manage to do so with very little compromise.

The cliché promises that 'you learn by your mistakes'. Even with years of therapy it is almost impossible to change how you see yourself and how you feel about the world. At best you learn

new ways to tackle the problems that churn you up and bring
out insecurity.

Who am I today?

Who did I used to be?

Who will I be tomorrow, or the next time that you see me?

1

Bombay Scream

My first trip to India was a purely spiritual expedition. I followed the predictable path that leads one to search for the meaning of life, or at the very least some kind of spiritual security blanket. In the back of my mind I hoped that I would become a more spiritual person, and I certainly became more aware of my own feelings and, more importantly, those of other people.

The most essential aspect of that journey was the opportunity to spend quality time with myself, away from my career and familiar things. Leaving on Boxing Day 1989, I travelled with my then boyfriend Michael Dunne and Nayana, a bone-thin Krishna devotee who had persuaded me to check out India in the first place. I'd met Nayana, whose real name is Daniel Haber, some years earlier in New York. Daniel is a Jew who defected and as camp as a rhubarb sling. We stayed in the cheapest guest houses, ate simple food and, because no one recognised me, I could take in all the beauty and sadness around me.

The trip and the spiritual quest allowed me time to reflect on my early years growing up and I realised that I was lucky my parents weren't racist, envious or small-minded. In fact, they were always unpredictable. When you thought Dad would be really angry he could surprise you by just shrugging his shoulders.

Dad has never really grown up. His biggest fault is his inability

Straight

to take responsibility for his actions and to admit he is wrong. I think an awful lot of his anger towards my mother stemmed from unresolved issues he had with his own. He grew up in a house dominated by women and his mother was a tough cookie, a real matriarch who ruled the roost.

I suspect that when he came to marrying, he sought out a vulnerable person he could dominate. My mother had ended up in Woolwich when she was sent away by her family in Ireland after having my eldest brother Richard out of wedlock, and she was grateful that anyone would take her in, as my dad did in 1958. Her own mother Bridget Glynn was very domineering, and it seems to me that in those situations you either run towards what you fear or overcome it by making someone else suffer. Though I have to say my granny Bridget was fantastic, always sizing up to my dad: 'You might scare my daughter but you don't scare me.' God rest her soul.

While I thought about my family in India I also took on board how hideous the previous few years had been: the breakdown of my relationship with Culture Club's drummer Jon Moss – which he only acknowledged publicly a couple of years ago – had caused the band to grind to a halt. I was consuming more and more drugs, as were the rest of the group. This period was followed by the madness of my friend Marilyn and I swanning around the world spending money like it (and I) was going out of fashion. We spent a lot of time in New York where drugs were as easily obtainable as chewing gum. And then heroin took hold.

I first met Marilyn when a whole crowd of us were extras in the new-wave film *Breaking Glass* in the late seventies. We were in a pub in Finsbury Park close to the Rainbow Theatre, and Marilyn kept bending over in front of the straight blokes, revealing a tampon string hanging from his knickers. His sick humour lured me in.

History has wrongly painted Marilyn as the reason I started taking drugs. Often he would be the one trying to quit and I would be the one turning up with a cache of narcotics. Drug use is an (ill) informed choice: you can drag a horse to water but you can't make it break-dance.

If you asked my friend Philip Sallon – who has remained both a reliable and unreliable force in my life since I was barely sixteen and first saw him doing his deranged munchkin locomotion on a podium at my first ever visit to a gay club – he would insist that Marilyn was out to destroy me because he was jealous of my success. Philip also maintains that we were bad for each other, and that is probably closer to the truth, though amid the craziness there were moments of total joy. I loved Marilyn and I still do, but the best moments we had together were while living on the bread-line in various squats in London's West End, watching the stars from the gutter.

The drug fest came to an abrupt halt in the summer of 1986 when the media backlash occurred with headlines such as THE SHAME OF JUNKIE GEORGE and the *Daily Mirror*'s fox-hunting classic: FIND HIM!. When I made the *News at Ten*, my father and my manager Tony Gordon hatched a plan to kidnap me for my own safety. Thankfully it never happened.

The *Sun* broke the story after my brother David gave it to the paper for free: BOY GEORGE HAS ONLY EIGHT WEEKS TO LIVE. This was followed by Richard Branson's intervention, then arrests and convictions. Then deaths started to pile up as our collective drug problems kicked in: the casualties included the artist Trojan, shoe designer John Moore and model rep Louise Powell.

It got too close to home when my friend Michael Rudetsky's body was found at my house and another clubbing friend Mark Vaultier – who used to stand at the door of the nightclub Taboo holding a mirror up to people's faces asking: 'Would you let yourself in?' – died from methadone poisoning at the home of Mark Batham, whom I'd known since schooldays.

The day Mark Vaultier died, a bunch of us had been arrested while walking down the street at 10.30 in the morning. After we were all released Mark drank an entire bottle of methadone. Apparently he felt guilty about my arrest, because he had attracted the attention of the police in the first place, which only added to my sadness and deep sense of loss.

I knew then that I had to stop and went through the very hideous process of kicking heroin. I was lucky because my family offered so much support.

My friend Bonnie Lippel was also an important force around the time of my addiction. Having moved from New York to become my housekeeper she found herself embroiled in almost every drama and moment of sadness. Philip would always refer to her as 'the demented fan' and Bonnie was just as quick to put him down.

Bonnie could be hysterically funny, like the time she answered the door to a prying journalist and told him her name was Blanche Dubois. Neither of could believe he printed her comment and her fictitious nom de plume.

Bonnie was and still is a dear friend and I have much to thank and love her for.

Somebody asked me the other day: 'If you had your time again would you avoid drugs?' My response was: 'I'd take less drugs.'

What you do to yourself is personal, however stupid it may be; smoking a cigarette, eating meat, we're all on chemicals of one sort or another. Getting caught is the greatest crime. Many of the people who were writing stories about my drug intake had serious addictions of their own. At the time of my arrest there was a prominent showbiz writer who was trying to bring me down while to my certain knowledge shovelling cocaine up his own hooter.

It's important to remember that in making the decision to use drugs you do affect others around you. You hurt those who love you and that's reason enough not to do them. My addiction was shocking to the public because I appeared so level-headed, but it's also important to look at why people use drugs. Behind the public façade I was riddled with insecurities and when success failed to eradicate them, I had to find something else. No one wants to hear an ex-drug abuser say they liked taking drugs, because it sends out a bad message, but we have to accept that people take drugs because they enjoy them. However, very few people are strong enough to keep drug use under control. Eventually the drug starts to control you and that's where the party ends.

Even after I started to embrace Buddhism with Michael, I carried on drinking and necking the odd tab of ecstasy. Acid house was a great moment for me. There were no stars and I could drift around clubs with very little hassle. Long before the trend for superstar DJs and super clubs like Ministry of Sound and Cream, the scene was about the music and the illusion of unity on the dance floor fuelled by ecstasy. It helped me get a sense of myself as a real person again and focus on why I started making music in the first place.

I've been asked a lot: 'When did you really know you were famous?' It's a bit like that hardy perennial: 'When did you find out you were gay?' How do you know? Well, you walk through a school playground or a disco and complete strangers either hug you or hate you.

So, having scored a solo hit with my single 'Everything I Own' and debut album *Sold*, I turned to the post-acid-house dance culture and created my own solo project, Jesus Loves You. After being dismissed for years as pop tripe I received respectable reviews for my music; the first Jesus Loves You single, 'After the Love', was even made record of the week in the *NME*.

All this occurred around the time of that first Indian trip, where my initial cynicism was replaced by valuable lessons about myself. Just being in India, where many of the comforts we take for granted are out of reach, makes you forget the petty stuff that clogs up your life. Visiting an ancient temple really does leave you feeling engulfed by a higher energy and existing without soft toilet paper raises entirely different emotions – but is a powerful experience, nonetheless!

After the trip certain questions remained unanswered. The Indian caste system gives those in the higher echelons an excuse to be cruel to the poor, even though the laws of karma suggest that people who live in poverty or with disabilities are suffering for bad activity in a previous life. In reality it's just a way of policing the impoverished and maintaining the superiority of the wealthy.

Often we'd see dead bodies lying in the road, but people just stepped over them. If we gave money to beggars, we'd be accused of encouraging them and fuelling the problem. Nayana told me I was being 'naive' until I reminded him that I was actually paying for him to travel around the subcontinent. The attitude to beggars in India is certainly harsher than it is at home, but many people in the so-called 'civilised' West are just as guilty of not caring.

Although I was glad to get back to the material world, I brought back a degree of wisdom. I realised that no religion or faith is without its faults or qualities. It is the often wrong-minded or convenient human interpretation of faith that is the problem. I also came to the conclusion that however alluring a certain doctrine may be, it wasn't possible for me to follow a path without constantly questioning it. I feel strongly that we should all try to respect the beliefs of others, even those that condemn the gay lifestyle (which is pretty much all of them).

Some of the most seemingly normal and sweet human beings have blurted out shockingly ignorant things in my company. I've even met a few right-wing gays at dinner parties. In my opinion a right-wing homo is a bit like a vegetarian butcher.

You can spot a militant Muslim from a mile away but there are just as many hard-core Christians who blend in while harbouring hateful thoughts. That old adage 'love the sinner not the sin' may seem sweet until you remember that they think you're damned to Hell.

2

A Judy Garland In The Shirley Temple
Part II

My second trip to India later in 1990 was a very different experience. I went to perform and record in Bombay with the West India Company, a band formed by Blancmange's Stephen Luscombe and Indian percussionist Pandit Dinesh.

Stephen has a deep knowledge of Indian music and culture while Pandit is a dab hand at most instruments and was able to communicate with the musicians, who all had unique ways of cutting deals to play on our sessions. The project involved working with the legendary Indian songstress Asha Bhosle and a singer called Hope, a wholly inappropriate name for someone so negative.

My good friend Mike Nicholls came along to make costumes for us with designer Rachel Auburn, who – when she ran a clothes shop with Mike – was well known for slipping speed into her Japanese machinists' coffee. Those poor girls didn't have a clue. 'I stay all night, Rachel, finish everything, no tired at all.'

I returned to India less dazzled and more cynical about its spiritual potential to transform me. I still believed India to be a deeply spiritual place but understandably most people there were too busy struggling for their own survival to be concerned about my spiritual well-being. I'm quite sure people like me seemed utterly ridiculous to the average Indian.

Having Rachel and Mike in tow was indicative of my more relaxed attitude towards being elevated. Rachel may have been overt in her disregard for spirituality but Mike was just as irreverent in his silent way.

Rachel wouldn't think twice about openly spiking my belief system whereas Mike would tread more lightly until he was sure of not being unnecessarily rude. I'm sure both of them took the piss out of me when my back was turned however. Mike is the kind of person who appears to be more pliable than he actually is. Give him a JD and Coke or a spliff and you'll soon find out the truth.

I first met Mike during the Batcave days of the early eighties and then reconnected with him through my fraught friendship with Caron Geary aka MC Kinky, who became my musical sparring partner around that time.

Mike had a workspace in Caron's house in Crowndale Road, Camden Town, and he'd often run up outfits for us both.

Mike is very different to Caron and I, who not only wash our dirty laundry in public but wrap it around other people's heads. He is extremely secretive and proud and it took me years to discover just how colourful he really is.

GLAMOROUS PUNK

He is tall
Charming
Secretive
Astute
All the boys find him cute
He is devilish

I feel like I've known him forever
And now
Having spent good times together
I can say
I love him
He is a good friend

There is real trust now
He tells me things
That change
My perception
His darkness
Is reassuring
Like a handsome brother
Sometimes
A sister

He is stylish
Never camp
On everything
He puts his own stamp
An ardent Punk
Ambitious
Proud
When he drinks
He gets real loud
And sweet
He's got big feet

I never know what's on his mind
It is quietly busy
I worry
That I talk too much
We are both needy
Expressing this in very different ways
He is queer
Not one of those shallow gays
He smokes dope
All through the day
He floats
Smirks
Plays music loudly

He looks like a straight boy
He could pass
I am told he has a pretty arse
He says
'It's one of my best features'
Then
Delivers a line from a John Waters classic
A bit camp
Not too much
My friend Mike
Can be very butch
A streak of contradictions

He has left New York
The empty room
Hopes to see him soon
Like
We do
The bag of weed too
Dean & Deluca
Not pumpkin
Or Sushi
Mike hates them
Silently stubborn
And choosy

There is more
I don't write it down
He is so private
It might make him frown
And pout
He is wired
A little boy when he's tired
Gold glitter around his eyes
Punk slogans on his ties
His long legs strapped together
I think I will love him forever

One of the things we had in common was our love of India's innate campness. We were always referencing that great scene in John Waters' gross-out art movie *Female Trouble*, when Divine discovers her daughter Taffy has joined the Hare Krishnas: 'If I catch you downtown dressed like some kind of fool chanting and bothering shoppers, I'll give you consciousness when I knock you unconscious!' And the other favourite line: 'What have these people DONE to you? Have you been brainwashed or something?!'

We arrived in Bombay during the monsoon, and the mixture of thundering rain and foggy heat was almost unbearable. We stayed in a small house with a bunch of servants who could be summoned by a bell on the living-room table. Hope loved to ring that bell and shout: 'Boy! Come here, boy!' When Mike and I decided to remove the battery, Hope's colonial aspirations were briefly thwarted.

Stephen is a lovely bloke, but always looks as though someone's stolen his last bit of chocolate. One of his steely glares could stop an Indian wedding band in its tracks. Rachel, who is now a popular DJ and producer, was part of the original crowd who haunted the legendary nightclub Taboo.

Rachel was also a close friend of the extraordinary Leigh Bowery, whom I played in London and on Broadway in my show *Taboo*. Actually, Leigh shagged Rachel, and that's how we all found out that his knob looked like a huge bruised banana. There was even a rumour that her son Jack was Leigh's child, but it was just one of the many which spread like a fire in the Australian outback having been started by Leigh himself. Leigh often spent hours on the phone spreading or embellishing second-hand gossip. Sometimes he'd be talking away into the receiver but there was nobody on the other end, even though he'd claim to have been speaking to anyone from Steve Strange to Joan Collins.

Rachel was the star of that Indian trip. On Lord Krishna's birthday there was a huge celebration at the Hare Krishna Temple on Juhu Beach, where I performed 'Bow Down Mister'. The audience was made up of wide-eyed Indians who had travelled far and wide from remote villages and were very bemused by the boy in a turban and heavy make-up. As Mike said: 'It's all very *It Ain't 'Alf Hot Mum*.'

The scene backstage was equally surreal with gurus desperately trying to avoid Rachel. 'Get her away from me,' muttered one as the Indian press and cameramen captured her strutting around in a see-through, flesh-hugging white dress.

Rachel and Mike were staying in a small stone room in the temple, smoking wacky baccy and drinking alcohol; Rachel had purchased a huge bottle of vodka and smuggled it in. Every time she raised the bottle to her lips to guzzle, a devotee would – with perfect timing – walk into the room; they thought she was the spawn of Beelzebub. Within the Krishna movement women are subservient, or very quiet at least. Occasionally we would come across the odd female devotee who stood out from the rest, but they were viewed with suspicion and often had a history. And any of the devotees who had a 'reputation' were usually friends of Nayana, including one called Naratam, who Rachel allegedly seduced. Apparently he had been celibate for twenty years and as soon as Rachel heard that, while we were driving into Bombay in a big dilapidated American saloon car, she wrapped her legs around his shoulders. Then, in the centre of the city, crowds formed around her as she weaved in and out of the colourful market stalls with the rain making her dress even more transparent. I loved having Rachel with us because she was the perfect counterbalance to all the heavy spirituality.

In a studio close to the temple we spent our days recording, including an Indian-style take on Abba's 'I Have a Dream' with Asha, but we never got round to completing it. The song was later covered by Westlife.

Working with Indian musicians was a real eye-opener. One time we took a break to watch Asha record an album with a forty-piece orchestra. The arrangements were so complex yet it was all cut live, straight on to six tracks, which is so primitive in comparison with the way we work in the West.

What a strange bag of tricks we were. Pandit always chirpy, Hope desperate to be a diva, Stephen like a moody Northern housewife, Mike and Rachel with hashish smirks on their faces and me being driven mad by people on the street because my picture had appeared in the press: 'Karma, Karma, Karma . . .'

Unlike that first Indian experience, which was very low-key because I was just a tourist, this visit had been announced publicly and there was a buzz in the air. We were invited to parties at posh places where we saw the ritzy side of the city and the opulence contrasted drastically with the intense poverty.

One house was particularly stunning. Once owned by Salman Rushdie's family, the walls were lined with antique temple doors, everything was made of silver and gold and there was so much food it was obscene. We wanted to take some out to the beggars in the streets, but the waiters wouldn't let us into the kitchen.

The guests at the party kept asking Hope to sing but she created a fuss: 'Oh, I can't, my throat's so sore.' But it was obvious she was lapping up the attention and the next time I saw her she had stripped down to her bra and was hollering 'Georgia on my Mind'. Rachel had her period but rather than get moody she decided to get even. She removed her panties and wrapped them around her wrist, asking guests to smell her new perfume. Luckily, only Mike and I had any idea how grossly she was behaving and when reminded of the incident, Rachel insisted it had never happened.

One day, Mike, Rachel and I found a young kid on the street who had been badly bitten by a dog. We brought him back to the house but the Indian staff screamed: 'He can't come in here.' We ignored them and called a doctor who we had to bribe before he would treat him.

Incidents such as these made me question India's spirituality. Once, after we had spent an hour with a top guru in the Krishna temple, Asha invited me to dinner, asking if I ate beef or 'a little chicken'. I was shocked, because she was supposed to be a vegetarian and had been praying with the guru, but it's considered Western to eat meat and lots of wealthy Hindus were at it. I declined her offer but realised that some Hindus are just as selective as Christians.

After that trip, I didn't see Asha for about ten years. Then Stephen took me to see her perform at Wembley Stadium in 2001. There was a brief photo call before she took to the stage and she was so rude. 'Why are you wearing that silly hat?' she asked me. 'You are so fat.' I really wanted to tell her she looked like a hag and that she was twice my size but I just walked away. I watched her perform for a while and she sounded like a sixteen-year-old. She was amazing but I was so upset by her bad manners I couldn't stay.

I came back from that second trip to India with an entirely different view of what it meant to be spiritual – or what it meant to me. I realised that you could be spiritual without being part of an organised religion. This had nothing to do with the way the devotees had behaved. In fact, I still have good friends in the movement, including John Richardson and his lovely family. John was the drummer in seventies pop group the Rubettes, and is someone I regard as truly spiritual. But if I said that to him, he would be humble and say: 'It's a work-in-progress.' People who meet John say he has great energy and that he radiates kindness.

I found it particularly hard to reconcile Indians' spirituality with their views on the gay issue, and couldn't find it in myself to see my sexuality as an affliction. The whole notion of detachment was also tough for me. How could I detach from people I loved? So what if they were going to die eventually? I know that everything is impermanent and that the material world is a rat race, but isn't it better to stay in it, to try and live a decent life and teach by example? Surely it's better to clean out a river, do charity work or support the welfare state than sit on a mountain contemplating your navel?

Of course, spirituality can become a drug in itself. After I came back I went around telling everyone they should be more enlightened, which must have pissed a lot of people off. I do feel that there is an arrogance to spirituality. Some people use it as a way of looking down on others: 'I have a hotline to God.' Can anyone take Madonna's spiritual ranting seriously? If you are truly spiritual, surely you don't need to keep telling everyone about it. If you do, perhaps it's yourself you're trying to convince. Spirituality is something you do, not something you say you do. It's all very easy to read a few books and digest ancient wisdom and take it as gospel. So much of the stuff I came across was clearly metaphorical and had no connection to the world as it is today.

There are certain eternal truths in any age, and surely the best is: 'Do unto others as you would have them do unto you.' It's fine for people to follow a spiritual path and live in ashrams but that doesn't make them better than those who choose not to. It's about how you treat others and how you carry yourself on a day-to-day basis. It's about generosity of spirit.

In my home I surround myself with various religious deities because they remind me to respect all faiths and never to be disrespectful to anyone's beliefs. I try not to blaspheme or say things that offend the faith of others. I am weirdly superstitious about people dissing God. One recent dilemma of mine was trying to find a wall space among my religious talismans for a painting I bought that had 'Fuck You, Hate You' written on it. I just couldn't have Buddha staring at it, so the painting ended up behind a door.

John Richardson told me that one of the top Krishna gurus had said I had done the movement a great service by writing 'Bow Down Mister'. Apparently I had 'served Lord Krishna well'. I was very touched by that and if that makes me superstitious, who cares? I am superstitious. Even if I don't believe everything I'm told, I discount nothing. I think those who refuse to acknowledge anything they can't prove are just as annoying as those who buy into something without question. Who does Jerry Hall think she is when she says things like 'Yoga is so over'?

To be honest, my initial interest in Krishna devotees was purely fashion-based. I was lured by the vivid colour and the ritual. The first time I visited the temple in Soho Square I felt very awkward as they banged drums, chanted and danced like lunatics. Then they unveiled deities dressed in glittering costumes that would have made Labelle proud. It was like seeing Ziggy Stardust for the first time.

To a non-believer – which I was at the time – it sounds ridiculous to bestow such value on inanimate objects, but to a devotee those statues are symbolic of something all-powerful. It's not so ridiculous when you consider how much value a fashion victim puts on the latest Marc Jacobs handbag. The human ability to place value on inanimate objects is not simply spiritual. We are all guilty of doing it, every day of our lives.

3

My God's Bigger Than Yours

You can never really win an argument with a spiritual convert because they'll always find a genius piece of doctrine – or some clever quote about 'moving into the light' – to shut you up.

I discovered this to my emotional cost a couple of years ago when I met a guy who I'll call Sexy Sage (well it does sound like a Beatles song and he definitely belonged in the Yellow Submarine). He was as fit as anything! He was so bloody handsome, physically my ideal man, and later when we talked he professed to have a deeply spiritual side.

A bunch of us went out for a drink after the shoot and somehow we gravitated towards each other. He told me he was into tantric sex, so I joked: 'How fucking selfish. Isn't that just withholding valuable fluid?', adding: 'I'm into Tantrum sex myself; when I don't get it I have a tantrum.' My irreverent attitude made him laugh and the more we talked the more it seemed we had a very similar attitude to life.

I invited him to an awards ceremony as my guest a couple of weeks later and there – despite claiming to be currently celibate – he took some woman's phone number. I was none too pleased about it and spikily said: 'It's not very polite to take somebody else's phone number when you're on a date.'

To which he replied: 'I'm not on a date.'

To be fair to Sexy Sage he told me early on he was straight, which in a sense meant that he was accepting there was some attraction.

As a measure of how whirlwind our friendship was, within two weeks of meeting him I wrote him a gushing but very honest poem about how much I adored him. It would have been the perfect time for him to run but he didn't. Around the same time he gave me a picture he'd found in India. It depicted a lion biting the genitalia of a sword-wielding deity. After he gave me the picture he kissed the palm of my hand. Not surprisingly I wondered what he was trying to tell me! When I showed it to my therapist Jamie, he said: 'This man appears to be emotionally immature. The message of the picture is that he doesn't think he can handle your emotions.'

Despite this warning, I started to see more and more of Sexy Sage. I knew he was complex but I enjoyed his company; there was so much to like about him. He had impeccable manners, and was the epitome of the perfect gentleman; he never, ever freeloaded. I'd meet him for meals all the time and speak to him constantly on the phone. There were so many danger signals in terms of where our friendship was going but we both ignored and encouraged them.

When he went on a trip to Egypt I didn't hear from him for about two weeks, which drove me insane. When he finally called I behaved like a stroppy girlfriend. He told me to chill out so I said I never wanted to speak to him again and slammed the phone down. Of course my behaviour was just an attempt to get a reaction, and it worked. He called me back and said: 'Why are you prepared to give up our friendship so easily?' After that things were much better between us, and my favourite times with him were when we were alone, whether at his flat, my place, or having dinner.

To start with I found his spiritual aspirations admirable although some of what he believed was quite fantastical. He actually said he wanted to transcend the mundane physical form and enter the astral plane. His reasons for abstaining from sexual activity were supposedly to do with preserving energy and his life force. Why was he so keen on preserving his life force if he told me he hated being alive? Sometimes he would be deeply negative, going on about how humanity is vile, and how we had fucked up the planet. It may sound shallow to say it, but I would often think: 'How can someone so handsome and sweet, with everything going for them, be on such a downer?'

Sexy Sage would claim that he enjoyed debate, but like most spiritual people, he hated to be outwitted. He was into a mixture of transcendental meditation, yoga and tantric sex, yet this was coupled with a relentless appetite for partying. Often we'd have weekend benders and I'd drag him to gay clubs like Crash and the Orange, which opens at 5 a.m. He was always cool with it.

For a few months we conducted an unconsummated, full-on romance. There were times when he held my hand and was physically affectionate, but there were always clear physical boundaries, if not emotional.

One night he came to meet me at Teatro where we all went drinking after performances of *Taboo*. At the time Mari Wilson was part of the cast and that night, royally sloshed, she announced: 'I'm really falling in love with you George.'

I heard him whisper: 'I know how you feel.'

After a night's clubbing he drove me home and proceeded to tell me about a gay experience he had when he was 18. 'I've tried it,' he said, 'and I know it's not for me.' He was trying to engage me in a conversation about it, and I, for obvious reasons, wasn't interested. He seemed aggravated that I wouldn't discuss it and as he made tea in my kitchen he kept pointing at all the pictures of men on my fridge, asking: 'Who's that? Who's that? What's his name??'

Another time he said to me: 'Why were you born a man?' I used to put that down to bad luck, but it's not really a question you can answer, is it?

Another time he said: 'The last taboo between us is sex.' As you can imagine, this behaviour aroused all my senses.

I constantly discussed my relationship with Sexy Sage during therapy, but didn't involve any of my friends. Mike Nicholls knew Sexy Sage through a mutual friend, and was probably the only person who shared my torture and joy. Mike and I have a similarly disjointed way of looking at the world, in particular sexuality. Mike was aware that the situation was making me quite deranged, but knowing me as he does, he understood that any practical advice would fall on deaf ears. I knew that my friendship with Sexy Sage would most likely end in my tears, but I'm very wilful and while there was a modicum of hope I had no interest in logic.

One night we went to Nag Nag Nag for Sexy Sage's birthday and again I became jealous because he was talking to some girl. I stormed out and went home. Sexy Sage called, said I'd ruined his birthday, and added: 'That's it.'

I immediately jumped into a cab to his flat and spent twenty minutes ringing the bell. When he finally appeared he was aggressive and cold. He accused me of having too much 'negative energy'. I was in tears and could see that he was finding it difficult to show any compassion whatsoever.

At one point he punched the wall, and suddenly I saw my father. I kept apologising and eventually he begrudgingly let me in. I sat in the kitchen alone for fifteen minutes while he pottered around and then I got up and left. For a while after that our only contact was via email. He wouldn't answer my calls apart from one time, when he said he was sorry for having misled me.

Of course, that was complete bullshit. I think Sexy Sage had bitten off more than he could chew, and in the harsh light of mundane existence his spiritual posturing was revealed as nothing more than a smokescreen.

Just before we finally fell out he mumbled something about 'needing to deal with past abuse'. I advised him to see a therapist and he did. I was the first person he called after his first session, and he was in bits. He didn't tell me exactly why he was so upset. A few days later he was like a different person, announcing arrogantly: 'I don't need to deal with the past. I don't need therapy.'

I hounded him with emails questioning his belief system, which I guess must have driven him even more nuts. It was an opportunity for me to use my gift of words and my own wealth of both spiritual experience and cynicism.

One day he turned up at my house and asked me to stop emailing him. 'What do you hope to achieve?' he asked. What I needed were answers. I couldn't understand how someone who claimed to be so enlightened couldn't rise above a problem which he had wilfully helped to create. I said: 'You've got a short memory. What about your promise that we'd be friends for life?'

The saddest thing was that this man was actually a very well-mannered, kind and considerate person. Despite the fact that he had emotional problems, he was hard to dislike in any way. I cared about Sexy Sage so deeply that I could have remained friends with him and overridden my desire for a relationship. The situation with Sexy Sage, and the disappointment I still feel, harks back to my need for resolution. However evolved you are, there are always people you cannot connect with, but when you've invested so much time and emotion in a friendship it seems odd to trash it so readily.

Just like my dad, who always talked about love, loyalty and sticking together no matter what, Sexy Sage had the patter down but couldn't deliver on his seemingly heartfelt promises. Perhaps it's foolish of me, but when somebody presents themselves as sincere, I want to believe it more than anything in the world. The sad thing is that you don't meet many people in life who are truly sincere.

When anyone tells me they are spiritual these days I immediately think: 'Show me, don't tell me.' Even the Buddha said: 'Question everything, believe nothing.' I'm more inclined to put my trust in him.

SOMEWHERE IN DALSTON

Somewhere in Dalston
He is angry
A face of rage
Punching
Yelling
Not in the least bit spiritual
Or
At one with the universe

Who is he angry at?
Himself
No
You

This stuff needs to come out
I am thinking
I am scared
Feeling rejected
He rages
'I won't put up with this bad energy'
Then don't
I say
I walk away
Sad

He dives against the elements
What is he looking for?
As he goes further down
Deeper inside
Himself
Breathing
Stretching
Absorbing ancient wisdom
Denying
Connecting
To
A
Higher power
Not
God
Something bigger
An all consuming power
With strange names
Strange rituals
Leading to inner calm
Apparently

Now
Far from peaceful
Close to tears
Refusing to express
Anything honest
He is nothing like Buddha
More like Jesus
Being crucified
He doesn't want to feel like this
Still
He does
What about friendship forever?
Love for life
Empty rhetoric
Empty words
'You read me all wrong'
He says
No
I read you all right

Sexy Sage once raged at me: 'You've only rummaged around in the spiritual drawer,' suggesting that, because he had bought into it hook, line and sinker, he was somehow more elevated.

There have been times in my life when I've found that ordinary gestures of sweetness can be the most spiritual.

For example, when my brother Gerald was arrested for the manslaughter of his wife Jill I felt that life could get no darker. When it happened I spent a few days at my family home in Woolwich. I managed to arrive before the media descended and sat taking phone calls from Gerald's ex-girlfriends. Every single one of them said to me: 'I don't get it. Gerald was never violent.' The compassion for my brother was really intense but at the time I was riddled with pain and couldn't think clearly.

When I returned to my own home in Hampstead, I found it hard to face the world. I was worried that someone might say something derogatory about Gerald. Everyone knew what had happened because it had been splashed all over the press. When I finally went to the local shops, I was treated with a politeness and compassion I didn't expect. It was then that I decided to think very carefully before making quick judgements about other people. Who knows what the grumpy lady in the newsagent's has had to deal with before coming to work? I also remember a line from a movie I saw around that time where Richard Gere says: 'Good people do some really bad things.'

I'm not suggesting I'm some super-sensitive saint, but that experience opened a window for me. I know Gerald will always suffer and live with his guilt and I wish I could do something about that. Jill's mother has been amazingly compassionate and is living proof that some people can absolutely be described as truly Christian and spiritual.

Often, one has to experience tragedy in one's life before setting off on the spiritual quest. Giving your power to an unseen force is perhaps naive but fantastically romantic. I have described my journey to India as 'a Wizard of Oz experience', because, like Dorothy, I discovered that you don't really have to leave your own backyard to find faith. That's right; I was a Judy Garland from the Shirley Temple. In fact, you don't have to go to churches, temples or even meditate. You can attain faith in Sainsbury's, trust me!

When I was coming out of my spirituality phase this mad hippie healer said to me: 'Everything that goes on outside is just a mirror of our internal world.' Sadly most humans don't develop emotionally beyond the age of seven. I wonder how much healthier the world would be if the education system added emotional intelligence to the curriculum? I also believe that teachers should be encouraged to have regular therapy themselves because many of them seem to have an unhealthy contempt for children. If you come from a home where screaming and violence is an everyday occurrence the last thing you need is more of the same. My own teachers constantly called me useless and a poof.

Therapy and spirituality can help you become more rational and overcome emotional obstacles but I don't think you can ever really change who you are. These days I am always being asked 'Are you still spiritual?'. I never know what to say. I like to think

I have faith. I like the idea of pantheism, the belief that God is in everyone and everything. Maybe God is actually the human race and the biggest mistake we have made is separating ourselves from that possibility!

When I see those stickers that read: 'When Jesus returns will you be ready?', I hope for his own sake he stays where he is. If he were to reappear he would suffer yet another crucifixion or be locked up in a madhouse.

Most of us have had our hearts broken many times but we don't give up on love. So those who say they feel God are no more lunatic than those who say they feel love. Maybe looking outside of ourselves for the answers to life's puzzles is our biggest mistake? Falling in love is the most illogical experience: you project and assume all manner of things which have no connection with reality. It's the same with religion. You hear stories about Krishna dancing on a snake in the middle of a lake, and when you're in love you often feel like you're dancing on a snake in the middle of a lake. In fact, hasn't Kate Bush written a few songs about it?

Whenever you have a relationship with God through an organised religion there are far too many conditions. We should all be able to conduct a personal and unconditional relationship with whoever we think God is. Organised religion is a brilliant means of policing society and filling people with fear. If you look at the spiritual centres of the world – India, the Middle East, Jerusalem – they are racked by conflict and violence.

I once read that to deny God's existence is just as foolish as to believe in it. As for the Devil, apart from being responsible for soft rock, he's an essential part of the human psyche – after all 'devil' is only 'lived' backwards, and 'evil' is 'live' spun on its head.

For me, God is the collective goodness of humanity, which is rarely in sync. Sometimes I wish He'd just part the clouds and scream: 'Desist!'

4

Coloured By Numbers

There are still days when I make Joan Crawford look like Mother Teresa but my life is slightly less neurotic now and I attribute that to two things: my regular therapy sessions and the feng shui system known as Nine Ki which I have followed for sixteen years. I have been in therapy for several years now and my therapist Jamie is a blessing, although sometimes I have to be reminded who the patient is. Very few people can read me as well as Jamie.

Sometimes I use my sessions to vent my spleen or I might just tell jokes. With Jamie I have genuine dialogue and he is expert at reading my body language. It's amazing how a simple body posture can speak reams. I met Jamie through a friend about a year before I actually booked my first session. Sometime in 1995, I was in a vegetarian café and we bumped into each other again. He asked: 'Aren't you the one who needs help?' and I said: 'Yesss!!!!'

I remember once quizzing Jamie on what type of therapy he practised. His reply was: 'Mainly the type that's effective.'

Therapy doesn't change who you are or the way you feel deep inside. At best it can teach you new ways to approach problems and express yourself appropriately. That's not to say that you don't lose it occasionally but it also teaches you to forgive yourself in most cases, apart from murder and gratuitous shoplifting.

Therapy is also an opportunity to talk to someone intelligent and objective. If anyone had told me ten years ago that I would end up in regular therapy sessions I'd have laughed in their face. The most powerful sessions are the ones when you think you haven't got a care in the world. That's when you end up in buckets of tears trying to piece your life back together.

I grew up in a household where only out-of-control emotions were ever expressed. Real problems were suppressed or dealt with within the family, which meant they were never dealt with!

One of the most confusing pieces of advice Jamie ever gave me was: 'Go out there and get your heart broken.' After Jon Moss, my longest love affair was with drugs and I had taken myself off the relationship market. I was terrified of being rejected and hurt, and yet all I could talk about was the desire to be loved. Jamie was trying to explain that rejection, however painful, was part of the process. Believe me, I've read all the books: *Feel the Fear and Do It Anyway*, *The Road Less Travelled*, the lot. People can put their belief into any of the theories, but, like religion, I think belief is a poor substitute for thinking and talking.

I wouldn't call myself religious, although I don't think you can ever escape the religious convictions passed on by your parents. My mother and father were always described in the press as 'staunch Catholics'. Mum would often take us to church when we were very young, and all of us kids went to Sunday school, but it was a way of getting us from under her feet. Mum and Dad were hardly strict about us practising our faith.

Maybe having six kids to feed took precedence over faith, or maybe it was because, like a lot of people, they lost respect for the Church, as more of its indiscretions were made public. After my mother's mother passed away I discovered the horrors of her teenage years in a strict Irish convent. If she wet the bed she would be made to wear the wet sheet for the entire day and they were regularly made to feel disgusted with their femininity.

My ex-boyfriend Michael was raised by the Christian Brothers in Ireland and suffered physical and mental abuse. That high-handed morality often creates the very thing it seeks to eradicate. Those who are the most disgusted by sex are often the ones who are the most consumed by it.

I'm not suggesting that my parents were disgusted by sex, but from the little my mother has told me it was more dutiful than sensual. In fact, that was one of the things which ended their marriage. One day my mother woke up and decided she had had enough and moved into a separate room.

My parents never talked about sex even though they clearly had plenty of it. We were never told we would go blind if we masturbated and it's not as though we were raised in a Dickensian atmosphere, but there were no open expressions of affection. I remember when, at sixteen, I kissed my mum on the cheek, she asked: 'Who've you been hanging out with?'

Earlier, at the age of eleven, I found a porno mag in a skip and hid it under the living-room sofa. My dad found it, and rather than have an intelligent discussion about it, he ridiculed me in front of a room full of people. The refusal to sit down and talk sensibly about these issues has left me with all kinds of obsessions about sex. If sex is only ever portrayed as a sordid or embarrassing subject, one tends to separate it from love.

Like most males, if I'm in a relationship and my partner doesn't want to have sex four times a day I take it very personally. I've had to learn to be affectionate with my partners without expecting it to spiral into frenzied fornication. This issue is magnified in gay relationships not only because of the levels of testosterone involved but because gay men tend to have no emotional education whatsoever. Most of us discover ourselves through sexual activity, which is why there is so much emphasis on it in the gay community.

Our society accepts in principle that one in ten are gay, and yet even in this so-called liberated age there is no acknowledgement or preparation. If a parent knows their child is going to be disabled, essential arrangements are made. I don't believe anybody is born with a defined sexuality, but perhaps some children have more of a propensity for homosexuality. Heaven forbid that should be encouraged in any way whatsoever!

That's why the current debate about gay marriages is so ridiculous. There is no emotional infrastructure and yet gay men and women are expected to slip into matrimony with ease. Obviously some couples are successful but society makes it difficult.

As a teenager if anyone touched me I would be defensive. 'Get off me!' I'd yell. After all, what was the point of physical contact if there was no sexual intent?

If the average man thinks about sex six times a minute, I think about sex six times a second! Ironic when you think about how I've been portrayed . . .

Of course nothing matches my romantic libido. I can be terribly cynical about love but I am also mindlessly optimistic and stupidly romantic. In relationships I also take solace and direction from Nine Ki. It's a physical form of feng shui, the art of designing and arranging your living and workspace to allow good energy to flow with ease.

The Chinese and Japanese will not erect a building without consulting a feng shui expert. A large bank was once erected in Hong Kong but it was discovered that it blocked the flight path of a dragon and part of the building had to be restructured. If you are laughing at this point, stop and ask yourself how much Western mythology you embrace.

I discovered Nine Ki after a chance meeting with a woman called Dragana Brown and her partner Simon, who are now very close and dear friends of mine. Drags, as I call her, worked at one time in a French eatery called Richoux near my manager's office. We used to have band meetings there and it was very eighties, the type of place where Joan Collins would lunch after sauntering straight past the queue as if she was still on the set of *Dynasty*.

I had just started eating macrobiotic food and would often have lunch at the East West Centre, which Dragana was also managing. Drags and Simon were writing for a macrobiotic magazine and asked if they could interview me. When we got together I started interviewing them. I discovered that Simon was a shiatsu masseur and booked a session. When I found out that they practised Nine Ki I was really fascinated. At the time I was travelling so much that I was worn out mentally and physically. Drags explained that our bodies weren't designed to be flying around in aircraft and that endless travel had a serious kinetic effect.

Nine Ki dictates that you have a set of three numbers based on your birth date. Mine are 317. These numbers simply relate to the year, month and day you were born and explain different aspects of your character. They also tell you which emotional energy dictates a particular day, month or year.

We often find ourselves attracted to people who are wrong for us in much the same way we crave food that is bad. Using Nine Ki you can work out how best to communicate with a partner or even to end a relationship. Of course, I've never used it in that way because I hold on fast no matter what the forecast!

When I first got into Nine Ki, I was with Michael and discovered that our zero communication was because our emotional Nine Ki numbers were at odds, as well as our earth elements. One of my earth elements is water and one of his is fire. What does water do to fire? Extinguishes it. He was always saying: 'You think you're better than me!' And all I'd done was ask him to wash up!

Even knowing we were crap at communicating I couldn't let Michael go. In a way we had a parent/child relationship. I was trying to be the father neither of us ever had, and I was also the only person who cared for him no matter what he did. When he was heavily into drugs – for the last couple of years of our relationship – he treated me terribly and yet I always knew his behaviour was not malicious, but a cry for help, and that he was a good person.

Nine Ki makes absolute sense to me. You can't separate the way you feel emotionally from your physical well-being. People often talk about their emotions as though they are kept in a separate battery pack, to be switched on at will. It's the same with sexual energy. I love it when people say: 'I feel absolutely nothing,' which is an impossibility. Mum has a great line which was always directed at me: 'You could cause trouble in an empty house.'

On that same subject, if my mum was in a bad mood when I was a kid, I could feel it as soon as I opened the front door. Her sadness would permeate the entire house. That's another reason why I don't underestimate the power of energy. I consult with Drags and Simon whenever I'm about to make a long journey. They tell me whether the direction is good, neutral or dangerous in terms of the energy. It has no bearing on how you travel, whether you fly, sail, walk or roller-skate, but if you continually move in bad directions you can build up a surplus of negative energy, which then has a physical impact. It can also make you accident-prone.

Drags said about this guy I dated briefly called Jeff that he was in a low-energy year and that he should improve his diet – and stop snorting cocaine. When I told him, he wasn't particularly impressed. The next time I spoke to him he had his leg in a cast after being hit by a car.

My interest in Nine Ki drives my management to the brink of insanity. I am constantly turning down lucrative offers because the travel direction has the wrong energy. I've even flown in different directions from the rest of the band on tour, via other countries, to get to the same destination. My manager Tony still thinks it's ridiculous, but then he doesn't eat pork because he's Jewish. I don't eat pork because it's cruel. Surely that's a more reasonable position to take?

Now I have a system that makes me focus on the finer things in life, because there is an invisible energy which runs throughout the universe; through your body, the food you eat, your home, your workplace and the air that surrounds you. It's readily accepted in the East, known as ki in Japan, chi in China and prana in India.

All of us, whether we relate it to energy or not, have days when we wake up and the world seems completely on our side. Then there are days when it seems that nothing can go right. There are also certain years when we feel more insecure, have lower energy and can't work out why. Equally, there are years when we are on top of everything and can do no wrong.

Western astrology can also be used to explain these natural patterns. I believe astrology to be very accurate and people are often exactly like their birth signs. I am completely a Gemini:

> Roses are red,
> Violets are blue,
> I'm schizophrenic,
> And so am I.

Those who write off astrology as rubbish often do so because their star sign has rendered them deeply cynical and far too practical. You might also find that these people are often useless at expressing emotion and prone to be black and white about most things. Usually they're called Aquarians or Virgos. Jon Moss, a staunch Virgo, calls therapists 'the rapists'.

The black American folk singer Richie Havens has a great song about the entire horoscope, detailing the traits and the energies which occur with each star sign:

Gemini, who is… I think, I think, I think so much I wish I
   could stop thinking;
Cancer, who is… I feel, I feel, and there are no words that
   describe how I feel, ever;

Nine Ki has slowed everything in my life down and it means that journeys have to be planned. I won't just jump on a plane because someone offers me a fortune. If a DJ gig or a tour are offered and they do not fit with my Nine Ki, I just wait for another offer. In most cases something always comes along to replace work I have turned down.

Nine Ki also suits me because I am not really driven by money so it allows me to choose work carefully. Even though I am basically self-employed I have a manager and agents and it is in their interest to keep me working. I am conscious that I have obligations to those who earn a living from the work I do, but if I surrendered to the amount of work I am offered I would have no life. Even if Nine Ki turns out to be total hocus-pocus, it has been beneficial by removing a lot of stress from my life.

There are a lot of insights to be gained from the particular set of numbers each person possesses. Madonna, for instance, is a 683, a powerful combination which goes some way to explaining why she seems unstoppable. There's no coincidence that Michael Jackson, who was born just 12 days after her, is also a 683.

I can't think why it springs to mind but the line from the John Lennon song 'Across the Universe' – 'Somebody up there likes me' – seems appropriate for Madge. Before your hackles rise, I'm not about to tear her to shreds or suggest she has no talent. If anything, Madonna is in league with the planets and has an abundance of powerful energy on her side. Her Nine Ki numbers indicate that she is quite sure about what she wants and will rarely stop until she gets her way.

Madonna is not really an artist in the same way as Prince or Joni Mitchell are. She is a triumph of marketing. Perhaps that is a stroke of genius in itself? People always say she's a brilliant businesswoman, but trust me, at that level of income she hardly does her own accounts. Her great achievement is staying successful to the point where even the worst failure could not dampen her legacy. She has survived more assassination attempts on her career than any other living pop artist. Regardless of whether she touches any of the truly great performers, she will be remembered like a Sinatra.

I have always found Madonna fascinating but I'm not one of those people who respect success for the sake of it. Why should I? Arms dealers and warlords accumulate fortunes but I don't respect them. I am more inclined to respect someone for having great ideas, for challenging ignorance or for stirring up real emotion. If Nina Simone had never written another song after 'Mississippi Goddam' or 'Four Women' it wouldn't have taken away the timeless genius of those masterpieces and if Lou Reed had only recorded 'Walk on the Wild Side', he would still be remembered for capturing a huge, glittering moment.

For young girls coming of age in the eighties Madonna represented a new type of female power. Some even regard her as one of the great feminists. She was, for many, a ballsy chick who was in control of her life and made her own rules. Maybe that's how she was sold to us, but therapy has taught me to recognise that she was actually an abandoned little girl who wanted to be loved. I wonder if getting so much love from her many fans, however lacking in true intimacy, has made her take it for granted?

I once heard a phone message that Madonna left this PR friend of mine who'd made the mistake of gossiping about Madonna's personal business. It was pure Joan Crawford. I tried to get a copy to make a dance track out of it, but Madonna caught wind of that and her manager called my manager and the whole joke became drama on toast.

I thought it was amazing that someone who protects her public image so fiercely would leave a message like that on an answerphone in Kilburn! It reminded me of the time I rang photographer Steven Meisel and threatened to smash his face in after some horrible photos he'd taken of me were printed in an Italian fashion magazine. He had promised those shots would be destroyed and had taken others that I loved. I played a bit of 'Do You Really Want to Hurt Me?' on Meisel's answerphone along with an angry message. I encountered him at a fashion show about a year later and he scarpered as soon as he saw me. By that point I was well over the drama and I ended up buying one of his photographs at an Aids fund-raiser, which he personally signed for me. So I guess we are friends again!

Those who crave fame are actually just desperate to be loved. Often they are so wounded that only the adoration of millions will ever convince them that they are worthy of love. The first time you are greeted by screaming fans the adrenalin rush is quite spectacular. The trouble only starts when you actually start believing it is real.

The world of rock 'n' roll and pop is a fantasy realm where you can be anything you want to be. It is a world of illusion, a place where reality and fantasy are blurred, where you can live in huge theme parks with monkeys and llamas. So Madonna's Nine Ki energy has made her a living, breathing cash register. If one of her albums sells 20 million copies and the next only sells 10 million, the public or the record company – and maybe even Madonna herself – may consider it to be bad news, but that's only because the type of success she aspires to is all about eclipsing itself.

When she published her book *Sex* in the early nineties I was asked for a quote by an American journalist. I said: 'The only thing left for Madonna to really do now is have a baby and find God.'

Either Madonna is very predictable, or I'm a closet mystic.

You decide.

5

Disco Monster Terrorist

At one point in the nineties I became better known as a DJ than as a singer, but few people on the dance scene knew that I actually started playing records with my friend Jeremy Healy way back when I was seventeen.

Freaks were low on the ground in my area and I first spotted the young Jeremy Healy bounding off a bus in his school uniform, set off rather nicely by a pair of thick-heeled sky-blue brothel creepers. I somehow knew we would meet again and sure enough we did.

And when we DJed together in 1979 at Philip Sallon's first club Planets in Piccadilly, it was – like most of my career moves – accidental. Philip only owned two records: *The Sound of Music* and something by the Beatles. Jeremy and I were the only people he knew that had record collections so we were given the job. There were no mixing skills required back then and often we were so drunk we'd forget the record had ended. One of the reasons we wanted to DJ was that the booth was raised, so we were up above everybody, the freaks in the pulpit. Later, in the mid-eighties I bought some decks, mainly because it was the trendy thing to do, and they were untouched for ages. Then, when I got involved in the early acid house scene in 1987/8, Jeremy was already a full-blown DJ, giving me mix tapes of music all the time. Back then he was really experimental and would mix all sorts of mental stuff together, rather like the music he does for John Galliano's Dior shows these days.

One night I was at a big rave party called Pushca and for some reason the promoters Debbie and Rick decided to chuck on a cassette tape in the chill-out room. Everyone was bored of hearing the same songs looped over and over so I complained and said: 'Why don't you get a DJ to play some old house and pop?' Debbie and Rick offered me the job. I was paid £300, my cab fare and all the drink I could consume, which was great because I was so nervous.

One night at Pushca I dropped 'Islands in the Stream' by Dolly Parton and Kenny Rogers for the fun of it and George Michael rushed on to the dance floor and started swinging his arms in the air like a madman (or madwoman).

Playing Pushca's back room was like going back to what I did at Planets. I'd jump around from early house such as Mr Fingers' 'Can You Feel It?' to 'Devil Woman' by Cliff Richard. It was really the start of the trash DJ vibe, where anything goes. In the early days I'd get fans coming to clubs who weren't into dance music and thought that I was going to sing 'Karma Chameleon'. It was always a bit of a battle to shake them off. Then I'd get the clever dicks asking for Culture Club tunes just to piss me off. I'd tell them: 'Sorry, I've only got the jungle remix of "Victims".' After a while I became accepted as a DJ and my spinning career really took off. I still get people turning up with old Culture Club albums and books at gigs but that's mainly in America, where they think my career ended after 'Karma Chameleon'.

Some people don't understand that DJing is a job and that you can't have a full-on discussion with them while you're working. I know people mean well but there is a familiar pattern that starts with: 'I just wanted to shake your hand and thank you for all the great music you've made.' Before I have a chance to say 'Thank you', they embark on a Magna Carta-style tale of how, when they were sixteen, they dressed up as me at a fancy dress party and won. Or they'll announce excitedly: 'I used to dress like you in the eighties.' To which I now reply: 'So did I, funnily enough.'

It's a bit like me telling Bowie that when I was sixteen my aunt Jan cut my hair like his but it went wrong and I looked like Dave Hill from Slade. I'm sure he'd be deeply riveted and tell me about the time he smudged his eyeliner backstage at the Hammersmith Odeon.

Despite the relentless aggravation DJing has provided not only a second career but a whole host of adventures. In the early days I certainly didn't think of it as a career. A whole bunch of us went to clubs together and when I started playing it provided jobs for everyone. Andria Law, who runs my DJ agency Red Parrot, had once done club promotions for More Protein, so when the bookings kicked in it seemed sensible to get her involved.

She had already started the agency before I came along and it was good to be working with friends like her and Johnston Walker, who was another die-hard clubber.

They still run Red Parrot and are like a comedy team. Andrea runs on Jamaican-cum-Spanish time while Johnston is the absolute opposite, punctual and terrifyingly caustic when things don't go to plan. If Johnston feels that a promoter isn't treating his DJs well, he will let them know in no uncertain terms and usually carries the rant all the way home on the motorway.

Our yearly trips to Ibiza are always entertaining. Not only does Johnston hate Spanish food but he's none too fond of their manana approach. If he's not berating them about the terrible food he's on to the Germans and their towels on the beach at 5.30 a.m.

Andrea and Johnston are always threatening to terminate their working relationship but they're like a joyously dysfunctional married couple.

By the early nineties super-clubs like the Ministry of Sound were in full swing and a residency there led to loads of successful mix albums. With Pete Tong of Radio One I sold millions of dance compilations, which heightened my DJ profile even more and secured heaps of international work. Pete and I had the biggest-selling dance compilation ever with *Annual 1* so the timing was perfect for me.

At the time I was working everywhere; Ibiza, the south of

France, Budapest, China, all round the world. I once played for a crowd of 50,000 in America, and also at all the big gay circuit parties, big drug-fuelled festivals for Muscle Marys. (For those who don't know, a Muscle Mary is a gay man who divides his time between the gym and the sugaring parlour, and, in an attempt to look like a construction worker, ends up looking like Jayne Mansfield.)

I was being offered absolutely ridiculous money for these gigs. I once DJed a rock festival in Denmark where I was on for twenty-five minutes between two bands, for which I was paid £25,000. Thank God I took along my Marilyn Manson and seventies records because that's all they wanted to hear.

One of my funniest DJ memories was playing the Fifty Years of Pizza Hut party with Seb Fontaine. The promoter asked for a house set, but something told me to bring my box of vintage records. When I arrived the dance floor was empty and Seb was looking rather perturbed. As soon as I dropped 'Dancing Queen' by Abba the dance floor was awash with taffeta ball gowns. Seb shook his head and said: 'You crafty bastard.'

Corporate gigs pay very well but they're no fun because anyone can play a bunch of old pop classics. Another time I was offered £50,000 and asked my agent: 'Are you sure they don't want me to take my clothes off as well?' However, I did the gig and retained my dignity.

I worked for Versace for a number of years. My first gig was for the man himself shortly before his death. Up until that point the soundtrack to his shows were Elton John or Queen albums. I sent him a CD where I'd mixed Pavarotti singing 'Nessum Dorma' over breakbeats along with an assortment of camp dance records. He was absolutely amazed and the show itself was fantastic. His shows were always glamorous, with glass catwalks and diamanté strung all over the floor, but this time the music matched the camp of the occasion.

When Donatella took over after Gianni's sad death she always had strong ideas about the sound. One time she was very stuck on this tune by Fatboy Slim with the radio-friendly title 'Fatboy Slim is Fucking in Heaven'. I went backstage to say hi and she emerged from her opulent Winnebago singing the words in her guttural Italian tones: 'Vat Boy Sleem ees faakin' een hea-ven . . .' It was a moment of high camp, to say the least. At that same show Elton John casually slipped her a watch completely studded with diamonds. Apparently it was for the beach. Nothing about the Versace experience was ever cheap.

Of course, there is a pecking order for celebrities at the after-show parties. If Cameron Diaz or Madonna were in attendance I'd always be shoved to a side table. Actually, I prefer the voyeuristic experience. One time both Prince and Madonna were invited and they circled the block in their limos for twenty minutes because neither wanted to be the first to arrive.

Once, I was summoned to meet Prince and endured the most embarrassing experience of my entire life. He complimented me on my earrings and not another word was spoken to anyone for a painful ten minutes. All the other guests were Italian, adding to the communication barrier. It was as if Prince was trying to intimidate through silence. Luckily a plate of carbonara arrived and Prince proceeded to fork-feed his glamorous wife Mayte. I used this as my excuse to escape and ran into the toilets screaming. It was especially upsetting because I regard him as a complete genius and I was praying that the rumours of his aloofness would be unfounded.

Working with the Ministry of Sound was great; it heightened my profile and I made a lot of money out of advances from record sales. Yet there was always a compromise: they would persuade me to put the big hit dance tunes on the compilations and I could add unknown or underground tracks which I loved and which helped to promote friends' records. It was a system that worked really well for a while, though it did get me pigeon-holed as a handbag house DJ, a term used to describe anyone who plays safe popular music. I've never done that. Even the dance music I made under the guise of Jesus Loves You was never by the book.

I reached a stage where I was having to compromise more and more on the Ministry compilations, then one night in 1996, I was attacked by the Ministry's security guards outside the club. Even though I was wearing an Access All Areas pass, they had insisted on pushing me to the back of the queue and made my girlfriend join a separate girls' line. I joked: 'Where are we, fucking Mecca?' The bouncer told me to shut up and I told him to fuck off. Next thing I knew I was on the ground being throttled, staring up at a huge poster for the *Annual 1* compilation I'd made with Pete Tong. Luckily a raging drag queen jumped on the bouncer's back, screaming: 'Let go of her! Leave her alone!' Just another reason why I'll always love drag queens.

I called the police but guess what? The exterior security cameras, which were supposed to be on twenty-four hours a day, didn't manage to pick up on what happened and the story emerged that the tape had been lost.

Funny that.

I was scheduled to record a new mix album for the Ministry the following week and obviously I refused to do it, not only because of the way I'd been treated, but also because the Ministry's manager Mark Rydell described me as 'a crap DJ' on national radio reports about the attack. He also said the Ministry had already employed Judge Jules as my replacement and that they were going to sue me for £25,000 for the artwork already prepared for the album.

My lawyer promptly checked the contract and discovered that they had to give me ten days' notice before employing another DJ, and were therefore in breach. All of a sudden it was worked out amicably. I was given more points and extra money and the album was delivered and released.

There was even a photo session with bouncers carrying me back into the club on a throne. But after that album my contract wasn't renewed and I was replaced by the more trendy Tall Paul. The Ministry is a very mercenary organisation and I realised that it was nothing personal, just business.

The whole super-club phenomenon has tailed off, and most of the big DJs of that era – like Paul Oakenfold and Sasha – are concentrating on America. When places like Gatecrasher and Cream opened, the dance-music scene lost the eclectic quality which was most exciting about acid house. The audience had become much bigger and started to dictate what was played by DJs.

On top of that all sorts of genres were created – trance, progressive, tribal and, worst of all, hard house, basically gay disco with a rocket up its arse for white boys who can't dance.

Crowds only wanted to hear things they knew; in the same way that a band moving from cult status to mainstream success often loses its edge, dance music became pedestrian. Who can forget the stream of appalling European dance records which clogged up the charts in the nineties? Pounding DIY rhythms with weak-voiced anaemic white girl vocals singing about trance stations, castles in the sky and other ridiculi.

I'd get kids coming up to me during a set and asking: 'Have you got anything we can dance to?' I'd say: 'It's not my fault you're a white boy who hasn't discovered his hips.'

The other cliché was: 'Have you got anything harder?' To which I'd reply: 'Wait till I've finished playing.' Jon of the Pleased Wimmin always had the best retorts. When asked if he had a particular track, he'd respond: 'No, but I've got herpes.' One time I was playing Manchester's Hacienda and did a car-crash mix. I had to duck down behind the decks in shame. Jon said: 'Well, at least they know you're here.'

I wrote a song about the state of dance culture called 'Sanitised' after a particularly horrible gig in Peterborough. It just seemed to be such a waste of energy and time. Dance music has become so bloated and corporate that now it's all about thugs with their shirts off who don't get it. They're not into funk or anything remotely sexy, just hard, relentless thud.

'Sanitised' starts with the declaration:

All you white boy-Kentucky-Fried-McDonald's-chomping-
    can't-take-the-bass,
can't-wind-your-waist motherfuckers,
I am not the resident,
My name is not DJ Give 'Em What They Want . . .

The dance scene in England is run by three people, one of whom is Pete Tong, who for years worked for a record company while having a national radio show. The stranglehold Radio One has over dance and pop music would be tantamount to insider trading in another industry. If you did what they do on the Stock Exchange you'd be behind bars.

But now the days of those DJ mega-gigs are over. I continue to work all the time, but it's never been about the money for me. I love clubs and I get to meet interesting people – and the occasional cute boy. There is also something appealing about being part of an interesting culture that is always contemporary and fast-moving. This feeds the other parts of my career. After all, the majority of my life has been spent in clubs.

For years I didn't get gay club bookings because, number one, they hate paying, and two, it's very cliquey. I didn't have an issue with playing the gay scene but no one wanted me because I don't play US funky disco. Most DJs tend to stick to a rigid style and I jump all over the place.

My saviour arrived in the form of Wayne Shires, who promotes London's hardcore gay club Crash. He took a risk booking me a couple of years ago, and hey presto! I'm playing for queers. I really hope we are entering a period of more eclectic dance music because the boys are much nicer on the straight scene, and they give me more attention!

These days I DJ regularly at gay nights such as Crash and Kinky Trade in London or Beige and Plaid in New York, not only because of the moribund state of dance culture but also because I've spent the last nine years travelling all over the world and I really just want to play more wherever I'm based.

DJing in America is very different. Even though dance music started in the States it has never taken hold like it has in England. One of the reasons is that there is an apartheid on youth in America. You need to be twenty-one to get into a club and that's why I attract old Culture Club fans to DJ gigs. You need a young enthusiastic crowd for a scene to thrive. My favourite gigs recently have been in Canada where you can get into clubs at nineteen; the difference is phenomenal.

In the UK I get kids saying 'My mum loves you', but they're not shoving copies of *Colour by Numbers* in my face. I don't want to be mean to those that supported me in the eighties but there's no point in coming to a dance club if you're not into the music.

It's virtually impossible to get hardcore dance music played on American radio stations, although there are specialist shows. Usually DJs have to blend the underground stuff with remixes of Mariah Carey and Missy Elliot. I suspect this harks back to the disco explosion in the seventies when people burned records in stadiums and wore badges saying 'Disco Sucks'.

Even punk began in New York but it took the British to exploit its potential and by the time it arrived back in America it had become watered down as new wave. You can buy a gun and join the army with ease but you're not allowed to go out and get bombed and dance at the time in your life when you really feel like it. It makes no sense that the American music industry ignores the commercial potential of dance. One imagines it's because there's much more money to be made out of traditional bands who can sell out stadiums and sell out to Coca-Cola.

Being a DJ has kept my ear to the ground in terms of new ideas. When you're in a successful band you tend to lose touch with what's going on. Once I started DJing a lot of records come to my attention which I wouldn't normally have heard. Also, if you want to avoid the obvious you start building up a catalogue of interesting music which then feeds you musically.

The only DJ gig I've thoroughly enjoyed in the last couple of years was Future Funk in North Wales. Any club with the word 'funk' in the title makes me comfortable because you know that people want to hear bass, and that makes my job more satisfying.

I don't think that my sets are too incongruous, although one review by an American dance journalist accused me of having no style. Maybe I should call myself DJ No Style? Getting it wrong is sometimes part of the fun. I'm not interested in listening to a DJ who has planned every element of their set to the last beat.

My favourite time for dance music was when Jeremy Healy was playing London's Subterania in the mid-eighties. He would drop Bob Marley's 'Could You Be Loved' right in the middle of a house set, which would set the place on fire. It's not as though my sets consist of Indian wedding bands over drum 'n' bass but I do play music I love regardless of genre. After all, DJ decks were created to allow mixing of all sorts of tempos.

On the whole, the dance press is dismissive of me – that's why they didn't come to see *Taboo*, let alone review it, which is weird when you think that it's all about the roots of clubbing. Dance music is the bastard child of the early electro played at eighties clubs like Blitz. The cool references for all those early Detroit house DJs are bands like Depeche Mode and Human League.

Certain dance magazines are always making pointless digs at me, despite the fact that I was clubbing before they were in Pampers. Last year one included me in the 'down' part of their barometer, saying: 'George's hats: Did we fight the acid wars for this?'

Most of them weren't even around when acid house started, so what was that about, space filler? I rang *Muzik* magazine and left one of my classic messages, including the line: 'If you write any more shit about me I'm going to come in and fuck your editor up the arse.' They ran most of it – except for the buggery bit – on their letters page with the comment: 'Be careful, George, or else you might really be a man with convictions.' And they're supposed to be cool. If they'd done their homework they'd have known I've already got two.

I've found my peers in the dance world are about as supportive as the ground after a major earthquake. I recently had a top five record in the dance chart with a track called 'The Psychology of the Dreamer', a collaboration with my friend Eddie Lock. There wasn't one lousy spin on Pete Tong's very important and powerful radio show and no interest from any of the dance rags. When Eddie went to Ibiza at the beginning of the season, a top radio producer confided: 'It's a great record but you've got zero chance getting it played with him on it.' So, when I am asked to collaborate with other artists, a part of me feels like telling them: 'Don't, I'm the kiss of pop death.'

Even Judge Jules had to gingerly slip 'Out of Fashion', the track I made with him, on to his Radio One playlist when it came out as a single last year, for fear of upsetting his bosses at the station.

And I had to commission my own mixes of 'Out of Fashion' to play in places like Crash.

The dance journalist Gavin Herlihey wrote that 'Out of Fashion' was 'bland' but then at the bottom of his review selected it as a standout track. Make your bloody mind up!

In the same issue he raved about Madonna's latest album *American Life*, describing it as 'brave'. If doing Pilates and drinking soy lattes is Madonna's idea of soul-searching, she needs to escape from her bodyguards more often. A measure of how bad things are in dance music is the fact that they are kissing the arses of those that have done the least for it, though Madonna is perhaps the exception because she has always understood the power of a groove.

Last year I played at the Dance Star Awards in Miami, where Paris Stilton (sorry, Hilton) was presented with the best celebrity DJ award. She simpered: 'I don't play clubs, just house parties.' By this I assume she slips on a Justin Timberlake CD.

Afterwards, Wigstock legend and world-class DJ Lady Bunny flounced onstage and couldn't help commenting that this was a direct insult to all the DJs who have spent years honing their craft. It was jaw-dropping to hear Lady Bunny be serious, but if the state of dance culture can make Bunny rein in her stratospherically vile wit we know we're in deep trouble.

6

U Can Never B 2 Straight

In gay circles there is a phrase which I abhor: 'Straight-acting, non-scene.' I personally prefer 'straight-acting, if non-seen'. The term refers to gay men who can successfully pass themselves off as heterosexuals and choose not to frequent gay venues. In their attempt to slip through the pink net they are in fact the queerest of the queer; they can pretend to be one of your mates without creating alarm, all the while wondering how to get into your trousers.

Throughout history gay men have acted and dressed in the masculine drag of the time to disguise their bent. Some periods have been more successful than others. In the seventies masculinity went a bit Googie Withers, with all the unisex garb and coiffured hairstyles, and yet it was still quite easy to tell who was straight and who was 'embarrassingly fashionable'.

It's only recently that gay men have successfully pulled off the trick of appearing hetero-exceptional. Straight men seem to have hijacked camp (apart from the final frontier: drag).

These days straight boys are afforded the luxury of adoring themselves in a way that was never possible in the past. I find it highly amusing to walk past a building site and see the name of a gay designer hugging the hips of a hod carrier; a stroke of genius that queer designers have infiltrated the area of the male anatomy that straight men are the most sensitive about, and most keen to protect.

You couldn't imagine Kevin Keegan sporting an Alice band in the seventies, but the last time I was in Ibiza it was the hetero guys wearing the sheer shirts and cockatoo haircuts while the gay men looked as if they'd come to fix your radiators.

A great example of this gender twist is the success of *Queer Eye for the Straight Guy*. We're fooled into believing we have four very individual gay men who represent a fabulously wide demographic, when in fact they're all poncey poofs into theatre and soft furnishings. The only shocking difference is that one has a bit more gel in his hair and those headphones slung round his neck (ooh, the urban touch). In my opinion the Village People were a far more authentic representation of gay culture.

Another thing about *Queer Eye* is that it presents gay men as non-threatening and, more importantly, non-sexual. The kind of queers you could safely leave your straight boyfriend with. It is noticeable that the guests are never too sexy and that there are no deliberate sexual overtones.

There should be no rules about how a gay man acts or dresses, but the desire to appear straight stinks of self-enforced homophobia. If you question a gay man who chooses to pass as a non-homo they will tell you they are 'just being normal'. But being normal is an act in itself, so the whole thing is cock-eyed. Generally, those types of gay men are the first to sneer at drag queens and obvious screamers, because they feel we are threatening their pathetic bid for assimilation. This goes right back to the days when Quentin Crisp was greeted at a gay bar in the forties with the line: 'Did anyone see you come in? Make sure no one sees you leave.'

Most gay contact ads require potential suitors to conform to these stereotypes and gay Internet dating sites seem to be full of queer-hating queers who don't want to be reminded of what they are. Excuse me, but what's so straight-acting about sucking a dick or having a cock up your arse? It makes no difference whether you're wearing marabou-trimmed slingbacks or a Hackett shirt.

The modern homosexual may yet prove to be the ultimate

threat to straight society, because at some point it will become impossible to distinguish one from the other, if it isn't already. You might say this is a good thing but you have to question why people are so keen to assimilate.

If you think that, by passing yourself off as 'normal' you will ease your passage (forgive the pun) through life, you're mistaken. You can't remove the sexual difference by modelling yourself on heterosexuals any more than you can understand what it's like to be pregnant by sticking a cushion up your jumper. You must remember that I don't actually think that terms like 'gay' or 'straight' mean very much or explain anything. I reckon we are all made up of equal parts of Rambo and Lucille Ball.

Homophobia is itself a form of self-hatred because it is a projection, based on the very real fear that somewhere inside the aggressor is a dormant nelly. When a homophobe attacks a gay man he is essentially trying to destroy the part of himself that he can't console, giving way to the social pressure to comply with preconceived notions of what it means to be masculine.

So many boys have lousy role models in their fathers. The most they learn is that the essential male attributes are aggression and a void of emotion.

It's interesting that gay men who outwardly act 'straight' are often the most voracious; so much of their time is dedicated to cock-sucking, mutual wanking and other forms of 'no-strings' sex. In private they personify the clichés, and yet they could prop up the bar in the roughest pub.

Their lives are ruled by their sexuality.

When I was a kid I hated football because it represented the last bastion of utterly straight behaviour. These days it is recognised that a significant proportion of soccer fans are gay, watching the big game in the local pub, going to matches and forming teams to play in the Sunday League.

Beckham may have opened the floodgates and suffered ridicule for his sins, but he was clearly on to something. Even the commentators are now spruced and styled in designer gear, as if to acknowledge this multisexual new audience. Many footballers have accepted that they are now objects of sexual desire to both men and women. Freddie Ljundberg stripped down to his undies to model for Calvin Klein and was a cover star for *Out* magazine in the US.

Even rugby has got in on the act. Now the gay audience has been provided with a mud-stud in the compact form of Jonny Wilkinson, who has been the focal point of a recent Hackett campaign.

Go to any gay pub and you'll see as many Hackett shirts as you'll see at Twickenham.

I think it's safe to suggest that straight is, in fact, the new gay.

A recent edition of *Attitude* magazine contained a poll of the UK's most influential homosexuals, many of whom revelled in the fact that these days you can be 'gay and normal'. Sorry for being perverse but I say: *Vive la différence*. I don't want to be assimilated to the extent that my bedroom habits are the only thing which separates me from the rest of humanity.

Just because a few queers appear on TV and we have more clubs, pubs, bars, sugaring parlours, shops, cropped tops and Will Young, don't think that suburban families are sitting down to dinner and debating whether Will is a top or a bottom.

For me, the sexual mechanisms of gay culture are the real stand-off. In a nutshell the issue is: cocks up arses. Straight people always think of gay men or women in a sexual context but they don't really want to get into the finer details. We have a community which moans about Peter Tatchell but will queue round the block to squeal along to Steps. Despite greater gay visibility, I don't believe the world has changed very much. Homophobia is like apartheid; in South Africa, it's not supposed to exist any more, but life there is still pretty much the same – the racism is as hideous as it ever was. Similarly, you can create laws to protect gays from violence and homophobia but you can't legislate straight people's emotions. The fact is that straight society is still fearful of gay culture and gay culture is constantly trying to appease that fear. When the age of consent for homosexuals was lowered to sixteen the prevailing panic was that gay men would be lurking outside school gates.

During the Clause 28 furore the Tory government cleverly

adopted the term 'promoting homosexuality', based on the nefarious suggestion that open discussion equals encouragement. Plenty of people are brought up with staunch religious ideas which they reject. Forcing somebody to read the Bible doesn't turn them Christian, or even into a Cliff Richard fan. Nearly all homosexuals are raised in heterosexual environments, so something ain't working.

The whole 'straight-acting' business is strange for me because I have always received more attention from straight men than gay men. Mind you, I have an uncanny knack for sniffing them out. My policy is to assume that everyone is a bit gay and work from there. When I DJed at the Sydney Gay Mardi Gras a couple of years ago, I managed to find the only straight guy in a crowd of 10,000 queers! I spied this guy, walked up to him and said: 'Hello. Are you straight?' He said: 'I'm afraid I am.'

I've often wondered where my sexual preference for straight men stems from – I like the term 'preference' because it's non-aggressive and suggests that who you decide to sleep with is no more important than whether you prefer Edam to Gouda.

It obviously has something to do with the macho environment I was brought up in. If you are raised in an atmosphere which consistently reminds you that you don't belong, and constantly confirms that heterosexuals are superior, the message has to sink in at some level.

It would be hard to find a gay man who is not emotionally traumatised by growing up in a world which forces him to suppress an essential part of who he is for most of his childhood. The fact that gay men are coming out at a much younger age does not compensate for the fact that until they do they are imprisoned by the culture they live in.

My relationship with my brothers and my upbringing in Woolwich had an energy of masculinity which still appeals. In fact, when I drink I can become very Woolwich and that scares me. There was an incident a couple of years ago when I punched a guy in a gay club and all I want to say about it is that it was a very expensive waste of my energy. I was furious with myself for giving in to my violent demons.

There is a vulnerability to straight men I find very attractive. If a straight guy has a repressed desire for other men (and many do), their vulnerability is often clearly reflected. These dalliances usually happen in an alcoholic or chemical haze, but they still happen.

I've always been attracted to vulnerable, wounded people, even though the resultant relationships can be relentless and the fallout very bitter. I've jokingly called myself a 'hetero hag', and it has been suggested that chasing after straight blokes is all about not getting what you want. Not necessarily, trust me. We don't always consider the sexuality of the people we find attractive, and you can't help who you fancy. Many men who insist they are hetero-sexual have a funny way of showing it.

Even if you are straight, think back to boys at school who were handsome and loved by everyone. Girls throw themselves at them and boys try to be like them. Straight men who claim they can't tell if another man is attractive are especially nauseating.

All men use each other to define their masculinity and standing in society. Look at the straight men who model themselves on the likes of David Beckham, or, in the past, Elvis and James Dean. There is something clearly homoerotic about this. The reason they do so is, of course, because they hope that they will be blessed with similar popularity and material wealth, but there's still a queer kink to it. Would Beckham be quite as popular if he were not so damn pretty? Hero-worship among men goes back to the gladiators (and I'm not talking about Wolf).

Desiring someone because they are physically attractive is no less shallow than being attracted to fame or power. All attraction is initially superficial. You don't walk up to someone and say: 'What a beautiful mind you have.'

Growing up I didn't think I was particularly special-looking. Hence the desire for transformation. Becoming famous was, I suppose, some sort of compensation for how I felt about my appear-ance, and also my self-worth. The downside of fame is that it attracts people for the wrong reasons. You create this persona in order to be more attractive and then become pissed off when people are attracted to it. 'Why can't anyone love me for who I really am?'

I know that a lot of the men who gravitate towards me are initially lured by my celebrity, and that knowledge doesn't make me feel any better. I know other famous people who simply don't care, using every aspect of their fame to get what they want. The trouble is, even if you think you've got what you want, you invariably discover that you haven't!

I go out of my way to debunk my fame and act like a regular person but that also puts people off. Men are sometimes horrified when they discover that I have ordinary feelings and can be just as dull as they are. For a relationship to really work you have to get beyond those initial obstacles, and when I do I'll let you know.

I wonder whether I have fully come to terms with my own sexuality. It's true I am more comfortable in the company of relaxed straight guys and I often defy their preconceptions not only of a gay man but also of a celebrity. The dalliances I have with straight guys tend to be traumatic, which makes me think that the panic they often express is a reflection of my own.

I've never felt that I've fitted into the gay community with its rigid rules about physical perfection to dress codes. And I'm not particularly interested in discussing Posh Spice's shoes on *Top of the Pops*. There are a lot of gay men like me who for one reason or another feel ostracised from their kind.

I HATE THIS DISCO

Is this disco
A pit of insecurity
Or what?
Some of the boys are really hot
Don't they know it?
Straight acting
Obvious
Viciously camp
Annoyingly camp
Bewildered
New to it

You always have to watch your back
In this disco

The boy you were talking to
Engaging with
Is talking to someone else
With muscles
And tattoos
The face on it isn't pretty
He looks good in his tight vest
They leave together

Lovers row
Those in open relationships separate
In search of fresh flesh
Another boy
Overly impressed
Are you really?
Yes
He follows you home
He is crap in bed

Star struck
He tells you
'I've only slept with two guys'
You strip him
And he's moaning
Your head
Between his thighs
You try to fuck him
'No'
Only the straight guys
Let you do that
And they leave quickly

This one
Is screaming
As you make him cum
Index finger
Wedged into his rectum

He won't take your dick
He loves your tongue
Completely in heaven
Salty
Plentiful
He makes that whimpering sound
That you love
Flooding your throat
Job done

I hate this disco
I still come
Every week
Never know
Who you might meet
Lots of competition
Better looking
Thinner
Fitter
Boys
'Hello'
It's him again
Shit
Can't remember his name
He doesn't really fancy me
Tells me I look young for my age
'Thanks'
Down with the underpants
More tongue
More cum
Fingers deeper
Maybe
This one's a keeper?
Love?
No
Just
Lust

Back in the seventies, when I first came out, the rules were different and at least there was some sense of the struggle gay men shared. When I came out at least I had the support of my family. I was only fifteen at the time. Dad was really cool while it was Mum who freaked out. I know now she was worried about me being abused or hurt. I thought I was more worldly than I was. Dad even gave me £60 for a pair of Vivienne Westwood bondage trousers, a gesture which was hugely significant to me, because, as Mum reminded me: 'I could buy a three-piece suite for that money'. He did go through a stage of cruelly ribbing me about not being a man but it was short-lived. I think most of his attempts to get his boys to be tougher were a little suspect because behind all the aggression Dad could be surprisingly sensitive and thoughtful. I understand that a lot of younger gays growing up in this slightly more tolerant age aren't interested in how their freedom was won. Soho is now SoHomo, with all its gay clubs, bars and shops, and if I was sixteen I'd probably think they'd always been there.

I'm not suggesting that there are no young politically minded homosexuals, and that there aren't battles still to be won, but, as with pop culture, there is no longer much sense of gay culture's history. In some respects there is a stronger argument for widening debate in schools about sexuality than all the drama about gay marriages. A gay man of my generation – and I'm no fossil – has very little in common with the young guys bouncing around to Kylie at G.A.Y.. Perhaps that is why I am far more attracted to the panic that permeates so much of straight culture. Or it could be that I just enjoy complicating everything; I have a very odd way of viewing the world which is probably why my life is so often at odds with itself. I know I'm guilty of losing myself in the drama that comes with these bound-to-end-in-disaster affairs. Holding on to the dream of how something could be is often better than the reality.

Recently I had one of those complex encounters in New York with a handsome preppy type called Ben. We met at the Bowery Bar. Just as the club was closing I spotted this gorgeous boy standing on a table taking his jumper off. He threw it across the club so I picked it up, approached him and said: 'Put your bloody clothes on. You're acting like an idiot.' I wandered off for a while and when I came back he was talking to some older guy, and I ended their conversation by saying: 'He's with me actually,' and pulled him away.

I only discovered he thought he was straight when we got into bed, such was his urgency to be penetrated. Had I been a less conscientious being I may have obliged but I knew it was the wrong thing to do.

After that night he called to apologise for being so drunk and asked what we had done. I said: 'You've got nothing to be worried about. I was the perfect gentleman.'

For weeks he kept calling and I kept missing him. Then I eventually invited him to see *Taboo*. After the show he came to the stage door to see me, and my dresser Alessandro told me he was with a girl. I decided not to meet him because I thought he was with his girlfriend. He called me at 3 a.m. and said: 'The show was amazing. It was like my life. That song "Stranger In This World", I'd love to play it to my mother.'

The next time I saw him, after endless back-and-forth phone calls, we talked about what had happened. He told me his life story and that night the act was consummated with consent.

His was a familiar tale: ridiculously handsome, a father who thought he was a waste of space and more secrets than Victoria. The sexual experience had been fantastic and very intimate, and yet the next time we spoke it was like talking to a stranger. The mistake he had made was allowing me to be intimate with him so he couldn't divorce that intimacy from the sexual act and blame it on alcohol. It wasn't the sex which terrified him, but the feelings he experienced that evening. Unfortunately for him he had met someone intelligent, sensitive and able to read him like a book.

When I attempted to discuss it he would only say: 'I'm confused, I'm confused.'

I told him: 'Children are confused, not twenty-seven-year-olds. You're ashamed.'

In the aftermath I wondered whether I had somehow connected with his panic, and wrote the song 'Panic' about him:

How can I compete with pretty girls and champagne?
All those disapproving voices that flood your brain,
And your father's voice saying, 'You should be ashamed.'
So why are you here with me tonight?

He told me during one of our last phone conversations: 'I'm really comfortable around you,' all the while sounding absolutely terrified.

Having recorded 'Panic' I got my burly black driver Mikey to deliver a CD of it to the mid-town bar where Ben worked as a waiter.

Mikey had never met Ben before, but instantly knew who he was. He handed the CD over, turned on his heel and left. He said the look on Ben's face was priceless.

Ben called and said: 'I can't stop playing this song. It's amazing.' Shortly thereafter, he changed all his numbers and left town, never to be seen again. Almost a year later I received an email from him. He said: 'I am clean and serene. A peace has come over me.'

I sent him an email back, saying: 'I'm glad you're not doing drugs any more, but you're still queer.'

Strangely enough, he didn't respond.

Around the time our relationship was hot-footing it into the abyss, I was performing nightly in *Taboo* on Broadway. It was hard not to draw a parallel between what was happening on stage – with our plot centring around a similarly confused gay/straight tryst – and what was happening in real life. I thought to myself: 'Twenty-five years on, and I'm still playing out this drama.'

To cap it all, one night the actress Glenn Close came in to visit a cast member. I don't usually bother famous people, but I asked her to write 'Don't get too Glenn Close' on an envelope. She sweetly obliged, a perfect summation of my fatal attractions.

In many ways the situation with Ben transcended sexual complications and seemed to be more about emotion, and in particular my relationship with my own father. In my childhood my dad was there physically but never emotionally. My mum would say to him: 'You never tell me you love me.' To which he would glibly reply: 'I'm here, aren't I?'

Perhaps the wounded child in me connected with the wounded child in Ben, and I wouldn't be surprised if he has similarly damaged relationships with women. A lot of men seek out a father figure in me, and I'm beginning to think I'm attracted to men who are as emotionally unavailable to me as my father was, regardless of their sexuality. A lot of my closest friends come from similar backgrounds and often it's not till you sit down and talk that you realise why you're drawn together.

There's no question that it's harder for gay men and women to conduct healthy relationships because we are judged harshly by the greatest father figure of all: society. When I was younger I only viewed life from a gay point of view. I now realise that many of my straight friends also struggle when confronting this central issue of combining heart and mind. I'm beginning to see that most human problems are more emotional than they are sexual. Again the two cannot be separated; they work in cahoots. I guess living without emotion would be just as traumatic as living with it.

A man like Ben could never feel comfortable introducing someone like me into his world because of the judgements that would be made about him. It's fine for him to drop my name like he dropped his pants, but God forbid he actually acknowledge our intimacy.

It's not as though I have no mercy towards him or the problems that he and others like him face, but it annoys me that the gay man is always at fault and cast as the predator. Sexuality and sex in general are often used to avoid dealing with the heart of the matter. If society stopped judging homosexuals in purely animalistic terms maybe we would be able to function better emotionally.

There is a direct comparison with the female struggle to be seen as emotional beings. Women of my mother's and grandmother's generations were simply baby-making machines. In Ireland the priest would visit women to see if they were pregnant and not using contraception. There was never any discussion of their feelings. By focusing purely on sex you suffocate emotions and make it a huge issue. In this respect gay men and women are still in the Dark Ages.

Just before the war kicked off in Iraq I picked up a soldier one night outside Heaven who was about to head out. I was getting into a cab and he smiled: 'Hey, you're Boy George.' I responded: 'Ten out of ten for observation.' He asked what I was doing and I joked: 'Hopefully taking you home for the night.' He jumped right into the cab.

Philip was there, nudging me and saying: 'Are you mad? He looks really rough!' I was thinking: 'Well, exactly.'

Back at mine, I made him tea and we chatted for a while. He was clearly a little inebriated but seemed quite gentle. He told me his father was a policeman who had harangued him into joining the army because he had been in trouble with the law and was off to Afghanistan the following morning. In bed, he was aggressive, clearly uncomfortable with his queer desires and far from sweet. I enjoyed it, though after sex he was grumpy and cold. I really wanted to ask him to leave but instead we fell asleep. In the morning I had forgotten that he was there until I felt this stiff thing rubbing against me. Soon enough we were at it again.

I made him tea (again) and left him watching the TV while I showered. When I came downstairs, he was gone. I looked around, thinking he might be hiding in a cupboard with a knife, but he'd done a runner, taking my digital camera with him. Doubtless he stole the camera to console his shame.

Whatever the encounter, whether it is charged with emotion like it was with Ben or a kamikaze shag with a Scottish soldier, it often feels like a problem without a solution. I'm always being told I should look for a nice gay man I can settle down with, but they come with their own set of Louis Vuitton baggage.

I always turn boys into songs because songs last longer. What a fantastic and complex specimen the male species is. What an invention and so many different flavours.

Whoever created them deserves everything they don't get.

7

Unfinished Business

At some point you have to stop worrying if people are only attracted to you because of fame. I guess in some twisted way it was designed for that purpose. Boys don't make passes at girls in glasses, but a whiff of fame makes them go insane!

Even when I was seventeen, swishing around London painted to the high heavens, I was adding pizzazz to what I felt was my dull self. I would rarely let any boy see me sans make-up, often rising before them for a quick overhaul. I guess I've been playing characters of one kind or another for as long as I can recall. I don't think of myself as famous but I can't control how others choose to see me and it's too late to try and undo my history.

Fame makes you suspicious of everyone's motives but I refuse to let it make me paranoid. The make-up, especially in the early days, was essential for luring those boys of 'questionable sexuality'. It helps them to delude themselves that I am more feminine than I actually am, despite the fact that I am more like a rugby player naked.

Fame wasn't a factor with Kirk Brandon. In fact, he was already a budding punk star when I first met him in the late seventies. I fell for him the minute we met and the fact that he had a girlfriend at the time didn't stop him pursuing me.

His band, Theatre of Hate, had a massive cult following and

very soon I was doing everything I could to promote them, trying to persuade press to come to gigs and designing posters and T-shirts. I would march into the offices of the _NME_ and demand that they reviewed Theatre of Hate gigs. Lord knows what they made of me in my Goth Goes Hollywood drag!

Kirk did his best to hide the affair at the time, although he was never that consistent; sometimes he could be openly affectionate in public and in front of the rest of his band. Our relationship was important because he was my first real love and meeting him sparked my desire to start my own group.

When I wrote _Take It Like a Man_ I decided I had to include Kirk. Long before the book was published, my co-writer Spencer Bright chased old friends and ex-lovers to corroborate my stories. One of them, who I renamed Gary in the book, went absolutely berserk and threatened to beat Spencer up, but being a journalist Spencer somehow persuaded him to meet. Of course, the guy in question denied we had ever been an item and described me as 'deranged and obsessed'. Reading the transcript of his conversation was both amusing and sad. I couldn't argue with the accusation that I was 'deranged', because I am, but at the end of their meeting, my old boyfriend told Spencer he would really love to see me again. Human beings really are insane. Or was it the fame thing again?

After I returned from my second trip to India, my manager Tony called to say that Kirk was trying to get in touch. I hadn't seen him for many years so I was intrigued to find out what he wanted. Kirk knew about my independent record label More Protein and was keen to get me to release some of his new material. We were mostly releasing dance stuff so Kirk's angst-ridden rock would not have been right. We spoke briefly on the phone and he seemed very amiable and centred, taking the piss out of my travels to India.

When I mentioned the book Kirk said he was not interested in being involved but didn't seem overly concerned about it. My attempts to get him to talk to Spencer were laughed off: 'I suppose the book is going to be full of a load of old lies,' he snapped. 'No,' I assured him, 'it will be full of a load of old truth.' To cover ourselves, we drafted a letter to Kirk making it clear that I would be writing about our relationship and that we were happy to change his name if he wanted, but he never responded. When the book came out there was no immediate reaction from Kirk and very little coverage of the gay aspect of the book in the media. It was drugs, drugs, drugs all the way. The gutter press is rarely interested in gay relationships unless there is a hint of tragedy.

Around that time I spoke to an old friend from the punk days, Angie Usher, who mentioned that Kirk was now married. For some bizarre reason I was upset and I went for a walk on Hampstead Heath to clear my head. As I walked, old memories resurfaced and I wondered why I was so bothered about Kirk being hitched. The phrase 'unfinished business' came to mind and I realised that was probably why I was so stirred up. There's a real difference between my relationships with Kirk and Jon. I still see Jon and can rationalise what happened between us. But when Kirk and I split after about six months there was no resolution. He just came up with the same old crap: 'I need time, it's not you, it's me.' Then there was a gap of a few months. We started seeing each other again but pretty soon it was over for good. I didn't encounter Kirk for years, which was weird because I had been so madly in love with him.

We looked great together, him with his rockabilly thing and me with my punky look. It had been a big time in my life but then Culture Club took over and Jon and I got together. Jon constantly slagged Kirk off, calling his new band Spear of Destiny 'Spear of Mid-European Angst'.

That day on the Heath I started humming a melody and by the time I got home I had the basis for a song called 'Unfinished Business'. I was about to record my album *Cheapness and Beauty* and decided to include it; most of the songs on *Cheapness and Beauty* were autobiographical and related to subjects covered in my book, like the CD which accompanies this one. When the album was finished I decided to include pictures of the people who inspired those songs, as well as the likes of Quentin Crisp.

I used an old black-and-white snap of Kirk and me, with the lyrics to 'Unfinished Business' printed across it. The lyrics are

pretty cutting and direct but they relate to how I felt when Kirk
dumped me:

> You liar,
> You coward,
> You sleeping fool,
> Don't you know that secrets kill?
> Heaven and hell are right here on earth,
> Decided by your own free will.

8

Vanity Case

Kirk was furious when he saw his picture in the album booklet and heard 'Unfinished Business'. The song, not the book, convinced him to take me to court for 'malicious falsehood', so, in the autumn of 1996, I was served with a writ.

On the day the case opened in April 1997 I'd arrived back in the country at 7.30 a.m. from a DJ trip to Australia. There was no need for me to be in court but I made the decision to attend for the entire showdown. I came home, showered, had a cup of tea and went along. I knew it was going to be an ordeal that shouldn't be taken lightly.

When I first saw Kirk in the courtroom he didn't make eye contact, but he did glance defiantly in my direction, looking nothing like the handsome, cocky rockabilly that had swept me off my feet so many years before. I'm sure he felt the same about me. I was no longer the skinny, androgynous ladyboy he had fallen for, but of the two of us, I thought, I had fared better. Well, I would, wouldn't I? I couldn't help thinking Kirk's hair could do with a good bleaching!

The case started with Kirk putting his argument to the judge. He was litigating in person – because the solicitor and counsel dropped out – which made it all the more surreal, particularly since he did his best to sound like Rumpole of the Bailey. It was all 'I put it to you', and he seemed very out of his depth (and his mind, for that matter).

His first witness was his ex-manager Terry Razor, who had never really warmed to me. I remember meeting Terry outside the offices in Bayswater he shared with the Clash. I was all punked up and looking very 'woman' with my crimped spiky hair. The look on Terry's face when he saw me and noticed that Kirk was holding my hand! His grunted 'How are you?' shot at me like a bullet. I was already pretty well known on the London scene; Terry knew my face and thought Kirk should keep well away from me. He had a very macho image and was known for his anti-establishment posturing.

In the courtroom most of the questions Kirk put to Terry were pointless; how could he say that we were never lovers? No one could prove that for sure. It was obvious that Kirk was trying to use Terry to prove that the allegations in the book had forced him to cancel a tour. Razor became increasingly curt with Kirk because he kept him in the witness box for a very long time, asking hyper-pathetical questions.

In contrast to Terry, the rest of Kirk's band had always been really friendly towards me. Stan Stammers, the bass player, was forever asking me about our relationship and it was Stan who told me that one of their classic singles, 'The Original Sin', was written about me:

> Since you came in my life,
> I've had to rearrange my whole mentality,
> My sexuality.

Luke the drummer was the most gorgeous boy in London at the time and, in fact, I had a complete crush on him. Steve Guthrie, who played guitar, was Kirk's best mate and let Kirk live in his house in Hayes, out near Heathrow airport. When I encountered Steve in court as another of Kirk's witnesses I was surprised and wondered what he would contribute. When he took the stand he was clearly uncomfortable and didn't say an awful lot. His job, it seemed, was to confirm that nothing physical had occurred between

Above: 60s family gathering. My sister Siobhan in Mum's arms with (clockwise) brother Kevin (in glasses), me, my brother David and our nan Bridget Glynn.

Right: Favourite shirt. Me in the early 70s outside our house in Joan Crescent, Eltham, with (from left) my friend Denise Higgins, Siobhan and Kevin.

Above: Mum, Siobhan and my niece Maggie and nephew Zak.

Right: My dad.

Above left: Photobooth heaven with Andy, 1976.

Above right: Sans eyebrows at the Carburton Street squat 1978.

Left: Rockabilly Alien, 1977.

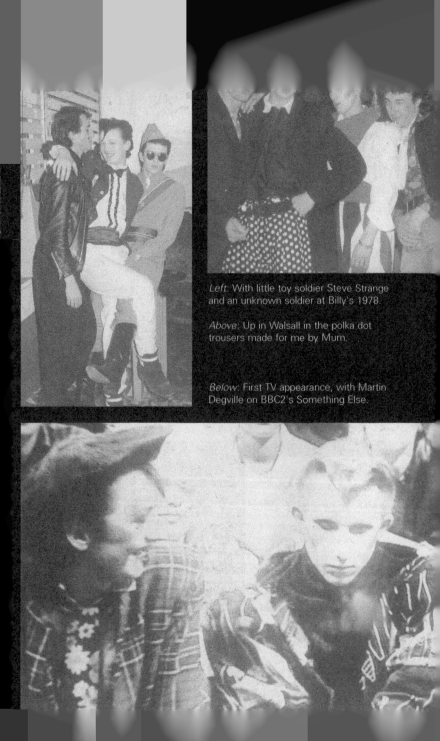

Left: With little toy soldier Steve Strange and an unknown soldier at Billy's 1978.

Above: Up in Walsall in the polka dot trousers made for me by Mum.

Below: First TV appearance, with Martin Degville on BBC2's Something Else.

Left: On the bed with Kirk Brandon.

Above: Jeremy Healy in tanned Ibiza DJ mode.

Below: Martin Degville and I leather-trousered up in the Midlands.
Inset: Princess Julia.

Above: With Jane Kahn, Patti Bell and others, 1978.

Left: Still taken from one of John Maybury's early art movies.

Below: Holiday snap of Jon Moss in repose.

Right: Culture Club mid-80s. Note disdainful glare off camera.

Below: With my friend and make-up maestro Paul Starr.

Below right: Dread bouffant Marilyn in sweetness-and-light mode.

Above: Encounter with a heroine: Quentin Crisp and I in New York, early 90s.

Left: My manager Tony Gordon and ex-boyfriend Michael Dunne.

Kirk and me, which was a bit sad, since I had slept in the same bed as Kirk in Steve's house, and Steve had even protected me during a public fight with Kirk.

We were always rowing in public. One night I went to the Camden Palace and caught Kirk kissing some girl. We had an argument and Kirk pushed me. Steve jumped between us saying: 'You don't have to hit him, he's only ever tried to help you.' I left in floods of tears.

Steve was even with Kirk the night we finally split up for good, and saw how distraught I was. After Kirk sped away on the back of Steve's motorbike, I walked in the rain all the way to Steve's house and he made me a cup of tea and put me to bed. Steve was always bailing Kirk out and his stint in the witness box seemed to be him performing just another one of those services.

When the judge, Justice Douglas Brown, asked Steve: 'Do you think Mr O'Dowd is a good man?' he replied: 'I used to think so.'

Trust me, the feeling was mutual. At one point Steve smiled at me but I was too appalled to react.

I imagine that Steve felt that I was wrong to have written about my relationship with Kirk. Why is it only OK for straight people to write about their relationships? If I'd been a girl there would have been no fuss. I would have been labelled a bitter old slag and that would have been the end of it.

One day after a lunch break I walked into court and saw my old landlady, Jean Sell, sitting there stony-faced. You know the way you instantly say 'Hello' to people you recognise? I did so, forgetting for a second that I couldn't stand the old trout. As I spoke she swung her head round and gave me the most spiteful glare and I realised that she wasn't there to collect her rent.

I had briefly lived in a windowless room in Jean's flat during the eighties. The deal was that I would run errands and clean up in exchange for rent but Jean quickly became sick of me. In fact, she only asked me to move in on a whim and she regretted it five seconds later.

It transpired that Jean had been on her way to work that day in court, and after reading about the case in the paper had jumped off the bus and rushed to offer Kirk her aid. The smirk on Kirk's face as he quickly took a statement from her was like that of a little boy who'd been given a lifetime supply of chocolate. He thought Jean was his piss de resistance, but on the stand she was as weak as a Steps dance routine.

Jean claimed I had cried on her shoulder pads because Kirk wouldn't have sex with me. She was absolute in her conviction that we were never a couple, radiating dishonesty and bitterness with every utterance.

The judge didn't believe a word she said, and in his summing-up stated: 'Miss Jean Sell seemed to be purely motivated by revenge.' He also told Kirk that she was such an unreliable witness it was very ill-advised of him to have brought her into the courtroom in the first place. Strangely enough I don't have any bad feelings towards Jean, even if it might read that way. I just thought: 'What a silly cow.'

Throughout the seven-day hearing I was convinced I would lose. Not because Kirk had right on his side — we had absolutely been lovers — but because I thought that the weight of the establishment would come down heavily on me just for being Boy George. I misjudged Justice Douglas Brown. He was old and therefore, I thought, would probably be homophobic. Instead he proved to be very clued up.

During a description of a famous photo of me with Kirk, the judge said: 'Would that be the photograph where Mr O'Dowd is dressed as a nun?' As people tittered he said: 'Settle down, it's not that amusing.' I thought it was hysterical. More comedy was provided when several of Kirk's ex-girlfriends took the stand in my defence. Scottish Jenny, the girl I stole him from, was indignant. When Kirk accused her of being motivated by jealousy and revenge, she snapped: 'Why would I be jealous of you? I've got a lovely husband and gorgeous kids. I'm only here because you're lying.' When she left the stand she was still seething, muttering to herself in her thick Scottish brogue: 'Jealous?! The cheek of it!' Jenny proved what a truly decent person she is. After all, she had a perfect right to be angry with me, but she'd moved on and was only motivated by decency.

Next up was Naoma, who dated Kirk after we split up. She

told the court that when they were going out together she had found a photo of me in Kirk's wardrobe which provoked a major row. She also said that they could never go anywhere I might be because Kirk told her I would cause a scene. At least he was right on that score!

Angie Usher was another witness for me. She had dated Stan Stammers and they shared a flat with Kirk so Angie was terrified about taking the stand because she was very fond of Kirk. But she got through it; I was so proud of her.

I first met Angie when she worked in Top Shop. Street Theatre, where I worked, had a concession there and I stupidly asked Angie if she was a sex change. I was always doing that to girls just to wind them up and she was most put out. One of her mates, Gay John, came into Street Theatre to punch my lights out but it was all smoothed over and we became good friends.

The most important moment came when Kirk was cross-examined. He casually let slip that he had shared my bed one night and Justice Douglas Brown picked up on it immediately and interrupted: 'Mr Brandon, there is no mention of this in your original witness statement.' Kirk responded: 'I didn't think it was important,' to which the judge replied: 'It is most important. You describe Mr O'Dowd as evil and obsessed. Why would you get into bed with such a person?'

He also asked Kirk what he was wearing that night and Kirk said: 'A thick jumper and shorts.' I nudged my lawyer Gary Lux: 'Yeah and a bleeding pair of chaps.'

Things became more surreal when Kirk questioned me. Gary advised me against making eye contact but I was determined; if I didn't, it would look like I had something to hide. Having read from a section of my book, Kirk furrowed his brow and asked: 'You admit that you and your friend Marilyn dressed up as girls to get off with straight men?' I wanted to say: 'Yes and it worked, didn't it?' But suppressing the desire to be amusing, I said that the dressing up wasn't just about that. We didn't wear false breasts but, yes, we attempted to look as glamorous as possible. Blokes would come up and say: 'Hello, love, can I buy you a drink?' Nine times out of ten they would still buy you one when they realised you weren't a female. It seemed ridiculous to be telling Kirk stories he knew inside out.

The judge asked me to explain further, so I told him what we did wasn't like Kiss or Gary Glitter, clothes and make-up worn purely for performance. This was how we lived and dressed day-to-day, whether clubbing, riding the tube or nicking a slab of cheese from the local grocer's.

At one point during my testimony I told Kirk: 'I don't understand why we are here. All I said was that I loved you. That's hardly offensive. I didn't go into sexual detail, just said that we went out. You know it's true, so why are we here?' But Kirk carried on with his ranting.

My barrister, playing devil's advocate, asked why I chose to write about our relationship. I told him that, although it was quite brief, it was a very important moment in my life. A lot of people asked me the same question and, after all, I had given Kirk an opportunity to change his name verbally and in writing and he'd ignored me.

In the late seventies there were often snippets about Kirk and me in the back of the *NME* and Kirk presented a bunch of these press clippings as part of his case. In fact, they worked to my advantage because they showed we were an item.

From Los Angeles Stan Stammers kindly provided a statement on my behalf and I found out later that a diehard Kirk fan called Spider was trying to get in touch with me to do the same. I met Spider in a club after the court case and he said: 'Kirk's a total idiot,' even though he still had his Theatre of Hate tattoo on his neck.

There was a long arduous wait while the judge summed up and I sat in a room with Gary, my manager Tony, a girl from Virgin Records and a huge plate of uneaten sandwiches. Normally I can munch through any crisis – earthquakes, failed tours, bad relationships, even the odd dodgy styling moment – but this time I truly believed I was going to lose everything. A terrible prospect when you consider what a lousy time we'd had between the sheets! It was hardly my kingdom for a horse-dick.

Despite my pessimism, Gary was confident we had won because Kirk hadn't been asked to wrap up his argument. Gary was right.

In his ruling the judge said 'this sad case' would never have come to court had I not later become famous. He also said that I had not been malicious in writing what I knew to be the truth.

Justice Douglas Brown concluded by saying that Kirk was a likeable man but his allegations of malice were hopeless, adding that the witness statements indicated Kirk had 'inclinations' and these, combined with the 'opportunities' we had in our shared bed, gave him reason to believe our relationship was indeed sexual.

Legal costs were awarded against Kirk, which meant that he owed £200,000 to Virgin, my publishers EMI Virgin Music and the book publisher Sidgwick & Jackson. He said after the case that he would appeal, maybe taking it to the US, but I haven't heard a peep from him from that day to this.

In the end it all came down to money.

Even though I won and costs were awarded to me, it was a strictly moral victory. Kirk was bankrupt and, because he had litigated himself, was not liable for the costs, so I had to pay £60,000 plus. The chances of me getting the money back are nil, but I don't care; it's not as though I really want it. What a fiasco. If Kirk had needed money that badly I probably would have given him some, not because I felt guilty but because I still cared about him. I felt sad and there was no sense of triumph. Throughout their reporting of the case the daily press had continually hinted I would lose, but they soon changed their tune when I was vindicated. But I didn't go out and celebrate with loads of champagne. Instead I jumped into a cab and came home with feelings of disappointment in Kirk and the so-called sexually liberated society we don't live in.

What's my view of Kirk now? Really, he's a bit sad, but I don't feel sorry for him – he does a pretty good job of that himself. I guess that even to this day, to maintain sanity he has to believe he was right. And his friends would have justified their defence of him by believing that I shouldn't have written the things I did.

9

Confidence Trick

In many ways Kirk is typical of a lot of the men I've been involved with. They are happy to be seen with you at the time but develop a loss of memory when they buckle down to straight life.

Not unlike Gavin Rossdale, who was the love of Marilyn's life for a number of years. When I wrote about their relationship in my last book I did so because he had a similar effect on Marilyn as Jon Moss did on me.

Of course, when Gavin's rock group Bush became huge in America in the nineties, the last thing he wanted to talk about was his bisexual past. Everyone, including Marilyn, was amazed that Gavin of all people became a bona fide rock star but I never begrudged him that success because I'd always been fond of him and still think he's a really sweet bloke.

I first met Gavin around 1983, when he was about seventeen and an absolute beauty, very flirtatious and ambitous. Steve Strange and I gave him a lift home from the Embassy Club one night. Steve was careful to drop me off first, thinking he might nab him. To my amazement Gavin remembered where I lived, even though it was pitch black when I got out of the car. A couple of days later I saw him hovering around in the street outside my flat. I was flattered if a little unnerved and didn't invite him in.

The next time we met was at Kate Garner and Paul Caplin's

warehouse space–cum–studio in Great Titchfield Street in the West End, which also served as the offices of Kate's group Haysi Fantayzee. Marilyn was being managed and housed by them and by this time Gavin was his boyfriend. I couldn't believe I hadn't moved quicker! But it seemed to me their relationship was as fraught as mine and Jon's.

That evening, Marilyn was being particularly vile to Gavin and I sat with him in his car while he poured his heart out.

When I was writing *Take It Like a Man*, Bush were well on their way to rock stardom in the US and he appeared at my house in Hampstead with the intention of persuading me not to include him and Marilyn. I agreed to leave out some stuff about him but I wasn't prepared to lie. I guess I was a little self-righteous because Jon was still refusing to accept that we had been lovers and in my mind there was a sense of 'Why should they get away with it?'

Then, when the book was published, Gavin was asked about it in *Rolling Stone* and said: 'George thinks everyone's gay.' That's true by the way, but beside the point in this case.

I didn't understand why he cared. It's not as if Marilyn was a hideous gargoyle. Marilyn was so feminine and Gavin was just as stunning; it was all very Mick and Bianca. Gavin's attitude made me wonder what had happened to all the great, ambiguous rock stars. Back in the seventies, people like Bowie, Bolan and Jagger had a ball playing with sexual boundaries. No one was quite sure if Bowie had slept with Jagger (though they have both denied it) or Iggy, or if Bolan really had an affair with Mickey Finn. And, after all, Bush were pretty much modelling themselves on Nirvana and Kurt Cobain was hardly uptight about sexual issues. He was a godsend in the macho rock world, wearing dresses and singing lines like: 'What more can I say? / Everyone is gay.' To me, Kurt Cobain was the last great rock icon, equally as exciting as Bowie, even to a jaded old queen like me.

I had another run-in with Gavin when I told *People* magazine that his girlfriend Gwen Stefani was 'Marilyn with muscles and breasts'. It was no put-down – I think Gwen is beautiful and extremely cool. Before the article was printed Gavin again stormed round to my house, ranting and raging. I asked him if he had actually read the interview. He hadn't. He calmed down when it was published because most of it was devoted to my crush on Adrian Young, drummer in Gwen's band No Doubt. You know: me and drummers!

I didn't go to Gavin and Gwen's wedding in 2001 but Marilyn showed up and was his usual graceless self. I heard that Gavin's mum went over to say hello and Marilyn snarled: 'Do you mind! I'm trying to pull this boy!' Oh well, at least you can rely on Marilyn to be charm personified.

I felt Gavin could have saved himself years of drama by just saying: 'So what? Marilyn was a babe.' To be fair to Gavin he helped Marilyn out financially on a number of occasions and he has never, ever been derogatory about gays. I don't think Marilyn has ever really got over Gavin and he's even joked to me: 'You don't miss your water till your well runs dry.'

There are some men I would describe as peripherally gay and others who are completely bisexual and up for it. Peripherally gay blokes rarely suck dick and often they won't be overly affectionate or engage in intimacy such as kissing. They usually lie back and let you do all the work.

Of course, I accept that you are what you believe you are and some men can best be described as 'terminally heterosexual'. If I decided to call myself Napoleon and convinced enough people, I would sure as hell be Napoleon.

10

She Was Never He

I have spent an awful lot of my life wondering how or why I became gay. What came first, the chicken or the Fabergé egg?

I find the subject of sexuality extremely fascinating because whenever you come up with what you think is a good explanation another comes along to contradict it. It certainly beats talking about the weather.

I wasn't always direct about my sexuality when I first became a pop star but I've never wished I was straight or been ashamed of my preference. From a very young age I knew there was something different about me and other kids helped enormously by calling me vile names. By the age of fifteen, when I was out to my family, I was already sexually active. Back then I firmly believed that I was born gay, that it was just some twist of fate. I suppose it was easier to put the blame on Mother Nature, because I didn't have to take any responsibility and could play the victim: 'I'm gay because whoever was working the human conveyor belt sneaked off for a quick smoke.' I was like a toy that had been manufactured with an arm missing.

I now feel there is something wonderfully empowering about accepting total responsibility for my queerness and wearing my pink crucifix with pride, maybe even colour-coordinating it with some matching sequinned platforms and a his-and-hers shift dress.

Many gay men get very upset if you suggest that they may have chosen to be gay. This is perfectly understandable because we have been raised to see ourselves as victims of an unnatural disaster. It also provides bigots and homophobes with ammunition because, if it's a choice, in their ignorant eyes, it's one you can unmake. I really feel that sexuality goes beyond nature or nurture and is just another spice in the scented wok of humanity.

I don't think anyone actually wakes up one morning and says (to quote comedian Julian Clary): 'I'd like a nice big cock up my arse.' I suspect that it's more of a subconscious process that can be sparked by various events. I once viewed sexuality in black-and-white terms but I now see it as a grey area with pink spots. The most interesting conversation I've ever had about this subject was a brief but illuminating one with transvestite comedian Eddie Izzard. He described sexuality like a ruler, with homosexuality and hetero-sexuality at opposing ends and bisexuality slap in the middle. There are those people who are absolutely terminal in their sexual choices, and they appear exactly at the beginning, middle and end of the ruler. The rest of the ruler's gauges make up the remainder of rich, complex and diverse options. I think Izzard is a fine example of a person of indefinable sexuality and all the more fascinating for it. Like many people I was guilty of branding him a closet, but you can see how comfortable and honest he is, and proof positive of his excellent theory.

Just because you choose not to act on an impulse that doesn't mean that impulse doesn't exist. We are all made up of a multi-tude of sexual and emotional possibilities, most of which we'll never ever act upon. Society has taken something wonderful, pleas-urable and instinctual and reduced it to a formula. It's not unlike what has happened with faith, which is gorgeous and glorious and about love of humanity. Religion has made that systematic. Even if somebody chooses not to operate within a religious structure, it doesn't mean that their faith is of any less value.

It is the denial of the possibilities of sexuality which really frus-trates me. How can you not find what you are attractive? Masturbation is still playing with a penis, even if it's your own.

This line is always effective. I recently said it to a straight DJ friend of mine. He looked at me and gasped: 'Why do you always have to twist everything?' Maybe because everything is already twisted!

I know that I'm emotionally needy and sometimes my desire for love is so overwhelming it acts like a gust of wind. There are times when you want something so bad you end up pushing it away. I never really believe anyone who tells me they love me and I play stupid games to make them prove it. I am also insanely possessive and jealous and would happily strangle someone for making a move on my partner.

This could be one of the reasons I don't operate too well in an exclusively gay environment because other gay men are only too happy to try and steal what's yours. The atmosphere in most gay clubs is sometimes far too sexually charged for my liking and a lot of gay men will engage with your physicality long before they engage with your mind.

Like many gay men I am attracted to obvious beauty and fall for guys who are neither my physical nor emotional equal, but it's safe to say that regardless of one's sexual preference we often hook up with partners with whom we have little in common. In my case that covers a lot of people!

I would say that I place more importance on love than I do on my career but as you get older it becomes harder to deal with love's complications. I find the gaps between relationships have widened with age and I tend to bury my emotions in my work – songwriting is an excellent way of working out the difficulties I have loving and being loved. When you go out deliberately looking for love you rarely find it. It often appears when you least expect it. I know I will never meet the kind of person I really want in the bars and clubs I frequent. I prefer mixed places to the hardcore gay variety. Many gay men are focused on fast-food sexual activity and even those gay men who say they want more have unrealistic expectations. They want a perfect-looking man under twenty-five or someone who looks convincingly str8.

I don't think I'm overly camp but like many gay men I can turn on an invisible high heel! I can look extremely feminine with the right amount of make-up but I am more masculine than most people realise. I don't think there's anything wrong with a bit of camp but it can be annoying in much the same way as exaggerated masculinity. Both are equally affected because no one is born talking like a barrow boy and I've never heard of a gay man leaving the womb singing 'I Am What I Am'.

I don't really know how some gay men attain the nasal tone that is associated with what I term 'the cartoon homosexual'. You don't meet as many of those cupcake queers as you used to, but there are always one or two lurking around. Hence the cliché: 'He's not queer, he's just theatrical.'

One of the reasons why sex is so important to gay men is that, for many, it is the moment of truth. As a child, even if you know you are attracted to other boys, you have absolutely no way of expressing it. If you do, you run the risk of even greater persecution than that which you inflict upon yourself. In addition, straight culture is horrified by the sexual aspect, and suppressing it only serves to heighten its importance for everybody.

You may be flummoxed by just how many different types of sexual bents there are. I know I am. Who can get their head round a respectable married heterosexual male who gets his jollies dressing up as a toy elephant? Such people are called fluffies in Britain while in America they call themselves plushies and there's sometimes a Disney connection. But isn't there with everything? I have absolutely no interest in dressing up as Daffy Duck (in the bedroom at least) but if Dermot Mulroney said: 'I love you, George, but will you wear this Minnie Mouse costume for me?' I'd go Looney Tunes.

The perameters of heterosexual sex have widened far beyond 'Brace yourself, Sheila, I'm coming in'. Even within so-called 'orthodox' sexual relationships, the goalposts are prone to be moved at will. What Jenny may allow might be wholly inappropriate for Sofia. As you can see it's almost impossible to label anything 'normal' any more, if it ever was.

Gays, lesbians, bisexuals, transsexuals and Transylvanians are only the tip of the whip. Is anyone really born with a natural taste for being locked in cupboards or asphyxiated? The desire to be tied up or beaten and the whole BDSM scene is obviously related to a more emotional rather than sexual deficit but the two are often connected (with a jump lead).

When I made that famous comment 'Sex? I prefer a cup of tea', on Russell Harty's show in the eighties little did I know how much significance would be attached to it. I remember my encounter with Mr Harty well and I also remember people telling me to watch him because he was crafty and quick. So was I!

It's amusing, looking back, to think that I was being told to be careful of a fellow homosexual. Let's face it, Russell's sexuality had a neon sign over it that flashed 'yes he is' even though he preferred to keep the truth under wraps. His denial and my desire to keep people guessing made us uneasy sparring partners.

I always prepare for interviews, not in the sense of planning my answers but choosing a particular outfit and trying to think of some twist that I can add to the moment. I went out and bought a white teapot, which was a visual cheeky wink to Harty and a warning that I could hold and pour my own!

I often became carried away during promotional opportunities, which were many and varied in the eighties. Just walking into a female toilet could guarantee a front page and I loved my column inches. To some this wrongly suggested that I was less interested in my music than I was in being seen, but I assure you that was never the case.

From day one it was almost impossible to separate the never-ending doubt about my sexuality, the way I dressed and what I said, from the musical offerings we were creating. In many respects, it made sense, since for me none of those things were ever separate. It was a case of: 'I am what I feel, what I wear, what I sing, what I say!' The historical analysis is that I was trying to create a non-sexual persona, trying to be safe. But the intellectualisation of the comment was pointless. I was a twenty-two-year-old gay man who actually had no problem being gay but realised other people did. Those right-on journalists who go on about how I should have been more honest didn't have to deal with the fallout. It's typical of the media – those who are looking in from the outside – to decide what's best for us. Once anyone famous admits to being gay they become the brunt of endless bad jokes. They are only ever referred to in a sexual context, they cease to have rows and start having 'dramas' and 'hissy fits', an argument becomes a 'cat fight' and their fists turn into 'handbags'.

The media always call for honesty but they are the ones who ultimately mocked me about being gay. If you want to avoid it you have to go to great lengths to never do anything that might be viewed as camp. Journalists feed off people's triumphs and misfortunes with equal relish but they never have to deal with the consequences.

Life in the closet is grim and those of us in the creative industries have an obligation to be honest and forward-thinking.

When I appeared on BBC1's political debate programme *Question Time* in 2000 another of the guests was Brian Souter, the entrepreneur who owns Scotland's Stagecoach transport empire. An advocate of Thatcher's eighties anti-gay rights bill Section 28, Souter has invested more than £1 million in a bid to keep the bill alive north of the border. To their credit the Scottish parliament overturned Section 28 long before that occurred in England.

During the debate I asked Souter whether I should be kept away from my many nieces and nephews in case I encouraged them to be gay, but he didn't appear to take on board the logic of my argument.

As for his heroine Maggie Thatcher, anyone who can state that 'There is no such thing as society' is patently beyond help. As I always say, Thatcher only had one good line: 'The lady's not for turning,' which I thought was very good advice. A couple of years ago while I was performing in *Taboo* in London I was invited to speak at the public school Westminster and then carry out a question-and-answer session without unnecessary restrictions on subject matter. Many of the questions from the packed hall of boys were about fame and Eminem but there were quite a few about sexuality.

I asked them to put up their hands if they thought they were capable of murder. Many hands were raised. I then asked: 'Who could sleep with a member of the same sex?' Only one hand went up, to a chorus of sniggers. The small ginger-haired boy aged around thirteen appeared unfazed. The point I made to them was that it wasn't important whether he ever did but it was extremely brave of him to acknowledge the possibility. As brazen as I was at that age, I wouldn't even have dared to raise an eyebrow if such a question had been posed during assembly at Eltham Green School.

I'm sure a lot of them left the hall thinking: 'Stupid old queen,' but it speaks volumes about society's pressures that, even today, only one kid in a couple of hundred would take that risk.

As I've already said, I find the sexual debate fascinating. And perhaps I'm guilty of shagging the arse off it. Mind you, if I don't bring up the subject someone else always does, usually straight blokes. And love them as I do, they have a tendency to assume many things. For example, no matter how unattractive they may be, they believe every gay man wants to get into their trousers. Then again, I'm kind of odd when it comes to attraction; given enough time I can find something attractive in most people, let alone most men. I can be swooned by talent, wit, charm, humour, a big nose, or simply the way someone walks. I like to think this is to do with emotional maturity, but my Nine Ki does delineate the highest libido of any given set of numbers!

I'm no size queen either. A boy I recently had a drive-by love affair with in New York kept asking me: 'Do you think I have a big bum?' He didn't want me to say yes, or 'That's the reason you're here', but I do love a sturdy rear end – though that's possibly too much information. But then this is my book.

You might ask what my fascination is with heterosexual men. Well, apart from the fact I deny their existence, they are often far more entertaining (and adventurous) than your common or garden gay gnome-o. However, their tendency to announce: 'Sorry, I'm straight, mate,' when you have simply asked for the time can be grating.

This aside, they afford me a lot of charm. As I've grown into my sexuality and adopted a take-all-prisoners approach, I get less aggression. Not long ago at Heaven a fellow comrade approached me with a note, which I suspected might be a 'you changed my life' confession. In fact, it read: 'You look much bigger in real life.' You always know where you are with a redneck; they can't help themselves. But someone who has shared your struggle has no excuse.

Our culture puts heterosexuals on such a high pedestal it's hard not to kneel and worship and the friction between gay and straight men ignites a dynamic all of its own.

One thing all men – gay or straight – share is the terrible business of our emotions being projected outward. Females share the tragedy of PMT or, worse still, what I call the PMDs – pre- and post-menstrual drama. Someone once joked: 'Women don't suffer from PMT, men do.' Luckily it's matched by the equally smart: 'Men don't suffer from premature ejaculation, women do.' Having the monthly clock, however distressful it may be, is what I believe affords women emotional edge. If men could be reminded once a month of their power and responsibility, the licensing laws would have changed years ago. Male emotion is often only expressed in the wholly inappropriate form of a hard-on. How many women, or sensitive gay men, complain they prefer breakfast in bed without the overgrilled sausage? Most males can't ride a bus without getting a hard-on, let alone display affection to a loved one, or even someone they hardly know!

The penis is the one part of the anatomy society has failed to suppress completely. Of course, we can't ignore those men who suffer from performance anxiety, but that even happens to the very best pop stars!

Generally, the male genitalia has an agenda all of its own and, like the loose floorboards of reality, is prone to spring up when least expected. I don't know about you, but my floorboards are always creaking. And if they're not, I'm ready to prise up a few nails to help them on their way.

My female friends are generally outspoken, if not deranged, and have no problem discussing sex and sexual issues. But I rarely hear them talking graphically about what they have done with men and you can trust me on this as an honorary female. Women may have become more ambitious and less prepared to accept traditional male bullshit, and some are willing to sacrifice elements of their femininity, but on the whole they invest a degree of emotion into every situation. And thank Eve for that.

Even in the twenty-first century, men continue to blow their own horns about sexual conquests and this often lacks the necessary wit, even when they are talking about those they have vowed to honour and respect.

Society slaps gay men with the double whammy: denial of emotion and sexuality. Straight men just have to contend with denial of emotion. I'm being simplistic, of course, because I couldn't hope to address the wealth of tragedy and torment endured by those forced into severe dysfunction or terrible abuse. Whatever the circumstances it all comes down to emotion, and suppression of emotion at any level leads to the same murky seas.

Straight men are so protective of their masculinity and act like their dicks and arses are the Koh-i-noor and the Crown Jewels combined. A lot of gays revere them in much the same manner. Sometimes I wonder if queers simply exist to remind the heterosexual that he is indeed superior. Who decided the rectum was more sacred than the vagina?

Even those of us who think heterosexuality is the greatest card trick of all have bought into this idea of superiority. After all, straight men provide children, put up shelves. Some even do dishes these days. In the back of their twisted minds, gay men have bought into this hook, line and stinker. And the years of brainwashing don't help either.

The oversaturation of gay imagery hasn't helped, because the devil is in the detail. *Queer Eye* says gay man = home furnishings à la Barbra Streisand. *Footballers' Wives*, even within its narrow margins, represents a much wider picture.

The advent of Aids has made straight boys more wary of experimentation. Illness has never been the greatest promotional tool, and a few male pop stars wearing eyeliner is hardly the glam rock embrace of queerness. And even then, it was a case of 'you come to us'. The likes of Bowie weren't dragging up at the Black Cap, but their gesture at least allowed a sense of celebration. The sun machine came down and we had a bit of a party.

For a little queer peacock like me in suburbia, the effect of the Bowies and the Bolans was cataclysmic. I have read snipes about Bowie's sexual about-turn since then, but you know what? – it wasn't Noddy Holder out there blurring the boundaries. As much as I love him it takes more than a top hat covered in mirrors!

Even if Bowie's claim that he was bisexual was a fashionable hoax, he marginalised himself for a sizeable chunk of his career. He took a risk that nobody else dared and in the process changed many lives. See what I mean by the devil being in the detail?

When I first came out I had an intense dislike of anyone camp, which, I had been taught, was the worst-case scenario. Now, as much as I defend Bowie, I also defend the likes of Larry Grayson, Kenneth Williams and the rest of those nelly fools. In their own fey way they shoehorned camp on to the agenda, and anyone who shoehorns camp on to any agenda is a friend of mine!

My loathing of camp was short-lived, and ironically occurred as I came out. It was suddenly halted by my then mentor Philip Sallon, who caught me being nasty to one of his simpering throng on a tube journey. As we were pulling into the gay mecca of Earl's Court on the Central Line, I was haranguing this boy among our crowd for being too obvious. Philip grimaced, as he is prone to do: 'You were only being vile to that queen because you saw your future.'

How true. Within weeks I was talking in full Palare: 'Bona to vada your dolly old eek,' and all that carry-on. Of course, I became bored of that particular form of gay expression and retreated to the middle ground where I remain to this day. Maybe, if the straight world had a more rounded view of us, we might have a more rounded view of ourselves. After all, we seem to put an awful lot of value on what straight people think of us. Part of this is due to the illusion of the existence of an all-embracing gay community. If we don't love ourselves, how the fuck are we going to love each other?

Even if there were some hippie gay revolution, you would still have to account for the fact that we are fallible human beings, but at the very least we should remember we are all refugees within our own culture. How could I, the son of an Irish refugee and a member of the great queer minority, uphold a prejudice against anybody?

Within the complexities of this rant lies my greatest dilemma, which you may not be surprised to find pisses in its own handbag.

Where's the glamour or mystery of living in an all-accepting happy-clappy society? There's nothing I enjoy more than seeing

Peter Tatchell hurling himself at Robert Mugabe or hanging off
the arm of the Archbishop of Canterbury screaming: 'It's an outrage!'

It's a fierce look and appeals to the troublemaker in me. I would
suggest, however, that Peter's biggest issue is actually personal and
that he would definitely benefit from half an hour on a bouncy
castle. In the grand scheme of things, what Peter is fighting for is
completely righteous, but by a funny old twist of fate, the end
result of all activism is a loss of individuality. Look at what the
Russian Revolution did for Soviet style. To quote dear old Quentin
Crisp: 'Never be on the tail end of a protest.' Like Quentin, I adore
a bon mot. Sometimes a neatly turned phrase can get to the heart
of the matter.

Of course equality is essential. For me, the argument about gay
equality is a human rights issue, and not a sexual one. It's convenient for society at large to keep it as a sexual debate, because the
in-built taboos and stereotypes can be dragged up to reinforce fear.
Our inability to see ourselves and others as individuals – regardless of our sexual preference, race and social standing – is actually
our greatest problem. That may sound a bit rich coming from me,
and although I've never been less than myself, I've always been
aware that I have everything in common with the rest of humanity.
That's why I got so much gyp from my gay compadres in the
eighties, who would diss me for being hetero user-friendly: 'Why
aren't you being more political?'

To some of us a flurry of ribbons makes as much of a statement as a placard. Isn't the best way to blow up a building from
inside? Do we have to throw the baby out with the boa for a
happy-ever-after Church-consecrated gay marriage and a mindset
which proclaims: 'We're just like you.' A centipede with an extra
leg is still a centipede.

But not quite.

11

U Can Never B 2 Queer

Back in the eighties, I was seen as the benchmark queer because I was the one plastered in make-up and wore androgynous clobber. George Michael passed for a straight stud but in fact it was he loitering around in bushes and public loos like some pre-war homosexual.

Privately he was every bit the predatory queer cliché and yet the entire universe couldn't see it, apart from me and my mother. And a French journalist who once said to me: 'Eezen't it a triumph for you zat George Michael 'az finally come out?' I was nonplussed. The journo was actually referring to his live rendition of Culture Club's 'Victims', which he once sang at Wembley Arena. This was long before he was caught in that LA toilet with his kecks down, wearing only a nicotine patch and a look of surprise when that LAPD cop turned out not to be a member of the Village People.

Don't you hate it when that happens?

For years queens on the London scene had openly discussed George's penchant for porcelain. It was really only a matter of time before he got caught and all the more shocking because he was so protective of his public image.

Being caught in a toilet could hardly be described as a glamorous moment and feeds perfectly into the notion that gay sex is desperate and seedy. Had he been caught making wild passionate love underneath the Hollywood sign, it would have been another story. Especially if it was after a Grammys ceremony and he was clutching an award.

Who knew that George was a thoroughly modern girl with an open relationship and everything! I'm afraid that's not something I would tolerate. I don't share my men or my chips.

In my opinion he only confirmed the idea that gay men are a bit rampant. Oh come on, why would someone in a relationship be cruising in toilets? There is absolutely no excuse when there are thousands of ways to meet other guys for gratuitous sex. Surely he knows how to work a computer? Thank God the cop showed up. George could never have come out to a glorious fanfare. He had to be caught, so that the air of him being set up gave the impression that he was a victim. The video for his song 'Outside' which followed the tawdry incident was played out like some sort of celebration of the newly liberated George, but he still kept it general, replete with a healthy selection of heterosexual couples joining in the alfresco grapple-fest. Was he saying we should all have the right to hump in the hedgerows, or was he, as I suspect, hedging his bets yet again?

My sniping at George has been relentless, but there's nothing new about faggots feuding. Pete Burns, whom I recently befriended after years of mindless bitching, joked that we were the modern-day Bette Davis and Joan Crawford and we admitted that behind the clawing we have always secretly admired each other.

Look at the hatred showered upon me by the likes of Holly Johnson and Jimmy Somerville. If that was about anything beyond plain old jealousy, it was the rather sad idea that in order to truly represent the gay community, you needed to be the right type of homosexual. The amusing thing about the whole business is that the gay community would much rather a Will Young than a well-hung.

The business of soliciting sexual activity in toilets is steeped in tradition and harks back to the days when public conveniences were the local gay clubs. There is no excuse for it now, but I can absolutely understand the attraction of a quick sexual transaction with a horny married man, although you have to see it for what it is: objectification at its most extreme. The terror aspect is also part of the thrill. I suppose you could say it's the cruising equivalent of skydiving. A lot of casual encounters, whether gay or straight, are about treating people like objects. We're back to the removal of intimacy, making sex a purely animalistic pastime.

If you think I'm making a judgement, I'm not. There's a lot of talk in the gay community about being 'completely free to express ourselves sexually'. I agree, but don't act like you're going to a temple to cleanse your spirit. As a kid I used to get a cheap thrill from reading the graffiti in public loos – 'Call John for rough sex' – along with those caveman-style etchings of the male genitalia. But that was back in the days when my sexuality was a naughty secret. Mind you, it's not as though I don't peruse that type of 'bog lore' these days! As we all know, there's nothing more sexy than repression. Wouldn't be a bad name for a cologne: Calvin Klein's Repression has a certain *je ne sais quoi*. A whiff of that and you'd know exactly where you stand.

I have no doubt had he not been caught, George would still be in the Closet Club Tropicana. His comment that he obviously wanted to be caught is of course true. To my mind, anyone who claims they can only meet guys in toilets is, forgive the pun, full of shit.

I first met the other George in the early eighties when he was briefly friendly with Philip Sallon (isn't everyone?). George used to come to clubs like Heaven with us. I never asked him if he was gay, I just assumed he must be. He would play Philip his early demos, and Philip would dispense advice, claiming, as he always did, 'I can spot a hit a mile off.' I didn't really get to know George that well but he seemed pleasant enough. Later, Philip would moan that he had dumped him as soon as he got a record deal. Actually, I think it was more about protecting his reputation, and hanging out with obvious queers was not a good look.

Around that time I was close to a black girl called Pat Fernandez, whom Philip nicknamed Black Pat – not one of his most original noms de plume. Pat and I were inseparable, but as George Michael became famous she traded in one George for another.

George and Pat could pass themselves off as a couple, and that's exactly what they did.

Who knows whether it was George's manager Simon Napier-Bell who advised him to leave the circus. It's quite usual for gay managers to tell their gay stars to disassociate themselves from nellies. I have met Simon a few times and he is great fun and a raging gossip but I'm not sure he knew George was gay at that point, so I suspect it was a decision made by George himself.

And, when he became a star, he was never that friendly if we met. I think he was terrified of me and my big mouth.

Years later I was told that George had described Philip and me as 'nasty vicious queens' and his friendship with us as a 'dark period'. I certainly don't remember it being that eventful.

I was always saying: 'He's gay,' because I couldn't stand the way George actively promoted himself as a ladykiller. It's one thing to keep quiet but another to deliberately paint a false picture.

One day I got a phone call from my friend Amanda screaming: 'He's done it, he's come out!' It was a false alarm because the interview in question was conducted by his friend, the journalist Tony Parsons, who also wrote George's biography. A close friend of George's had passed away and George was saying how much he loved him, not that they had been lovers. I remember thinking: 'What has to happen for this man to get over it?'

Shortly before the LA toilet incident, Parsons wrote a scathing piece about my rift with George. It was in reference to a comment I had made more than a year before and since then George and I had patched things up. I'd even been to a birthday dinner with him and Sarah and Keren from Bananarama. The timing was so odd and I was furious that Parsons had dragged up yesterday's news.

In his piece, Parsons said I was a hideous caricature of a homosexual, implying that George was a dignified one who chose not to flaunt his sexuality. He continued: 'One George went on to achieve global success and the other plays records to a few clubbers at the weekends.' Accompanying the piece was a cartoon of me as a fat lump of food waste. Writing about it does make me laugh now, and I don't care if you laugh too. It just seemed choice for a highly respected journalist to be using his privileged platform to attack me when it was his friend who was gilding the cliché. What makes it even funnier is George's gay evangelism since he came out: 'I am what I am.' Please shut up – somebody throw her a cerise boa!

I admit to a chuckle the morning the news broke but I didn't really give a shit. The media piled on to my doorstep and I joked: 'He's looking for love in all the wrong places.'

At the end of the day, the arrest was a good thing for George. What kind of life can you have if you have to hide what you are? I'm sure he's a lot happier now and that's the important thing.

At least I know why I was never invited to any of those Elton John parties in the eighties. I suppose that's something to be grateful for: 'You can bring Rose with the turned-up nose, but don't bring Lulu . . .'

12

Swallow Me

The current trend for boil-in-a-bag artists is frustrating for anyone who truly loves music. Young people are terribly complacent and it's a measure of how bad things are that Eminem is the height of outrage. What's so outrageous about being the cultural equivalent of a school bully?

That's why I recorded my White Label twelve-inch single 'Swallow Me', where I rapped about the great white saviour of hip hop.

Political correctness has stopped some folk from using certain words, but delete Eminem from that equation. In his song 'Without Me', Eminem calls Moby, who dared to slate him in the press, a 'balding thirty-six-year-old fag'. As Moby says, Eminem is attracting the attention of kids who are at an age where they could be terrified they might be queer. As for Eminem's response, I think: 'Madam, you protest too much!' He is very intelligent but he's a brat.

I can use the word 'fag' because I sleep with, and have relationships with, men, just as the black community can reclaim the word 'nigger'. But a white man using that term is asking for trouble. Eminem's success has put certain offensive language back on the map. I've had 'fag' shouted at me more times in the last couple of years than in the past decade, usually from kids.

Young kids these days are much more likely to use terms like 'faggot' because these words are pumping out of radio stations worldwide not only in hip-hop but also in ragga, where homophobia is disguised by terms like 'batty-boy' and 'chi-chi man'.

In 2004 Buju Banton finally apologised for records like 'Boom Bye Bye', which advocated the shooting of homosexuals. It took him ten years, and I reckon he only did so because it threatened his livelihood. Can you imagine a white artist being exonerated for such a crime with a simple apology?

Of course, it is important to acknowledge that most teenage boys don't need much of an excuse to be homophobic and Eminem's audience is mostly made up of teenagers coming to terms with their own sexuality, so he stirs up the innate paranoia which exists among that age group.

American rap music is without question a natural and understandable payback for years of racist oppression. For the first time ever in American black music history you have a self-contained black industry that is self-sufficient. Early MTV was slow in picking up on the rap explosion, so the black music industry created a situation where it could directly promote and sell itself to its own community. And Eminem is a testament to the confidence and power of that industry. The tables have been turned and black artists who, in the past, were part of a production line and had songs written for them have been replaced by artists who produce and write for themselves. Producers like Dr Dre, Missy Elliot and P. Diddy can also take their pick of new artists to nurture and polish for stardom. The big difference is that they are being nurtured by real artists who know the business inside out.

I admit that Eminem is good at his craft but musicians should confront stereotypes, not enforce them. He may only be saying what real people are saying in private, spouting racism and anti-Semitism, but those hateful views are not acceptable on record.

The success of Eminem proves how much the gap between the artist and the audience has shrunk. In theory it may seem like a good thing to tear down the walls between the famous and the people who make them so, but I wonder how much time Eminem spends chatting to his fans and making them tea?

Even with the best intentions, a career built on phoney realism is only a slightly more credible way of shifting units. As soon as an artist makes his first million, he can no longer claim that he's keeping it real. More like keeping it real estate. Likewise, J-Lo's line 'I'm still Jenny from the block' is possibly the most insincere and cynical lyric ever penned.

Rap was a genius invention and what it has done for black music in America can only be applauded. The reclaiming of the racist term 'nigger' is a cultural slap in the face to a country that was only freed from racial segregation in the last half-century.

However, rap's homophobic undercurrent is shameful when you remember how much black people have suffered. Surely, minorities should learn from their own pain and realise that suffering is not exclusive?

Rap musicians are most certainly today's most important cultural role models, yet they personify this contradiction, swaggering around in designer clobber, dripping in diamonds, gold, silver and platinum, referencing Cristal in their songs as they sit behind the wheels of expensive cars or lounge in designer pads. They compensate for these glamorous and camp excesses by being overly aggressive and brandishing guns.

The reason, I think, black artists in America are so keen to show off their wealth in what seems like an excessive manner is because most of these successful acts came from extreme poverty. This attitude has now bled into the black music scene in the UK and urban artists are no longer satisfied with boring old street cred. I wonder is the aggression just a way of hiding the embarrassment of being a little too flash?

I understand it because I grew up with nothing and it took me years to really respect money and to realise that it might not last for ever. Having so much success and money at such a young age, especially when you are not used to it, is very daunting. I was never one for flashing my wealth but I did spend it with complete relish.

If punk was all about anarchy, rap is all about avarice. Eminem is clearly trying to hold on to his street cred while being chauffer-driven for facials and mud wraps at the beauty parlour. Onstage, the truly ghetto fabulous will don the apparel of the street but behind closed doors it's all silk robes and cut-glass decanters.

You may say: why shouldn't someone who has grown up with nothing aspire to the better things in life? Eminem is every bit the poor boy made good and he embodies the American dream for all those trailer-trash kids who want a piece of the apple pie. When we look at America it is often the ethnic poverty that stands out but there are many white folk living on the breadline. In this respect, Eminem is a brilliant role model but he falls down in my eyes because he is trying too hard to be black.

A white boy entering the self-serving rap community has got to be very convincing if he wants to be embraced and considered credible. Rapping might seem easy to an outsider but to make it authentic you have to have a particular tone and all the moves to match.

Eminem has succeeded where all other white rappers have failed. Even if he has a handful of detractors, he is adored by the black community and worshipped by the white community because he is the first white rapper to get it right. In my opinion, it would be more of a triumph if Eminem added something new to the mix instead of just adding to the noise. The only reason Eminem is allowed to peddle his blatant homophobia is because certain hardcore sections of the reggae and hip hop community are unapologetically homophobic.

Once you become famous you realise that stars are just ordinary people with varying talents and often skewed political logic. I admire Elton John but I don't agree with his politics. I love his voice and hearing stories about his regular hissy fits but I think he is wrapped up in his legend, though in the pomp rock seventies stars were treated with greater reverence. Elton performing the duet with Eminem at the MTV Awards in 2002 is like me singing with Pol Pot. I think Elton John sang with him because he's so desperate to be hip rather than out of malice, but that's what happens when you live in a cultural bubble, full of fresh-cut flowers. Elton said that Eminem was one of the most important artists of our time. That's like comparing the Sugababes to Aretha Franklin.

It was a bad move, especially when Elton had just recorded a song about Matthew Sheppard, the American student who was killed by queer haters a couple of years before. Elton seems to be fixated with being trendy. He always knows who is up-and-coming but he can be quite selfish. I met him when I first formed Culture Club and was thrilled. We didn't become friends because he was still closeted back then and I was such an obvious queer. My reputation for saying the wrong thing assured that I would never get invited to his famous eighties parties.

Obviously when Elton befriended George Michael there was no chance of my being part of the 'velvet mafia', but when I had a hit with 'The Crying Game' in the US in the early nineties, Elton rang to congratulate me and we went out for dinner. I took MC Kinky and Elton was with some guy who had worked with the Rolling Stones. All through dinner he was grilling me about George Michael and asking me if George was gay. I felt as if I was deliberately holding my tongue and I said I didn't really know. It was a nice evening and afterwards I waved him goodbye in his Rolls as he blared my song 'Generations of Love' from his CD player.

At the dinner Elton gave me his number and I said I would ring him. When I did the number had been changed. I don't imagine for a minute he did it deliberately, but he could have let me know. The next time I saw him was at a charity event at a London restaurant. I told him it was very rude just to change his number and he seemed really uncomfortable. One of his friends seated at my table said: 'I'm glad you did that. He doesn't get enough honesty.'

I would have said the same thing whoever he was, but realised then that Elton was every bit the star and was probably used to having everyone at his beck and call. Still, it really changed my opinion of him.

When Elton recorded 'Sorry Seems to Be the Hardest Word' with Blue I made a crack in my *Express* column about them in the video looking really terrified of the big nelly on the piano, going to each other: 'Which one do you think he fancies?' A few nights later a friend of mine started a night at West End club Rouge, and asked me to sing a song during the launch party. David Furnish turned up with Neil Tennant, who told me: 'Elton's not very happy with you.' I responded: 'Who made him the headmaster?'

They started going on about the Eminem business. I told them that it was like the victim identifying with the persecutor and that they argued in favour of free speech but couldn't take it when someone spoke freely. Then I went off to the toilet. Suddenly there was a banging at the door. It was David, shouting: 'Why do you keep having a go at my boyfriend?'

I offered to talk to him when I had finished on the loo but he said: 'I've got nothing more to say to you.' The next morning the *Daily Mirror*'s 3AM gossip page ran a story saying not only that I had been booed during my performance – which is bollocks – but that I had run from David Furnish and cowered in a toilet.

Anyone who thinks I would run from David Furnish is a fool. The way people pussyfoot around Elton is really sad, but you create your own circle of friends. I don't dislike Elton and I'm sorry that he thinks I do, but if he can speak his mind and support Eminem's right to free speech, well, what more can I say? It's bonkers to be having a drama with Elton, one of my musical heroes. When I was listening to songs like *Daniel* in my bedroom at the age of fourteen I could never imagine I'd be having a media spat with him.

It's all completely Pinball Wizard, in fact.

13

Starman

As a kid Bowie had a huge effect on me. Not only was his music completely different from the rest of pop at that time, but also because he presented a complete package – the way he looked, the songs he sang, what he said in interviews.

When I was a teenager I was convinced that David and Angie Bowie sat around on oversized cushions all day while assistants paraded before them with gifts sent from admirers. They didn't eat like the rest of us. They drank from test tubes full of brightly coloured liquid or consumed food in pill form, like astronauts. During their lazy days they would receive visits from other stars like Marc Bolan or the camp one from the Sweet.

Because I had to go to school and do what I was told, the idea of living this sparkling bohemian lifestyle seemed utterly spectacular. I had no idea pop stars were just ordinary people who had to wipe their own arses. I didn't think about Bowie stubbing his toe on the bed in the morning as he rushed to the loo, or Angie screaming and slamming the fridge door because they had run out of milk. A lot of the romance that was once associated with fame has now diminished. The information age has given us far too much information. Now we see it all and know how most of it is done. Pop stars are just like us with more money and bigger bathrooms. I used to dream about having a pair of platform slingbacks like the ones Bowie wore when he performed 'Jean Genie' on *Top of the Pops*. It took me about eighteen years to get them and I had to have them handmade. How hard would it be to dress like Ronan Keating?

I remember writing to *Opportunity Knocks*, the talent show presented by Hughie Green, to see if I could go on and sing. I don't think I would have suited endless seasons on cruise ships but I was very young and naive. Now the type of artists that should be walking the plank are selling millions of records and showing off their beige sofas in *Hello!*.

Bowie recently commented that when he was getting into music back in the mid-sixties it was not considered a career opportunity. Anyone who said they were going to be a musician was told to get a proper job. These days it wouldn't be strange to see an ad in the jobcentre announcing: 'Pop star wanted'.

I realise that I am being snobbish but I guess, in some cases at least, snobbery is essential. You don't get any old git knocking up a painting and having it hung in the Tate. I suspect the art critic Brian Sewell would beg to differ, but there is at least some process a painter has to go through to achieve success.

Tracey Emin, whom I love and have known since she was a sixteen-year-old ragamuffin in Margate, was once asked by a journalist: 'How do you take to the suggestion that anyone could have put an unmade bed in an art gallery for a million pounds?' She snipped: 'They didn't though, did they? I did.' Can you imagine Britney Spears coming up with such a gun-slinging response?

If the general public wants to buy records by the Cheeky Girls or Bob the Builder, who am I to question them? There are plenty of things I have turned my hands to which I am not qualified for. I am sure certain writers at the *Sunday Express*, where I wrote my weekly column for eight years, were put out that I got the job. After all, they probably struggled through an English degree and I was kicked out of school with zero qualifications.

I grew up listening to just about everything from jazz to glam to Philly soul and reggae, and would buy any album with an interesting sleeve. In fact, that's how I discovered the seminal

Krautrock group Can but I won't pretend I played *Incandescence* over and over and that it spawned my interest in electronica.

I fell upon Pink Floyd and Black Sabbath while babysitting for my cousin Tina, but my musical tastes were completely indiscriminate – 'Yellow River' by Christie seemed as refreshing as the soothing croon of Ella Fitzgerald, early lovers' rock would sit alongside Cockney Rebel and there was no nonsense about which type of music was cooler. I just loved music because it came from a world that was so much more exotic than my own.

But Bowie – who I inherited from my older brother Richard – was the brightest vision in my youth and I believe he has had a greater influence on modern pop culture than any other musician. After seeing Ziggy at Lewisham Odeon in 1973 I was transfixed and then destroyed when I discovered that he retired two days later. How lucky was I to catch the penultimate performance, especially at the age of twelve? I went on my own, such was my determination to see the vision that was Ziggy.

Bowie's decision to kill off Ziggy in his prime was as depressing then as it seems wise now. One of the things I loved about him was that he constantly challenged the public perception of himself, and I thought that was what being a pop star was all about.

I've been lucky enough to have met David a few times, and when I did a webchat with him for his site a couple of years back he said he was 'absolutely knocked out' that I had covered his Ziggy Stardust song 'Starman', though I don't know what he thought when I did 'Sorrow' on the Christmas 2002 edition of *Celebrity Stars in their Eyes*! I'm the only celebrity to have won the show twice, but then that's no great surprise since the only thing I left school with was A-level Bowie. While in New York a couple of years back, I had dinner with David and Iman and a couple of guys from Christian Dior. I dragged along my friend Michael Cavadias – or Lily of the Valley as he's known on the drag scene.

I called Lily and said: 'What are you doing tonight?'

He replied: 'Nothing much.'

'Past tense,' I said. 'We're having dinner with Ziggy Stardust.'

I put the phone down and then immediately rang him back.

'Don't embarrass me or anything,' I told him. He replied drily: 'Oh, I'm just getting into my full Ziggy drag right now.'

I was terribly nervous all day because although I'd met him a few times I hadn't spent quality time with David before. He's super-smart, well read and up on everything – the latest, coolest music, films, art and popular culture. He's also very charming and has the ability to put everyone at ease while being perfectly comfortable with his legendary status. He was fabulous to Michael, who was actually quite terrified. I wasn't as nervous as I thought I'd be, but did keep thinking: 'Ohmigod, it's really him!' Iman is gorgeous and very down-to-earth. They get on so well it made me feel like I needed to fall in love.

David has amazing recall, and said that he clearly remembered the first time we met, at Le Beat Route in Soho in 1980, long before I was famous. This was during my freaked-out geisha phase, so I was wearing a kimono with my hair standing straight up in a shock above my head and heavy make-up. I was standing at the bar trying to exude cool when inside I was screaming: 'Ohmigod, David Bowie's here!' He came across and congratulated me on my appearance, saying that I looked like his friend Klaus Nomi. I came back with some witty riposte like: 'I've never been so insulted. I look like me!'

In fact, I'd never heard of Klaus Nomi, and went straight out and bought an album the next day. Then I saw him doing backing vocals for David on a video from *Saturday Night Live*. I thought he looked great, and realised I had been paid a compliment all along.

I've always thought that Angie was an underrated influence on David. She was with him from 1969 to 1974, through his most amazing transitions and some of his best material: *The Man Who Sold the World*, *Hunky Dory*, *Ziggy*, *Aladdin Sane*. When I told him that I was very impressed Angie had told me to fuck off as a kid hanging around outside Haddon Hall, the house they shared in Beckenham, he simply said: 'That was Angie's greatest line.'

In some ways I can understand the codness – my word for the animosity – between them. Like Jon Moss, Angie was part of a glittering pop moment, and acts as a constant reality check. A lot of hard-core Bowie fans love Angie. It seemed she was a pushy, ultra-hip chick who informed some of his best moves and they looked so amazing together.

I've communicated with Angie via email and found her amusing and charmingly brittle. I once sent her a poem I'd written and she promptly sent it back edited. Apologising, she said: 'Please don't be offended.'

Recently, Morrissey made the unthinkable fan faux pas by dissing Bowie during an interview. He claimed that the British public had fallen in love with Ziggy Stardust and not David Bowie. There have been too many spectacular Bowie moments since Ziggy for that ever to be true. For me some of Bowie's finest work eclipsed the glam years; the songs 'Word on a Wing', 'Scary Monsters', 'Always Crashing in the Same Car'. I rest my slingback platforms.

From what I understand, Morrissey fell out with Bowie during a tour, but just as there is a defined Bowie etiquette, there is also a clear Morrissey one. Pull a fox-fur stole out of your handbag or, God forbid, admit to a penchant for Cumberland sausage, and Mozza will send you to Manchester.

I heard he and Pete Burns had a falling out because Pete once turned up to meet him in some fur creation. I imagine Pete did it deliberately, which makes it all the more amusing.

Morrissey also fell out with Siouxsie Sioux after they recorded their brilliant duet 'Interlude'. Apparently, he said she was too aggressive, as opposed to passive-aggressive.

When I was having dinner with David that time, a chirpy young American boy approached the table and said: 'Hey, would you guys come and sing "Happy Birthday" to my girlfriend?'

I was about to rise to my feet when David told him: 'That's really not appropriate.'

There's the difference, and, I guess, that's why he's David Bowie.

14

Bitter & Chips

It's inconceivable to anyone who loves music to comprehend an artist of Bowie's stature being without a record deal. Yet Virgin Records, to whom I had been contracted since I was a spiky youth, dropped him because of poor record sales just a few years ago.

This was around the time they signed Mariah Carey for $35 million and did a similarly bonkers deal with Janet Jackson. It stunk of the worst type of disrespect, and it came as no surprise that they let me go in similar fashion.

I sent a letter to the MD Paul Conroy saying there was absolutely no point in continuing the relationship. They didn't exactly get down on their knees and sing: 'Baby, please don't go.' It taught me to expect no sympathy from rock 'n' roll. If you are an actor there is a union which watches your back, and even offers some provisions for those who fall on hard times. Maybe I was expecting at least some respect; after all Culture Club helped build the Virgin empire. I remember going around Europe as 'Do You Really Want to Hurt Me' was charting in various countries and visiting Virgin's temporary offices which were often someone's front room in Bruges or Basle.

Branson admits in his book that Culture Club paid for his airline. I remember trying to get a free ticket for a make-up artist to come from America to do a video and I was offered a lousy discount. I wasn't expecting him to say: 'Jump on any flight you like for free.' I'm not the kind of person who empties the minibar in a hotel room because someone else is paying.

The last album I did while signed to Virgin was *Cheapness and Beauty*. It was a departure for me in many ways; certainly more personal and brutishly gay than anything I had done before. I used hard glam guitars and worked with indie rock producer Jessica Corcoran, which led to lazy media observations suggesting I was trying to pass myself off as an 'angry artist'.

The first single was a cover of Iggy Pop and Bowie's 'Funtime', which picked up quite a bit of play on Radio One, mainly on the novelty value of asking listeners: 'Who's this?' Virgin had committed to following 'Funtime' with an equally aggressive track but when it only reached the early forties − which I was really happy with because I hadn't had a record in the charts for ages − they chickened out and went for the outwardly gay folkie 'Same Thing in Reverse', which was only ever played by Nicky Campbell, who was alone in championing it for months. In the US a radio producer said to me: 'This song has a fantastic melody but it's too gay.' After 'Same Thing in Reverse' bombed Virgin elected to put out 'Il Adore' − a song about Aids and death! − instead of sticking to the plan of releasing either 'Genocide Peroxide' or 'God Don't Hold a Grudge'. Obviously that didn't set the charts alight either.

This whole episode made me realise that when it comes to artists like Bowie or me, it's a case of: what do you do with the ex-superstar? You're doomed by your own legacy and the 'what if' factor kicks in. What if I came up with another 'Karma Chameleon'? You end up not with A&R but Umm & Aah; it's as though they are intimidated by your past and too lily-livered to tell you that your record stinks.

There aren't many artists who take well to criticism. If somebody had had the balls to tell me where I was going wrong I might have thrown a computer through the window and stropped off, but I would have sat down and listened to constructive suggestions.

Maybe it's stupidity or wilfulness, but I'm not the kind of artist who will do anything to have a hit record. I know I can hold a tune and if I was simply hungry for success I could have made it happen.

Sometimes there are conspiracies that align to convince you that something pig-awful is the best thing since Elvis. Equally, if a genius song or band receives a kick in the eye from the critics or the infinitely cool they whither and die.

Morrissey's triumphant return to pop iconography in 2004 is a case in point. *Maladjusted*, his 1997 album, was universally panned, and yet for me it was like a classic Bowie album, say *Hunky Dory*. Tracks such as 'Trouble Loves Me' and 'Wide To Receive' were some of his most romantic. Then there were the lyrics:

> So the choice I have made,
> May seem wrong in your eyes.
> But who asked you anyway?
> It's my life to ruin, my own way.

Or:

> I don't get along with myself.
> And I don't much care for anyone else.

I remember forcing friends to buy the album and reading the reviews and ranting: 'This is absolute bullshit!'

There are plenty of examples of artists who achieved nothing commercially beyond having the wrong or right hair-do, yet have outlived bands who were shoved up your rectum ad nauseam. And trust me, it's hard to add nauseam in that particular area. The New York Dolls, Velvet Underground, The Stooges, all of their classic images adorn T-shirts sported by the likes of Avril Lavigne and The Corrs.

I remember bumping into Andrea Corr in the lobby of a Parisian hotel. I was wearing a Marilyn Manson T-shirt and she said: 'Ooh, I find him creepy.' At the MTV Awards one year, after a spell-binding Third Reich-tinged performance of 'Beautiful

People' by Manson, I was approached by a famous young American actor who looked at me in disbelief, asking: 'You like that?!!' Obviously the beam on my face wasn't enough.

'It was pure oxygen,' I said.

The most prevalent example of this cultural about-face is the new-found worship of that filthy little Bowery hole CBGBs: you can't move for film stars, TV ads and pop stars sporting the club's logo. I haven't seen Her Majesty out hunting with the corgis in a CBGB tee, but it's only a matter of time before the stylists get to her.

If we are going to blame anyone for this hypocrisy the buck stops with MTV. I was one of the fools that went along and did a public service message for them ('I want my MTV') when all they played was country videos and everything by Rod Stewart. The rise of MTV and video-culture eventually brought pop music to the level of lowest-common denominator advertising.

Look back at Bowie's video for 'Life On Mars' and you see a bleached figure in a white room wearing an electric blue suit with matching eyeliner. It still captivates to this moment. The beauty of all of those pre-MTV videos is that the primary impulse was to sell the artist as a dream, not a can of beans.

The only music that has benefited from the rise of MTV is black music, which ironically was shunned by the channel for many years.

After MTV the biggest culprit is the stylist (excluding the late Ray Petri and the still genius Judy Blame, who could turn up with a bag of safety pins and a cork and create a fashion revolution).

Pop stars have always used image and designers have always hooked into musicians for the coolest exposure. These days the degree of influence of stylists has wreaked tragic distortions. Chuck enough eyeliner and a shredded Motorhead T-shirt on a stage school brat and hey presto! Instant cool. Not.

I almost wept when I saw Take That don Vivienne Westwood bondage pants.

The cunning of sixties managers rounding up hordes of

screaming girls now seems naive when you look at the blatant cynicism of today's pop.

The most impressive, yet simple outfit I've seen in eons was worn by my friend Nigel Nuts at the *Taboo* opening party in New York: just a simple black T-shirt with the slogan No Queer Dresses Me.

Writing *Take It Like a Man* and making such a personal album as *Cheapness and Beauty* forced me to think seriously about whether I really wanted to be a pop star again. This was around the time when I'd gone into therapy, off on mad find-yourself courses and drinking copious amounts of bancha twig tea.

It wasn't as if I had ever expected to be in a really successful band or to become a pop icon. Of course I loved it, and the attention was great, but, to be honest, my main concerns during those years centred around Jon Moss. Issues such as: were we sharing a hotel room that night or was he going off with a girl?

Perhaps I had accepted that something major in my life had come to an end. The songs I wrote in Culture Club were a living diary. *Cheapness and Beauty* was a kind of full stop. For a long time I deluded myself that Jon and I could pick up where we had left off. In a way the lunacy I had experienced with Culture Club and Jon had been replaced by shocking clarity. I briefly thought about a complete reinvention – a major diet, a revolutionary new look – but I didn't have the patience or the desire.

I'm not suggesting that I had no soul or integrity before, but I was certainly more concerned with surface things. I talked convincingly with a lot of heart, but I never entirely felt it.

On top of this I'd become more defiant about my sexuality and had started to grow into myself, perhaps a little too much for some people. I was always being called fat and a failure in the press, but it started to bother me less. Up until then it was as though I'd been a prisoner of my imperfections.

I did my fair share of StairMaster, aerobics and yoga but I always got bored. I would read the stuff that was written about Madonna, and no matter how many hours she put in at the gym, her looks were still pulled apart. She was either too muscular or too skinny; even hard-earned perfection has its pitfalls.

Having therapy made me more aware of myself and in a strange sense more accepting of my lunacy. Knowing why you do something doesn't necessarily stop you doing it. I'd grown up but also accepted that I'd always be a little insane.

Perhaps that's why I ended up going back to Virgin when I released my last solo album *U Can Never B 2 Straight*. The album was a collection of my favourite acoustic songs and a bunch of new ones. Virgin owned the majority of them, so it seemed a sensible move. They appeared happy to welcome me back, though in hindsight I realise I was being appeased as a way of securing the release of the *Twenty Years of Culture Club* box-set. *Taboo* had taken off by that stage, and it was a perfect opportunity for them to surf on that nostalgia wave and shift some back catalogue.

I was extremely proud of *U Can Never B 2 Straight* but wasn't expecting too much from it. I was just happy that it was out and that one or two people might hear it. They'd have had to look hard because Virgin waited two months to put up posters, and even then they plastered them around Hampstead, an old music biz trick to keep the artist happy. As it turned out they barely bothered to promote the *Culture Club* box-set either. I think Virgin was under the illusion it would sell itself and jump off the shelves into a million Christmas stockings.

There were plans to release a three-track Culture Club EP which included a really cool remix of 'Church of the Poisoned Mind', but Virgin also changed their minds on that. I made it available on the Internet along with the cover artwork, and put: 'Copyright out of control.' I heard later that Virgin were amused.

I felt that if they couldn't even flog the classics, it was pointless to keep resuscitating Culture Club.

15

Cheapness and Beauty

Over the past few years it may have seemed that my verbal out-pourings have been more prolific than my musical ones. Sometimes I wonder whether I have become too famous for just being a quip in a hat, but at the same time, I know that people like what I do musically, and as long as there is an audience – however intimate – I'm happy.

I work very hard. There was a period in the eighties, post-Culture Club, when I didn't for two or three years, but still led a lavish lifestyle. My manager Tony brought it home to me when he said: 'If you carry on like this you'll lose your house.'

At the time I was being a bit snobby about the work that was being offered because I thought it was beneath me. But then I thought: 'Fuck it, this is stupid, let's do it.' One of the first gigs I played after that was in France with Boney M, for a lot of money.

Those trips were made easier by the fact that I had a great band around me. I didn't have to fight over every decision. They respected me because of my musical history and it was reciprocated.

The main disagreements were always between myself and MC Kinky, who added a quirky element to our sound with her unique rapping and chatting. I met Caron at Fred's bar, off Wardour Street when she approached me and asked: 'Do you still work with reggae chatters?'

I replied: 'I haven't for a while, but if you're good, who knows?'

She ended up chatting in my ear over the club's dance grooves and she was very good. She gave me an acetate of one of her first recordings, 'Reggae Gone A Kinky', and it was most certainly toasting with a twist.

Her lyrics were outrageous and very gay-friendly, attacking the homophobic elements of the reggae scene. It fitted in really well with what I was doing and we started to record and perform together.

A lot of people thought Caron was my sister and like siblings we had a suffocatingly close relationship. Our exchanges quickly escalated into personal slanging matches and we both became very skilled at pushing each other's buttons. I don't think I have ever met anybody with such an ability to wind me up, and I doubt that I made her life a picnic.

The first track we recorded together was 'Kipsy', a song about a model rep friend who was busted for dealing ecstasy. That track caused huge controversy and the girl we wrote it about threatened to sue us. Instead she settled for some signed albums.

I'd told Caron the story of Kipsy's drug bust and she turned it into an amazing rap. Her lyrical and melodic skills were never in question but we both found it hard to make distinctions between professional and personal behaviour; we were together every single day for six or seven years and it took its toll.

She was involved in some of my favourite and, in my opinion, best music including 'Generations of Love' and 'Everything Starts With an E'.

The problems really started when she went on to record her own material for my label More Protein, which was backed by Virgin Records. Like most uncompromising artists she found it impossible to listen to anyone else's opinions, but blamed everybody else when things went wrong.

I always felt that if she had let others handle the music and concentrated on lyrics and melodies, it would have been a winning formula. Caron insisted on controlling every aspect and this resulted in a string of records which were almost great. No matter who she collaborated with, within hours they were labelled wankers.

Never for a moment could she consider that the problem was her attitude.

Caron's big break came when she worked with Erasure on their *Abbesque* EP which reached Number One. I always felt Virgin should have capitalised on the success of that record by having some cool remixers work on her tracks but our relationship with Virgin was very fragile at that point.

Unbeknown to me they were already planning to drop More Protein and within a few weeks I was called to a meeting which resulted in the label being axed. Because Virgin kept me as a solo artist they were obviously deeply embarrassed, and in an uncharacteristic gesture they signed the entire label and its back catalogue over to me.

I decided to continue More Protein as an independent and enlisted an ex-RCA guy called Ross Fitzsimmons to run it.

Ross and I had a meeting with Caron and asked her to stay with the label. Caron told me: 'You've done everything you can for me, I think I need to move on.' She was about to sign a management contract with a woman called Jackie Davidson who was very well-connected on the ragga scene, working with the likes of Shabba Ranks. His career had blown up not only in the UK but America as well. There was talk of Caron signing to Warner US and she was evidently excited.

Sadly, we got into a heavy contractual dispute. I was desperate not to lose her and offered her more than she was entitled to. That wasn't good enough.

She ranted: 'You're supposed to be my fucking friend!'

I responded: 'So are you, but you're quite prepared to fuck off with Jackie Davidson after all the work I have done.'

I really believe she thought that I was somehow in cahoots with Virgin and deliberately trying to hold her career back.

Despite the fact that we gave Caron her share of the Erasure royalties, she went into overdrive, telling everyone in London that I was a thief, and would scream 'Berry Gordy' at me in public.

She hired a lawyer who issued a writ ordering me to pay all the royalties to her. Once her lawyer read the contract, he dropped the case.

When that bid failed she went to the Musicians' Union and her father would call me up at all hours of the night. Nothing came of any of it.

Part of me wanted just to give her the money to shut her up, but I thought: 'Why should I?'

Caron wouldn't let it lie and tried to poison everybody against me, even going so far as to badmouth me in a record. For most people it would have been difficult to decipher her ragga rantings, but because I know Jamaican patois I knew that when she chatted: 'Check yer brudda, yer sistah' and went on to talk about 'yer junkie murderahs,' she was referring to me and my family.

The highlight of our feud was when I was arrested for aggravated assault. I'd seen Caron at a fashion party at Harvey Nichols and foolishly tried to make amends. Before I managed to get a sentence out she shrieked in front of everyone: 'You fat cunt! You ugly fat cunt! You thief!'

As she turned away I grabbed her arm but she pulled away and I left. The following morning there was a story about a pop star attacking a girl at the same party, so I called the police.

Along with my lawyer Gary Lux I went to Earl's Court police station where I was formally arrested and gave a statement. Caron had told the police that I had punched her in the breast, twisted her arm up her back and pushed her to the floor.

I knew there were surveillance cameras in the building and asked them to check them out. I also called Harvey Nicks to see if anyone working there had seen anything.

The charges came to nothing and after that I realised that there was no point in me trying to heal the wounds. I often see Caron looking at me scathingly across the dancefloor at Nag Nag Nag but I stay well out of her way.

There were many adventures before things became as ugly as they have. I'll never forget one time with Jesus Loves You, when we found ourselves playing a leather bar in Arkansas. It was snowing heavily outside and we had to change in the storeroom surrounded by whips, cock-rings and dildos. I laugh about it now but at the time I looked at the rest of the band and said: 'What the fuck went wrong?!'

Luckily I've always had the ability to laugh at myself. The same could not be said of George Michael. I'd never write a song called 'Amazing' unless it actually was. In Culture Club I constantly compromised and had to be deliberately ambiguous with my lyrics. Being a solo artist gave me the freedom to express myself completely and a brand new truthfulness shone through in my work. I try to write about love and relationships in an honest and unpredictable way, because love is rarely honest and always unpredictable. That's why my lyrics are often bittersweet and verging on caustic. Bob Dylan was once asked why so many of his songs appeared to be putdowns of other people. He said: 'Actually, they're all about me.'

Right on, Bob.

There's no greater example of this than his song 'Positively Fourth Street' – reportedly about Joan Baez – which is as emotionally stirring as her sweet punch back, 'Diamonds & Rust'.

I have used and continue to use my songs to convey messages to those I love or those who have wounded me. I know I often cross the line of what is acceptable in other people's eyes, but my art is one area in which I will no longer compromise.

In Culture Club the emphasis was more on chart-driven pop but even then I had my own peculiar way of putting my point across. Titles like 'Karma Chameleon' or 'Church of the Poisoned Mind', are hardly run of the mill. Even when I'm being accusing, or playing the victim, there is always a sense of romantic optimism. In any area of one's life the ugliest response is silence, the black hole of emotion. I always feel at my most empty when there is no desire to react. Only then do I know it's all over.

As a musician and singer-songwriter I guess I really found my feet when I met the guitarist John Themis in the early nineties, when I was recording stuff like 'Bow Down Mister'. Our partnership really came into its own as I started putting the songs together for my third solo album *Cheapness and Beauty*. All the songs on that album were about the people and situations in my first book, including Jon Moss, even though our relationship had ended many years before. The song 'Cheapness and Beauty' itself has the line 'Judas in blue jeans'. Guess who that is?

I'll probably always reference Jon in my songs and the same applies to most lovers, because they always leave behind a part of themselves. The past tends to rear its ugly head, particularly when one is feeling melancholy.

During the recording of *Cheapness and Beauty* John Themis was really good for me because he's technically excellent and also has a lot of empathy with where I am coming from musically. Like me he can bounce from style to style.

I hired John from an agency to play on 'Bow Down Mister' after trying out several guitarists and we got on like a house on fire. John is one of those people you can't help but warm to, unless your natural habitat is an Electrolux freezer.

I feel I've written some of my finest songs with him: 'If I Could Fly', which a *Melody Maker* journalist described as 'almost Brecht-like' (I mention this because such compliments are rare and shocking); 'Il Adore', which became a major song in *Taboo*; and of course, 'Unfinished Business', the song which landed me in court with Kirk Brandon. John is a rare talent who can also accommodate my lack of patience.

One other great thing about John is that if you want a Kazakh nose-flautist, John will inevitably tell you: 'Actually, by some strange coincidence, I played with Jason Donovan in the capital of Kazahkstan and we met this cross-dressing nose-flute player there. I've got his number here.'

Through John I met singer Zee Asha, a powerhouse vocalist and the closest thing to Helen Terry I'd met since Culture Club days. On tour Zee would always join me on the 'girly' bus, though she was more than capable of holding her own among the boys.

On the last Culture Club tour we almost got into a fracas with some drunken louts in Manchester, who thought it was highly amusing to repeatedly sing 'Karma Chameleon' at the top of their voices in the hotel bar. It's a joke that's not even funny to start with, so you can imagine how it began to grate as we tried to relax after a gig.

Things got heated when one of them came over and tried to further intimidate us by pretending to be friendly, offering to shake hands. Zee leapt to her feet, her chest puffed out, and sized up to the whole lot of them, like a seasoned Mecca Ballroom bouncer: 'You've had your fun, now sit down, mate. That's what you're gonna do.' They backed down immediately, and Zee proved that she is indeed an honorary geezer.

Zee is not unlike myself in her ability to switch from butch to femme with alacrity. Waking up with her on the tour bus one was never sure which role she would adopt. It's fair to say Zee is not a morning person, but even in her worst mood she's somewhat of an accidental comedian. Watching her strop off the bus like Peggy Mount on steroids would always crack me up. She was always sweetness itself once she'd been fed and watered and applied her various lotions and potions. Her company is as invigorating as her voice.

Equally hilarious is Linda Duggan, a pint-sized Irish girl with a voice of pure silk and a verbal repertoire that would shame a barrack room.

During the Culture Club reunion tour she would always come off stage singing: 'Everyday is like my arsehole . . .' On the tour bus she would keep us amused with her various invented characters and stories about people she'd worked with. I'm quite sure she has a few stories about me.

It was Zee who introduced me to Kevan Frost, an ex-Formula One racing driver-cum-British Airways trolley dolly. He came on board during the 'Cheapness and Beauty' tour of South America to play second guitar, percussion and provide backing vocals. Later, Kevan joined us for a tour of America. Halfway through, our bass player Winston Blisset had to exit pronto because there were complications with his wife's pregnancy, and it looked like the rest of the dates would have to be pulled. Kevan piped up: 'Do you want me to play bass?' It turned out that bass was his main instrument, but how was he going to learn the entire set in less than eight hours? He assured us that he could, and locked himself in his room to learn the bass parts. That night's gig went off without a glitch and Kevan proved himself the indispensable force he is.

While I continued to collaborate with John Themis I also started to write with Kevan, songs such as 'St Christopher',

'Wrong' and 'Julian', which appeared on *U Can Never B 2 Straight*.

'Julian' — and some other songs — were written about one of my biggest emotional time bombs of the last few years. I should have known it was going to end in tears when his opening comment to me was: 'Can I be your protégé?' Doesn't have quite the same ring as 'I can be your bodyguard, you can be my long-lost pal', does it? I was suckered by his beauty; then again I always am.

When my mother met Julian she said: 'Son, he's too young for you.' I was old enough to be his father but he seduced me with the skill of a seasoned adult.

He was amazing in bed and affectionate in the mornings — that's my way of telling whether a relationship will work. How wrong you can be. I fell for him like a suitcase full of bricks dropped from the top of a skyscraper.

Julian wanted to be famous more than anyone I've ever met. He worked me and said all the right things but was hideously calculating in the same breath.

We saw each other over a period of about six months but then things began to fall apart. One night I called the ivory tower where he lived and played the heartbreaking song 'God Give Me Strength' from the soundtrack to *Grace of My Heart* into his answering machine.

As I was about to put the phone down I heard a woman's voice. It was his mum. I thought I'd rung the wrong number but she knew who I was. 'You sound like you're hurting,' she said softly. I was. We spoke for three and a half hours. I thought she was an amazing woman.

I decided it would have been pointless to lie to her about our relationship. After all, she is a therapist and it turned out that she had less of a problem with her son's sexuality then he did. She said: 'Julian would never say he loved you if he didn't mean it. He's my baby, I know him.' It was easy to have a logical conversation with his mother, who is a Gemini and understood me perfectly. Expecting Julian, who was twenty-one at the time, to express himself was foolish. I imagine he later portrayed me as an obsessed queer and denied the whole thing.

I do think that he started to care for me but I was such a scary proposition that I have to take some responsibility for driving him away. I was always testing him to see if he really cared and it didn't help that he wanted our relationship to be a secret. I probably could have handled the situation better, but I had no idea I would end up feeling so much for him.

His capacity for fantasy was relentless. When I met him he was bragging about having thousands of pounds in the bank. I didn't make it an issue. I thought it was just youthful stupidity and an attempt to prove he was important. But I reacted badly to his rejection and a lot of quite acidic and accusing songs were inspired by what I was feeling:

> Why can't you pick up the phone?
> Oh how gutless can you be?
> Run as far as you can
> You'll never escape me.

It took me a long time to get over him and I used my social platform to hound him (don't get too Glenn Close). I did warn him when we first met: 'Mess with my heart and I'll mess with your head.' For a long time I would wake up and it was like the Kylie song, I couldn't get him out of my head.

I bumped into him by chance last summer outside Heaven, where he was trying to gain free entry. I got him into the club, so at least I was of use again, and it was the dignified thing to do, better than telling him to fuck off. He gave me one of those loaded, dreamy looks which begged the question: 'How much power do I still have over you?' I just thought: 'Don't even try it, mate.'

My writing on *U Can Never B 2 Straight*, as ever, mirrored my mood at the time. I was feeling reflective and possibly indulgent after the three-year nostalgia-fest with Culture Club. It brought me back to that space of no compromise. When I played Amanda Ghost the song 'Julian', she said: 'You can't, George. It's so personal.' This wasn't the first time I'd heard this line, but in some ways this was the best compliment Amanda could have paid me.

I first encountered Amanda – whose real surname is Gosein – through Philip Sallon, who was always insisting: 'You'd love her, she's very you, mouthy and opinionated.' Even if one isn't mouthy or opinionated to begin with, a few months in Philip's company will cure that!

Anyway, I met Amanda and we didn't really hit if off at first, but I was very taken by her cousin Ian, or was it Scott or Fabian? He had quite a few different names at the time as he was embarking on a pop career and felt Ian to be a bit of an unexciting pop moniker.

Imagine: 'Tonight! On Top Of The Pops! It's . . . Ian . . . '

Ian is a good-looking chap, quite the comedian and he has what can be safely described as an overactive imagination and libido. He would tell extravagant tales about how his career was blooming but you would always forgive him because his desire to be loved was as powerful as his desire to have his name in lights.

Amanda, on the other hand, was cool to the point that I imagined she had to get into the fridge to warm up.

As a kid her father Dave had pointed me out to her on TV: 'Keep away from people like that – he's an evil squatter.' Dave owned a few properties and had obviously read about my days as a non-rent paying house invader.

Over many nights playing Scrabble at Philip's or just waiting for him to get dressed to go clubbing, further attempts were made to bring Amanda and I together as friends.

One evening Philip forced Amanda to pick me up in her Nissan Micra on her way to his house and we both felt very awkward and ended up talking about bulk-buying toilet paper. Amanda told me her mum was a manager at a Macro Warehouse in Enfield and when I informed her I had a Macro card I somehow became just another human being.

Amanda actually said: 'Oh, you're quite normal really.'

Years later, friendship in place, she told me that at first she had found me bitchy, which was amusing since she was no princess of politeness.

I discovered her to be sharp-witted, highly educated, moody

as hell and expensively dressed for someone who was at college and was paid peanuts for working the door at Philip's hugely successful club which ran weekly at Bagley's in Kings Cross.

Of course, when Amanda and I became inseparable Philip started to rage: 'She's a social climbing bitch.' All hell broke loose when Amanda admitted that her aspiration to be a fashion journalist was actually a way of biding time until she could become the next Stevie Nicks. While engaging in a sing-a-long at Philip's flat Amanda revealed an eloquent vibrato and an ability to play the guitar. I told her right away that she should make music. This news gave Philip more ammunition and he insisted that Amanda had just befriended me to speed up her rise to fame, sniping: 'See if she doesn't drop you like a ton of brocks once she gets somewhere.'

It's true that Philip was left out of things, but then he refuses to go to restaurants – 'I can't be around food because I just can't stop eating' – or the cinema: 'I just can't sit still.' The fact is that Amanda and I had more in common and didn't see why Philip had to be informed of our every move.

Once, while on holiday in Cyprus Philip started one of his 'Amanda is Satan' routines and I lost it and screamed: 'You wanted us to be friends so stop slagging her off. I'm not listening to this bullshit anymore.'

As it turned out, Amanda and I remained firm friends long after she signed her first record deal to Warner Music in the States and we are still best friends as she is about to sign her second deal.

Some of my favourite times with Amanda have been during our numerous trips to New York to stay with her sister Tracy who moved here after a weekend visit in the mid nineties. Tracy is on the team at my new photographic agency PMI and I have been made to feel part of the family by the entire Gosein clan.

These days Amanda lives in London with her TV producer boyfriend Gregor Cameron and, despite Philip's warnings, we are fiercely loyal to each other, sharing many of the same views on life and an equally twisted sense of humour.

U Can Never B 2 Straight garnered the best reviews of my

career. In terms of being personal there was no longer any kind of veil. Songs like 'Julian' ooze bile.

Around that time I performed at London's premier gay venue G.A.Y. singing songs from *Taboo* with the cast and chucking in a couple of Culture Club classics. I sang 'Julian' and after the show Philip said: 'Why did you sing that? It was like when you used to put on records at Planets to piss off boyfriends!' I'd play 'Who's Sorry Now?' or 'Drop Dead' by Siouxsie and the Banshees: 'Drop dead, you fucking little creep . . .' He was wrong. It was more about my need for self-expression, but yet again my timing was well off.

As a lyricist, the person who inspires me most is Joni Mitchell. Sometimes I listen to her lyrics and I just want to give up. I love her response to an audience request for 'Big Yellow Taxi': 'When a painter paints a painting, it's done. No one asked Van Gogh to paint another *Starry Night*.'

I was really pleased when Joni came to an acoustic show I did in LA in the early nineties. The gig itself was a horrendous experience, because the crowd talked loudly through every song. I stopped the band and said: 'You lot are fucking rude. If you want to discuss your shopping, fuck off outside and do it.'

Joni came backstage afterwards and said: 'Hey, I love you for bawling the crowd out. People are such assholes.' Having that support from her was incredible.

Depth of honesty is something I admire in any artist. That's why I love Dylan or Morrissey at their most vitriolic. Of course all such songwriting, like Dylan says, is really just transference. Often, as writers, we are trying to make sense of things we cannot console within ourselves. A fine example is John Lennon. By all accounts he was a clever dick, constantly trying to humiliate others, and yet in his music he yearned for world peace and social harmony.

And what about Prince, The Artist Formerly Known As Get A Personality? He has written some of my favourite songs, but can't hold a simple conversation. I don't buy into his shy persona. Shy is for librarians.

When I met Morrissey he was just as superior because I was considered a pop clown, charming the pants off the establishment. We took tea together many years ago in a Parisian hotel after being introduced by our record company Virgin France. It was a bit like a session with one of those psychoanalysts who never interacts. Morrissey's considered silence propelled me into overdrive. I couldn't stop talking and filling the many conversational gaps with drivel. After our meeting Morrissey described me as 'overbearing'. I guess there's not enough room in his life for two overbearing personalities. Still, I love him for so many genius songs and unique observations.

I realise that people think I've retired or I'm some desperate figure trying to claw my way back to the top of the charts. I would be lying if I said it doesn't anger me that Radio One won't play my music but I don't let that put me off writing and recording. If anything I overwrite. Left to my own devices I'd probably record an album a month.

The *Taboo* soundtrack – which I mainly wrote with Kevan – included 'Out of Fashion', one of the two songs I recorded with dance combo Hi-Gate. Through my DJ work I've got to know a lot of producers and remixers, so when Judge Jules decided to make the Hi-Gate album he asked me to contribute. He and Paul Masterson sent round a couple of tracks which I left untouched for a while, because Jules's music is quite hard and aggressive and I assumed I wouldn't like it.

Drunk one night I played them and discovered they were luscious and melodic, and wrote the lyrics almost immediately. They called one of the tracks 'Fashion', but I figured Bowie had covered that territory, so I decided to call it 'Out of Fashion'. When it was finished I realised it also fitted perfectly into a major scene in *Taboo*.

The other song I wrote for Hi-Gate was 'Poverty', which they thought was too personal because it's not only about warmongering but was also another one about my relationship with Julian.

> There's money in religion
> There's money in war
> There's money in arms
> But no love in yours.

I wrote it a year before the war in Iraq kicked off, but it seemed fitting to come out during its horrific aftermath. Funny how things change: when Virgin announced they wanted to release 'Do You Really Want to Hurt Me?' I put up a fight, my argument being that it was too personal.

How you learn.

Even when I make dance music, not noted for its lyrical content, I try to use intelligent lyrics. I also add live instruments to give it an organic edge. Another example was 'Run', the single which came out with DJ Sash in Europe. Yet again, it was a song about Julian. For the video, Mike Nicholls made me a jacket covered with images of Julian's face which complemented the Philip Treacy hat painted by my friend Trademark, which also featured Julian's face and the word RUN trailing around the brim.

I'm quite sure Julian was both freaked and flattered by the attention and told anyone who asked him about it that I was an insane person. I actually auctioned the bedspread from the video on the Internet and received a text from Julian asking: 'Who did win my bedspread?'

Featuring Julian's face in the video was more humorous than vindictive. After all, he was desperate to be famous.

As well as the Sash collaboration and others, I've released lots of music under the guise of my alter ego The Twin, the afterbirth of an eighties pop legend. The Twin is a Leigh Bowery-cum-Bowie inspired performance-art piece with songs that are very dark and comical. I write with various people, Kevan, Kinky Roland, Richie Stevens and T-Total (my old New Romantic mucker Tasty Tim and his partner Seratino). Together we have come up with a hybrid which has electro, ragga and whatever the hell else I fancy.

The Twin has garnered a good reaction, sometimes from people who haven't liked any of the other music I've released in years. It's strange because it feels like I'm regaining the audience I had before Culture Club, especially when I played live shows at clubs such as Kashpoint, the Cock, London's Institute of Contemporary Arts and my favourite Nag Nag Nag.

A lot of the material in *Taboo* is based on my life before Culture

Club. With The Twin I've taken things which I discarded a long time ago and remixed them visually. Performing under a pseudonym has also meant that I can experiment and say things which wouldn't gel as Boy George. You could say it's the rancid part of myself which isn't palatable to a mass audience.

Via my label More Protein, The Twin issued four limited edition singles: 'Here Come the Girls', 'Elektro Hetero', 'Human Racing' and 'Sanitised'. We also released The Twin DVD which features videos, film shorts, live footage, remixes and previously unreleased stuff. In the summer of 2003 I organised Electrolush, an electro night at the Electric Ballroom with Adam Sky, the Droids, Jonny Slut, and Avenue D from New York. It was a great night. Not so much Woodstock as Oxostock!

One of my favourite records of the scene, and a floor-filler at Nag Nag Nag, was Avenue D's defiant 'Do I Look Like a Slut?'.

I met the two girls in Avenue D by accident when I was in New York. I'd been searching for them for months so that More Protein could license 'Do I Look Like a Slut?'. I happened to be in this bar and Debbie was working there as a waitress.

When I flew them over for Electrolush they stayed with me in Hampstead. One night Debbie dragged a cute Spanish boy back and even asked me for a condom!

No big deal for a spunky girl who sings:

'Suck on my tits,

I'm a dirty bitch . . .'

I enjoy being around them because they have such an irreverent attitude. When they left London they flew to Atlanta for a gig, and then drove some stranger's car all the way back to New York via Miami. I was like a worried mother – 'Make sure you take care!' – while secretly wishing I could tag along for the adventure.

I've also collaborated with T-Total on the covers album *Hang Ups*, which includes songs by Dusty Springfield, John Lennon and, of course, Bowie. During this time I did quite a bit of live work, gigs for the fun of it. I think performing in *Taboo* gave me a new, comedic edge onstage and really improved my confidence as a performer. When I played two consecutive Sunday nights at

Soho jazz club Ronnie Scott's I don't think I have ever chatted so much onstage, even calling Kylie Minogue, who was in the audience on the first night, a 'bitch' at one point! More importantly it was the first time in years that my set consisted of mostly new material.

As well as covers like 'Sorrow', 'Children of the Revolution' and 'Karma Chameleon', I also performed songs I'd recently written, such as 'Song for a Boy in Deep Water', 'Cookie Jar' and 'Together Alone', a duet with Amanda Ghost. It's always a gamble playing new songs live. People want to hear things they know. It's a risk you have to take to move on.

A review for the first show at Ronnie Scott's was very hurtful. The worst thing about it was that it was written affectionately. Alexis Petridis of the *Guardian* said that Culture Club had never written a decent tune and that my lyrics were clichéd. The pay-off: 'Boy George is such a likeable character it's easy to forgive his musical shortcomings.'

I sent him an email asking him to list his favourite top ten songs. I didn't get a response. No surprise there. The following week another music critic wrote that my songs were great and that the show was superb. How the hell can you judge your worth on the opinion of one person?

Over the last year I've worked with other dance artists such as DJ Erick Morillo and breakbeaters Dark Globe. I enjoy collaborating with people like this because they have a solid base in dance music and are open to new ideas as well.

Everything I've ever done musically has been borne out of happy mistakes. Culture Club was lumped in with the eighties electro explosion but we were nothing of the sort. 'Do You Really Want to Hurt Me?' was a bit of a typewriter in a Renaissance, if you know what I mean. Even when I try to fall in line I always end up adding something incongruous.

I've never been an artist who seeks out the producer *du jour*. That's partly because I'm a control freak but also because I crave variety. One day I might pen a country and western song, the next I might be working with Dark Globe. I enjoy the diversity of my work because it suits my personality and I don't have to rely on past glories. Everything I've done in the past fifteen years has been called 'a comeback' but I haven't been anywhere to come back from.

I'm always being asked: 'What are you?' People don't know whether I'm a singer, a DJ, a newspaper columnist, a fashion designer or a dessert topping. It's hard for others to understand how annoying it is to be constantly referred to in the past tense. But then we live in a culture which is all too eager to pigeon-hole everything. When I was a punk, I used the term to describe what I was doing at the time but I never intended it to sum up my entire existence.

Sadly, we tend to become our jobs, our colour, our sexuality, our faith. When I showed an interest in Hare Krishna, people were desperate for me to define myself as a spiritual convert. I'm a magpie, a cultural sponge, I confess.

So, when I'm writing songs, I don't think about my audience's expectations. It's not as if I started my career thinking: 'I want my audience to be young, isolated weirdos who hate their parents and wear black nail varnish.' What's wrong with being a young cross-dressing weirdo who likes their mum? Perhaps that was the difference between me and the likes of Marc Almond and Jimmy Somerville. My gripe with humanity wasn't that particular and I learned very early on that just because somebody wears the same uniform as you, it doesn't mean you have anything in common.

I'm a huge fan of Marc's, by the way, but we've only ever exchanged nods in clubs and I always had the feeling he wasn't too fond of me. In the early nineties his boyfriend published an underground gay magazine called *Fist*. The tone was downright nasty and they'd print piss-taking articles about famous figures. I often wondered whether Marc used it as a way of attacking people he didn't like, because it's hard to imagine he didn't play some part in *Fist*. There were a couple of things printed in there which really made me chuckle; one particular piece called me 'Bore George'.

However, I was offended by another story about me injecting people with heroin and committing lewd sexual acts with George Michael. It was beyond humour and I was prepared to take legal action but decided it wasn't worth the hassle. However, I made it known on the London club scene that I was pissed off and that I believed Marc was involved.

Several months later I received a long fax from Marc ranting on about how I'd been slurring his good name by making unfounded accusations. It seemed completely random. I responded affectionately, telling him I admired his work and ended my letter with a twist on the Soft Cell hit: 'Say goodbye, wave hello.' I never heard from Marc again. Whether he was involved or not, I'll never know.

Last year Marc started working with my favourite musical collaborator Kinky Roland and started DJing and remixing. It seems our careers have taken a very similar path. Often when I call Kinky he will joke: 'I'm the filling in an eighties sandwich!'

Kinky knows I'm a huge Marc Almond fan and he assures me the respect is mutual. That's good enough for me.

It was terrible to hear the news of Marc's motorbike accident last autumn, just as it was heartening to hear how soon he was on the road to recovery.

Another strange pop encounter occurred in the early nineties when I almost lost my mind and had a production meeting with Pete Waterman. He was nice enough but it was clear we had nothing in common. I realised I wasn't prepared to have a hit at any cost. And I look lousy in gold lamé shorts. You see, for me Kylie Minogue's about-turn was a mistake. She tried to go out on a limb and when that didn't work she immediately switched back to giving people what they wanted. I really believe you should never be dictated to by your audience. When you start out the audience revels in your fresh appeal and then they expect you to repeat yourself in perpetuity.

You have to escape the cycle – it's the creative equivalent of breaking rocks in Siberia.

16

Don't Mind If I Don't

Of course, I've vowed many times never again to open the Pandora's box that is Culture Club. Right now I feel I could resist it for a very long time, but it's best not to make promises I may not keep.

I have discovered whatever you do, people try and drag you back to the past. I understand that a lot of people have a romantic investment in my history, but how would they feel if I forced them to wear their school uniforms for the rest of their lives?

Shortly before my first trip to India I embarked on a reunion project with the band. We holed up in a studio near Brighton and penned a collection of new songs. I don't remember any really great tracks coming out of it. There was one called 'Beautiful Fool' which had something, but the rest had a distinctly desperate and old-fashioned feel to them. Even so, we ended up in the studio with veteran producer Peter Asher and wasted a vast chunk of Virgin's money. I was bang into the dance scene and felt that the production sounded eighties in the worst possible way.

We were supposed to continue with the project after I returned from India and I was pretty enthused because I'd written some wacky tunes on my travels. One of those songs was 'Bow Down Mister', which seemed to write itself after I had taken a dip in the sacred pool Rhada Khand. I felt the song had a bit of a 'Karma Chameleon' feel to it, and because of the spiritual references it

was a more uplifting update. The band got together aga[in]
small studio in Chalk Farm and tried to carry on where [we left]
off. I had one of my famous rows with Jon about nothi[ng] [in]
particular. I guess we still didn't know how to channel all [our]
excess sexual energy! I did my usual: 'Fuck you all, I hate t[his]
band, I'm leaving,' and that's exactly what I did.

It was to be seven years before we were all in the same room
again. In that time the only contact I had with any of them was
with Jon, after I read an outrageous interview he gave to a Jewish
magazine in which he claimed I had once said: 'I wish your
mother had been gassed by the Nazis.' I was so angry I rang the
journalist and said: 'How could you print something like that
without speaking to me first?'

She was deeply apologetic and it transpired she was actually an
acquaintance of Jon's, and had simply taken him at his word. I
told her she would be hearing from my lawyers and the magazine printed a retraction in its next issue, but whatever, a lot of
Jewish people in north London – where I live – had already read
that lie. Admittedly I can be vicious, but I was fond of Jon's
mother. Aside from gasping in pure horror when she first set eyes
on me, she had always been very sweet – although I knew she
didn't always approve of me. I guess Jon was so irked about *Take
It Like a Man*, this was his way of wreaking some sort of revenge.

It was strange. I'd read the article in the morning and that same
afternoon, as my sister was driving me to the West End, we pulled
up alongside Jon in his car at Swiss Cottage. He smiled at me
and I flashed back a look of sheer hatred. Within minutes my
manager Tony Gordon was on the phone, saying he'd just received
a really freaked-out phone call from Jon.

When I told Tony what Jon had said, he went silent. Later, he
shrieked at Jon: 'What were you thinking?!' For me it was so
outrageous it was almost impossible to take seriously.

There is a strange connection between us all which matches
the madness that prevails every time we get together. I wouldn't
call it love, maybe affection or even blind loyalty. I do feel that I
owe them something. After all, I wouldn't be writing this book
if I had never met them. Would I have made it without them?

That's a question which comes to me again and again but it
doesn't really matter, because we did it together and you can't
change the past. Not even God can do that!

Without Roy, Mikey and Jon, and all the fun, hatred and chair-
throwing that comes with them, who knows? It was sad to see
Spandau Ballet squabbling over royalties. To my eyes there's nothing
more tragic.

So, having said 'never again' repeatedly, I somehow found myself
in New York with the whole sick crew in the spring/summer of
1998. We had appeared as guinea pigs on music channel VH1's
band profile series *Behind the Music*, which was just starting out
then and went on to become huge. The storyline was the usual
'They had it all and they fucked it up', and it focused mainly on
the bad stuff about our break-up. After watching it you could be
forgiven for thinking there were no good moments in our time
together. I guess the public prefers a cheap holiday in a pop star's
misery.

Since none of us were speaking at the time, we had all been
interviewed separately. Jon was still very much in public denial
about our relationship, while Roy was just plain bitter. Mikey had
always been the one who was constantly trying to reunite the
band. He talked about being left out of decisions and the divisions
created by my relationship with Jon. Still, he was his usual even-
keeled self.

On the back of *Behind the Music*, we were asked to perform
an unplugged concert for VH1 in New York. Virgin had been
completely uninterested in the band until VH1 made that offer.
Suddenly they were all over us, and released a greatest hits package
which included a live recording of the unplugged gig called
'Storytellers'.

Things started to escalate and we decided to reform Culture
Club. They got me on a good day, to tell you the truth. At that
point the only feelings I had towards Jon were defensive. After
all, this is the man who sat in a restaurant in Paris as recently as
1999 and said to a huge table full of people: 'I am one hundred
per cent heterosexual'!

Being around Jon again was awkward and stirred up a lot of

repressed feelings, especially as we rehearsed 'Black Money' with its poignant lyric: 'I believed that nothing could come between us, / Magic potions, you can save them for dreamers.' Our conversations were always clipped and kept to a minimum. There were many times when Jon attempted to be sweet to me and I would be horribly indifferent. I never allowed myself to be alone with him for too long because it felt so awkward. There was none of the fire which had once inflamed our entire relationship.

At the time of the relationship I was described as asexual, when in fact my sex life with Jon was rampant. We would often have sex before going onstage. We even had sex in the toilets at Whitfield Street Studios while recording the strings for 'Victims'. Many of our most electric sex sessions occurred after we fought. I think with Jon it added to the excitement and as much as he always blamed me for starting the rows, he was just as guilty. Looking back I think there was a lot of frustration because our relationship was all or nothing; either frenzied activity or silence. So many women were after Jon, especially once they found out we were a couple. I also received my share of attention and we were both terrible flirts. Jon would go mad if he thought I was after someone and I would lose it if he as much as smiled at any woman.

I'm also sure Jon used most of his time away from me to satiate his heterosexual cravings. He often went to Israel on holiday and I know he was not faithful. But I never cheated on Jon until I knew for sure. And when I did I made sure they were at least six feet tall!

I was so physically comfortable with Jon, I couldn't imagine feeling that with anybody else. I looked at other people, of course, but until that point I didn't fancy anyone as much as I fancied him. When I flirted with other men it was always a way of winding him up.

I've never been good at letting anything go and that probably explains my stubbornness with Culture Club. Even in the heyday we carried on, however unpleasant things became. We worked relentlessly over a four-year period and we were often totally worn out.

After spending weeks touring America we would be expected

to fly straight to Europe for a press junket. Records would come out at different times around the world and we tried to promote them in each country as near to release as possible.

Work meant that Jon and I were forced together and even when things were hideous I still wanted to be near him. Outside of work Jon and I led pretty separate lives. If we spent an evening together we would maybe have dinner, have sex and then Jon would leave. He would say he couldn't sleep or make some other excuse.

I never really felt like I had a proper boyfriend. Often in hotels we would have adjoining rooms and Jon would go off and sleep in the other room and leave sweet notes. I never felt comfortable about it. I have pretty much every note he ever wrote to me and many of them end with: 'You know, I love you, I hope you understand.' I spent a lot of time thinking Jon was ashamed of me but I suspect he was more ashamed of himself. Jon was never tactile except during sex and he wasn't interested in affection after the thrust of passion.

I don't hate Jon, though I imagine if we were ever to talk honestly to each other without all the clever-dick rhetoric, there'd be a lot of tears to wipe away. I'm certainly not in love with him any more, I'm sure of that. I don't know what I feel, although it's quite obvious I still feel something. Even after all the songs I have written about us, about love, it's impossible to really nail emotion. Whenever you try and make sense of love, it crescendos into cliché.

John is now a family man. The first time I saw him with his wife Babs and their baby, they were having a full-on row in the street. I was with some friends walking through Berkeley Square to a restaurant and didn't realise who they were until they were on top of me. Jon was first to acknowledge the irony and said: 'Bloody hell! Bet you're loving this!' Tiny children are a godsend in such situations. They tend to fill you with the joys of life!

Since then I've got to know Babs pretty well and think she's a very cool person. There has never been any awkwardness between us. Once I heard Jon berating somebody on the phone. I asked him who he was talking to, and he said: 'Shut up. I'm talking to

Babs. Mind your own business!' I said: 'You're so fucking rude, you haven't changed a bit.'

While Culture Club were successful my relationship with Jon created two camps – forgive the pun. Mikey and Roy were often left to fend for themselves, although Roy had a not-so-secret weapon: his wife Alison. Mikey was the sort of person who would only ever complain if egged on by Roy. After all, Roy co-wrote most of the songs with me, and was understandably sensitive about his contribution not being recognised.

Mind you, I once watched Roy talking about how 'Do You Really Want to Hurt Me?' was written and thought: Really? He wasn't there. Mikey came up with the bass line and I wrote the words over an old reggae B-side in my friend's flat in Cleveland Square. But Roy does like to rewrite history. The first time I sang him 'Karma Chameleon' he started banging pots and pans, going: 'Yee-ha! You must be joking! That'll never be a hit.' Funnily enough it paid for quite a few of his houses and cars. All the other members of the band would whinge because I received the bulk of the attention, except, of course, when that attention involved having to spend an entire day answering the same questions from journalists. If it was a national TV appearance, say the *Tonight Show* with Jay Leno or a high-end interview with *Rolling Stone*, there was never any quibbling. But endless idents for KLTM or whatever appealed to me even less, but nevertheless I did them. I guess you could call Roy's wife Alison Culture Club's Yoko Oh-no. For a long time it seemed she was the stirrer of the hornet's nest. Stuff like the classic: 'You deliberately sang over Roy's guitar solo in "Miss Me Blind!" As if I had time to be that calculating. I was far more concerned about whether my hat would fall off or I'd go off-key. After a while it became clear that Alison was, more often than not, speaking on behalf of her husband. Roy would rather shave a lap dancer than endure a confrontation. When he did occasionally erupt it was spectacular and very personal: 'You think you're fucking God! Go on, fuck off and go shopping!'

Mikey would always say: 'Do we have to scream at each other? Can't we just sit down and talk calmly?' It's not that he didn't have opinions but he hated all the shouting and mindless drama.

Mikey is Mr Laid-Back incarnate. Remember, this is the man who failed to show up to our first video shoot (for 'Do You Really Want to Hurt Me?'). He is always late for everything. The band would be panicking to get to the airport and Mikey would still be in his room, massaging coconut butter into his skin, music blaring, without a care in the world. He was the bane of our many tour managers' lives, whose job it was to rally the troops. Mikey would often end up having to catch a separate plane and then there was the time he missed the bullet train from Tokyo to Osaka. In Japan they barely get the British thing, so forget about the Jamaican five minutes.

Even when he did things like that, his boylike charm would win you over. Out of us all, Mikey is always the one pressing for us to reunite and tour. Although the money is obviously a concern, I genuinely believe the thing Mikey enjoys most is being up on stage chugging that bass with the rest of us.

17

Shirley Temple Moments

In the summer of 1998 Culture Club toured as part of an eighties package which included the Human League and Howard Jones – because we hadn't performed together for a decade and felt it was wise to rope in some other names.

Since Howard Jones had scored more hits in the US, the promoter decreed that the Human League should go on first, a decision they weren't too happy about. I don't think they were that chuffed about supporting us in the first place.

When the tour kicked off at the Chastain Park Amphitheatre in Atlanta that July, it certainly wasn't so much a rainy night as a frosty night in Georgia. I greeted Human League frontman Phil Oakey by saying I was delighted they were on the bill. He squeezed out a smile and gave me a frugal handshake, starting as he meant to persist.

One night before a gig I could hear their Northern mithering through one of the air vents in my dressing room. I couldn't resist standing on a chair and having a drop of eaves. Although I couldn't hear exactly what was being said, I picked up stuff like: 'It's a bloody cheek! Well, fook them!'

Midway through the tour I bumped into Phil outside one of the hotels and complimented him on the previous night's performance. Stony-faced he said: 'I was singing completely flat. We were terrible. I don't give a fook, me.' I'm not opposed to indulging in a bout of the misery guts routine myself, but Phil Oakey seems to have trapped himself in a deadpan, 'speak as I find' persona.

In 'The Things that Dreams are Made of', Phil laments:

> Everybody needs love and affection,
> Everybody needs cash to spend.
> Everybody needs some protection,
> Everybody needs two or three friends.

I'm a major fan, and went to one of the Human League's first London gigs when they supported Gary Glitter. I remember being mesmerised by their stark stage set-up and, of course, that futuristic Veronica Lake fringe. I went straight out and bought their first single 'Being Boiled', and I remember playing my mum their creepy version of 'You've Lost that Lovin' Feeling' and hearing her say: 'That's disgraceful! They've ruined that beautiful song.' God bless those glory days when you could piss off your parents with a pop song.

The first time I heard their classic 'Don't You Want Me' I was working in my clothes shop the Foundry off Carnaby Street. All day Radio One had been announcing the premier of the new Human League single. About ten of us crowded around the shop's tiny transistor, and broke into dodgy eighties dance moves. I thought it was a brilliant pop song and I have always loved their ability to make even the most mundane experiences transcendent.

Only three days before that eighties package tour came to a halt at the Wisconsin State Fair, vocalist Suzanne Sully tottered into my dressing room plastered and said: 'We've got a mutual friend. He's gay and he said we'd really get on.' It was a little late to start playing happy families.

On that tour, the person I locked horns with most was Roy. Now divorced and having been sober for four years, I think he decided to unleash his inner rock god. He was drinking and indulging in all the clichéd rock 'n' roll perks, dragging girls back to the hotel or even ordering hookers if he got desperate. Kevan Frost, our second guitarist, was woken one night by a rubber-clad

mistress out of whose holdall spilt all manner of pervy parapher-
nalia. He quickly directed her to the room next door, and claims
he heard Roy groaning in – and probably on – ecstasy. His girlfriend Casey even had to put a stop on his credit card when a
bill arrived for £8,000.

Jon kept himself to himself. One afternoon on Virginia Beach
we were all sunning ourselves on a private deck, while he sat in
his room, curtains closed, reading a book.

Onstage there were always two performances going on; my chirpy
persona to the audience was at odds with my Linda Blair-style asides
over bad playing. If Roy's guitar wasn't serenading Alsatians, Jon's
drumming was either high-octane or dirge-like. So I was always
cursing Jon onstage: 'Wanker! You're fucking useless!' Their attitude
was: 'People love it. Who cares if there's a bum note here or there?'
Sometimes I felt like I was in Def Leppard, especially when Roy
walked onstage in nylon track pants and a naff football top. He'd
shout: 'Pull the birds! Pull the birds! They love it!'

Acting like meatheads appeared to be fashionable at the time.
Augmenting the group with musicians who I had worked with
– John Themis, Richie Stevens, Kevan and the thunder-voiced
Zee Asha – increased the testosterone-fuelled behaviour. Some of
them clearly found Jon and Roy's stupidity mildly titillating. When
Jon is on form he can be highly entertaining, but when he starts
niggling people, it can be relentless.

Steve Honest, our tour manager at the time, was temporarily
close to Jon. It turned out, in fact, that the girl Steve was seeing
had been a former lover of Jon's. Rather than do the gentlemanly
thing, Jon started bad-mouthing her.

I don't think he realised how serious Steve was about her, until
Steve lamped him the night before we were due to leave for a
tour of Australia. I was on my way to rehearsals in a taxi and
received a phone call from Kevan telling me that it had all kicked
off. Apparently Jon's needling had gone too far, and Steve punched
him in the face and then picked up a chunk of his drum kit and
threw it across the room. The rest of the guys in the band broke
the fight up and Steve stormed out, screaming that he was going
to cut Jon up.

It was difficult for me because I was fond of Steve, but I had to accept that bringing him on tour was a recipe for further disaster. I spoke to Steve on the phone, and asked him to apologise, or at least make peace. That was clearly out of the question and Jon was adamant that he was out.

We became acquainted with our new tour manager, Ian, at Heathrow the following morning. He's a giant of a man and we were very lucky that as a last-minute appointment he turned out to be so cool.

Throughout the tour Jon used his ongoing war with Steve as inappropriate entertainment. At dinner he would pick up a knife and brandish it, saying: 'Cut you up!' I hate knives anyway, and it wasn't a joke to me. As far as I was concerned Jon was as much to blame for the situation as Steve. When I pulled him up over his displays of bravado he'd say: 'You're a bloody traitor.' On the one hand Jon claimed to be terrified about the safety of his wife and kids, and yet he made it a joke at every available opportunity.

You'd think that after all this malarkey I'd have stopped praying at the Church of the Poisoned Mind. But no. We embarked on yet another album, the inaptly titled *Don't Mind If I Do*. First, we recorded a reggae tune we had written some years before, 'I Just Wanna Be Loved'.

My manager Tony had always said it would be a massive hit and Roy was elected producer. I hated the result because it sounded flat and old-fashioned. As soon as Roy returned to Los Angeles I booked another studio and got Richie Stevens, a producer and drummer, to remix the song. Richie brought it to life and it went straight into the charts at number four – our first bona fide hit in more than a decade.

Although they refused to put 'I Just Wanna Be Loved' on their playlist, Radio One asked us to perform at their summer roadshow. I said: 'Fuck 'em if they won't support our record.' The previous year we had trudged down to Torquay for Radio One but that didn't seem to have much effect.

After the success of the single, we went ahead with recording the new album at Dave Stewart's studio, the Church. Stupidly, we allowed Roy to produce that as well, and it ended up costing far too much money. That would have been excusable if it wasn't so musically confused. It was our mistake to let Roy sweet-talk his way into the control booth. He'd been successfully producing film scores with Hans Zimmer and would spend hours concocting epic string arrangements which would have worked better in a bloodsucking scene from *Buffy the Vampire Slayer*.

None of us paid enough attention to what was going on in the studio. We only had ourselves to blame for the album being so disjointed. Still, it did go Top Five. But the second single, 'Your Kisses are Charity', performed badly and things started to deteriorate. The media fuss about our reunion was short-lived, although we pulled off a successful British tour with ABC, Belinda Carlisle, Heaven 17 and the (in)Human League.

Things really came to a head during the last US tour in 1999. It was badly timed and badly organised. Before we went on the road I had a bad feeling about it, and even tried to cancel the whole thing, but that would have resulted in a financial fiasco, so off we went. As I anticipated, it was a disaster. Not only were ticket sales lousy but Roy's rock-star antics reached Spinal Tap proportions. He couldn't even be bothered to turn up for the three-week rehearsals for the tour, because he had commitments in LA, but he promised not to interfere with my plans. I got Kevan's brother Matt Frost from Dark Globe to help make our sound more edgy, adding new technology to the live show. The programmed beats and keyboards gave us a more modern sound. We didn't change anything intrinsic but made it contemporary – the reggae beats now had a proper dub feel. As soon as we got on the road, the mouse roared. Roy started complaining immediately and Jon hated playing a stand-up electronic drum kit, as it made him feel redundant.

My view was that we had done the eighties tour and we'd made a new album, so what was the point in treading water? I'd say: 'If we're not going anywhere new musically, I'm not really interested in being part of this nostalgia-fest.'

Halfway through the tour Roy and Jon's moaning wore me down. I gave in, the programmed beats were dropped and we were back to pub-pop. At that point I had already decided I was never going to put myself through another Culture Club tour. I told my friends: 'If you ever hear me mention Culture Club again, slap me with a frozen cod until I come to my senses.'

I had my make-up artist and close friend Sarah Gregory on tour with me. She was always saying: 'You're as miserable as fuck. You don't need to do this.'

I knew I couldn't walk out during the middle of the tour because people had paid good money to see us, and they weren't party to our petty squabbles. Being on the road with a band is like going on holiday with a good friend. No matter how much you care about each other, and however awkwardly that translates, there are days when you would happily boil each other in a pot of hot oil.

Onstage during 'Karma Chameleon' Roy would shout 'Cum buckets!' and other random babble like a bawdy Northern comedian. During one gig in Boston his behaviour became so unbearable I started eyeing his bank of guitars and thought: 'I could so easily smash one of those over your head right now.'

A local gay dignitary had arrived to present me with an award. As a local TV crew attempted to capture the moment, Roy screeched in the background while Jon threw food around the room and approached the mayor, who was wearing a 'Silence = Death' badge, and said: 'Whassat mean?!'

After that Roy and I didn't speak for a week. Then one morning at breakfast he attempted to make conversation. He asked: 'Why are you intent on making this tour so fucking miserable?' I picked up my breakfast and moved to another table because I knew that if I had engaged I would have said one or two things I might not have regretted.

The tour ended in San Francisco with the indelible image of a bladdered Roy in my dressing room, swinging a bottle of Jack Daniel's and telling me: 'Don't forget who has the power in this band!' It was tragic that he thought I cared.

At least these days Jon is prepared to acknowledge that he loved me. He even said last year: 'I know most of George's songs are about me, but they're also about him.'

Touché.

In the end I was forced to accept that we were in the business of making music for very different reasons; I certainly didn't need the money but naively clung on to the dream that it could work again.

When the infamous Culture Club box-set was released at the end of 2002 it included a studio row I tracklisted as 'A Shirley Temple Moment'. It was recorded in 1983 while trying to record 'Victims'. It was typical of us to be working on a deeply romantic song while baying for each other's blood. I called Jon a 'spotty heterosexual cunt' and Roy stormed in and screamed at me: 'You fat bloody wanker! Haven't you got a party to go to?!'

In an ideal world we would have grown up and moved on from the petty insecurities of the early days. I guess it's true that rock 'n' roll renders you retarded for eternity. Roy, for one, seemed to have seen the reunion as his opportunity to settle old scores and assert his authority.

While in the middle of *Taboo*'s run in the West End, I agreed to a one-off Culture Club gig at the Albert Hall and a New Year's Eve shindig in Edinburgh. My decision to have Euan Morton – who played me in *Taboo* – open the set dressed in full eighties garb singing 'Do You Really Want to Hurt Me?' really irked the others. They were also none too pleased when I bounded onstage in one of my Leigh Bowery *Taboo* costumes: a crown of gravity-defying black rubber spikes and a chequerboard bustle dress.

My appearance – and their reaction to it – highlighted the fact that we have as much in common now as anchovies and double cream.

18

Everything Taboo

The idea for *Taboo* was originally hatched on the back of a barge one freezing cold night on the Thames.

Chris Renshaw, a director with a background in opera who was also working with Elaine Paige on *The King and I*, came to visit me while I was performing with Culture Club on the consumer programme *Watchdog*; we were doing everything we could to promote the second single 'Your Kisses are Charity' from our reunion album *Don't Mind If I Do*. (I suppose appearing on *Watchdog* was an indication that the single was about to go the way of the legwarmer. If something's up you find out during these types of promotional junkets.)

Anyway, Chris had read my first book as well as *Life of an Icon*, Sue Tilley's biography of Leigh Bowery, and had some kooky plan to put together a musical that blended the two stories.

I told Chris it was a cute idea. Although Leigh arrived on the London scene much later than the likes of myself, Philip Sallon, Marilyn and all the various strangers in this world, his story wasn't dissimilar, even if his wardrobe was larger.

At that first meeting with Chris it was established that *Taboo* would not be a roll-out-the-hits-type show, which made me very excited about it. He also wanted me to write a new score, which was especially appealing, having spent the previous three years steeped in nostalgia.

My first book had been optioned for a possible film project with the BBC. Some of their ideas were good; Julie Walters was in the frame to play my mother, which I loved – after all, she IS my mother. In typical fashion the BBC farted around. Despite commissioning several scripts and one expensive lunch, the project was eventually abandoned.

I wanted my friend John Maybury as writer for the musical. John had just directed his first feature, the Francis Bacon story *Love is the Devil*, and his close relationship with Leigh made him the ideal candidate. I had a meeting with John, who seemed enthusiastic, but not long afterwards I received a message saying that he felt too close to the subject matter. I imagine John made the mistake of discussing the idea with too many other people connected to that period and to Leigh, who had become a bit of a cause célèbre in the art world.

Shortly before his death Leigh had been painted by the artist Lucien Freud, and prior to that, his spell behind glass at the Anthony d'Offay Gallery had propelled him into the arms of the art elite. Still, I was sad that John had turned us down. Salvation came when Chris returned with examples of the work of three or four writers, including the one we plumped for, Mark Davies, a Liverpudlian with a bald head and a dry sense of humour who had written for the TV series *This Life*. I wanted to cover all the adventures and the people involved, the Princess Julias, the Philip Sallons, the Marilyns. I wanted to give them a voice and show what a strange, wonderful and often frightening time it was for all of us growing up. It was a chance to give credit to all the people who shaped my life.

Everyone thinks of the eighties as being a vacuous decade ruled by right-wing politics – which it was – but there was also a lot of magic which occurred throughout that period. During the heyday of Culture Club we were often accused of being Thatcher's Children, but it was more enforced adoption. We were really products of the seventies, everything from glam to punk to the dustbin men's strike.

It was Chris's idea to set the musical at Taboo – the eighties club which was fronted by Leigh and his sidekick Trojan – because it was the last gasp of hedonism that London clubbing had experienced. Leigh's club managed to attract all the old lags and a whole new family of young fashion freaks. It was hysterical, such a laugh, the dying vestiges of that out-and-out decadence which will never, ever happen again. A lot of the inhabitants discovered drag via me. The word 'freak' pops up a lot in the show, because the club was – and the musical is – a celebration of freaks.

But it's always worth remembering that every freak has a mother. When I met Marilyn Manson with his parents, he, in fact, was the normal one and I was struck by how nice he was. People are rarely as weird as you anticipate. There are exceptions of course: on meeting Courtney Love she reminded me of that mad snake in *The Jungle Book*.

I met Manson and Love at an MTV Awards after-show party in New York. I'd just finished chatting with Manson and passed Love on the way to the bar. She jumped on me: 'Oh my Gahhd!' I told her how much I loved her album *Doll Parts* and we chatted a bit about her time in England. Out of the blue, she adopted a serious expression and interrupted me, saying: 'I was actually in conversation with a friend. Do you mind?' I walked off, thinking: 'You psycho.'

Chris felt that Taboo was the final resting place of that kind of excess – drag, drugs and absolute contempt for fashion etiquette.

In order to fit in as many of those colourful characters as possible, we had to play with the time frame. Blitz culture kicked in at the end of the seventies, but Leigh didn't arrive in London from Australia until 1982 and didn't open Taboo until 1985. In the musical we placed characters like Steve Strange and Marilyn at the time of Leigh's club, and dragged him back to the seventies, because we always felt that he would have fitted in perfectly at Blitz. Our attitude was, if he wasn't there, he should have been.

The musical follows me from the time I left home in the seventies to my first trip to India, and we selected those who I felt were the most important characters from that time: Leigh, of course, with Philip Sallon, in a nod to Joel Grey in *Cabaret*, as the deranged master of ceremonies. Leigh's friend Fat Sue was a key figure, as were Steve Strange and Marilyn. Originally the script featured the role of Trojan, but because the London version of *Taboo* centred around my character, it was felt that he was extraneous to the plot.

There were also some composite characters made up from people we had known: the lead Billy, a confused straight boy and a social climber desperate to make a name for himself; his parents Derek and Josie, who were based in part on my own mum and dad; and the female lead Kim, a clothes designer who Billy falls in and out of love with. In addition there was Petal, a transsexual drug dealer and pimp based on someone I knew at the time, as well as a vile journalist called Janey and an assortment of prostitutes, cops and weirdos.

Soon we attracted the attention of producers. Andrew Lloyd Webber made an approach so I had a meeting with his people, including a friend of mine and Philip's, Tris Penna. One of the things which put me off them was that they were involved in the Pet Shop Boys' musical *Closer to Heaven*. I was worried not only that there were too many parallels between the shows, but also there was a chance that the *Taboo* project would be acquired and put on ice.

After talking to a few other producers we settled on Adam Kenwright and Michael Fuchs. I didn't want to wait around and they were ready to go.

The message of the show is about the search for acceptance by a bunch of people who feel ostracised and gravitate together to create an alternative family of freaks. After much work *Taboo* became a Dick Whittington-type story of a boy from Bromley – like me, but kind of straight – with an overly aggressive father and doting mother. He comes to the bright lights and enters the club world.

Sounds familiar?

19

Ich Bin Kunst

One of my main aims with *Taboo* was to show what an important figure Leigh was in the grand scheme of things. He was incredible, vibrant, twisted, like a ray of sunshine on the horizon, and I still miss him very much.

Leigh's biggest terror was pity. In the final weeks before he died on New Year's Eve in 1994, he said: 'Don't think of me as a person with Aids, think of me as a person with ideas.'

I first met Leigh when he made me some stage clothes in 1987. Of course, I'd seen him and Trojan around the clubs for years. How could you miss them? The first time I saw him was at the Camden Palace. He and Trojan turned up in their get-up of painted faces and noserings which they called Pakis from Outer Space. I can remember dismissing them because, to me, their style was nothing I hadn't seen or done before. I used to paint my face blue, green and yellow, often all at the same time. Once, I went out with a yellow face and a red neck and bumped into Grace Jones outside Heaven. She bellowed at me: 'Who cut your throat, honey?'

On closer inspection I realised that Leigh's styling was actually quite remarkable. Years later I went over to Leigh's kitsch council flat in the East End. It was surreal. Leigh was in his Benny Hill daytime look: shop-dummy wig and child-molester clothes, surrounded by all this swirling 1970s bad taste.

I had heard that he was an evil witch but thought he was a doll. Actually, I was in awe of him. Leigh made me two floor-length A-line coats. One was covered in gold hairgrips and the other had huge angel wings jutting out the back. They made me look fatter, which was probably deliberate. Leigh didn't have the same size prejudices as the rest of us. He celebrated his fleshy proportions and turned them into a gorgeous fashion statement.

I think that's what I loved about him most; he pushed it in your face. Like the night he swanned into Daisy Chain in a puffball face mask, sequinned boots and matching push-up bra. Except for those garish trimmings, he was butt naked. A fake vagina rug hid his manhood, which I am told was substantial. I remember staring at his big butt and thinking how brave he was and that he was quite sexy because of it.

He would cavort around places like the Fridge with his bum and stomach hanging out, exaggerating his body out of all proportion. At a time when everyone was body conscious and into gym culture, Leigh was a sight to behold with his arse out and belts around his stomach to make it look bigger.

The contrast of Leigh against a sea of muscle boys was completely incongruous. The rest of us use clothing and make-up to disguise our shortcomings but Leigh said: 'Fuck that,' and made his blemishes the focal point. He would create a costume that defied gravity. A big red crown of rubber spikes set off by a voluminous tutu and a perfectly made-up face, but with his muscular, hairy arms and legs exposed. There was always something masculine and contradictory about Leigh's drag. It was as if he always wanted to remind you that there was a man behind it.

It was amazing how scarifying he could be. I once walked around the West End with him and he was so big and his costumes were so threatening that the casuals and kids who would normally attack you wouldn't dare come near us. You can put most drag queens in a box marked inoffensive but Leigh was beyond drag. A case of man/woman/thing.

There is no question that Leigh was hiding himself behind all that spook drag, but still it was revolutionary. I suppose people thought of him as a ridiculous attention-seeker, which he was, but there was so much more.

There are loads of stories about him when he was younger, living at home in Sunshine outside Melbourne, avidly reading *The Face* and *Blitz* and picking up on what people like me were up to in London. He had watched from afar and when he arrived in London in 1981 he decided to take things further. He was a fan, but would never admit it. He was fiercely funny and when he came to my home in the late eighties, he said: 'Your house is very Joan Collins and your shoulder pads are too.' His quips were always well considered, and he did everything he could to disguise his Australian accent by adopting an affected tone, Oscar Wilde meets Zippy from *Rainbow*.

He wasn't interested in making his costumes more widely available, which I think he could have done and maybe made some money, because he was a very good designer. He was once asked in an interview how he would deal with somebody imitating his style. 'Well, I'd befriend them, follow them around and then wear them down until their spirit was completely destroyed.'

The idea that any old person could wear a Leigh Bowery design didn't interest him. Having gone through punk and the New Romantic period I, probably more than anybody, knew how hard it was to do something different visually. The characters that I had known and clubbed with over the years had done pretty much everything they could, or so I thought.

I called Leigh in the early nineties when I was putting my first book together, because I needed some dates and gossip. He was very charming and helpful. He asked me if the druggy section of the book would be 'horribly apologetic', adding in that heavily affected voice of his: 'You were fantastic as a junkie. That was my favourite Boy George period.' I laughed. It was typical Leigh: Miss Contrary, Scary Mary.

I would always go and see his shows, which were sold as performance art but were actually often just Leigh strutting around to the strains of Keith Nesbitt and Orville. One time at the Roxy club in Amsterdam, I watched from the VIP box as he was lowered from the roof to the stage by a pulley. He catwalked up and down,

Above left: With Mike Nicholls and Rachel Auburn on our way to India, 1990.
Above right: With Indian music legends vocalist Asha Bhosle and music producer Bapi Lahri.

Below: Mister bows down with the devotees.

Right: Up yours. Happier times with MC Kinky outside the gates to my house in Hampstead

Below: The band, from left: John Themis, Zee Asha, Jay Shorten, Richie Stevens and Winston Blisset with Kevan Frost's head in his lap.

Right: Kevan and John in wiggy stage outfits on the Cheapness & Beauty tour.

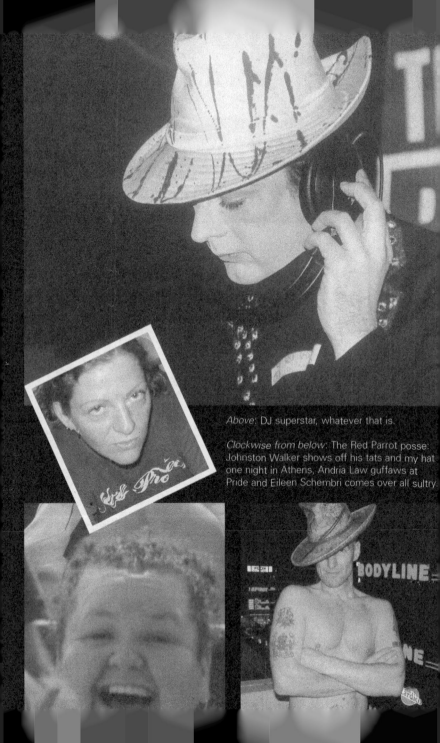

Above: DJ superstar, whatever that is.

Clockwise from below: The Red Parrot posse: Johnston Walker shows off his tats and my hat one night in Athens, Andria Law guffaws at Pride and Eileen Schembri comes over all sultry.

Top: My oldest friend - in so many ways - Philip Sallon with my best friend Amanda Ghost.

Bottom: Nine Ki adviser, macrobiotic cook and mother: Dragana "Drags" Brown and my godson Michael.

Top left: Inspirational original: a bosomy Leigh Bowery.

Middle: Gathering of the cast and crew of UK Taboo 2002.

Bottom left: Bald head and a dry sense of humour: Taboo writer Mark Davies

Below: Rosie O'Donnell makes an appearance in London with, from left, Drew Jaymson, me in Leigh regalia, Gail Mackinnon and Zee Asha.

Left: Pouting backstage with Julian Clary.

Middle left: Paul Baker tries to out-grimace Philip Sallon.

Middle right: Christine Bateman attends to my decolletage.

Bottom: Luke Evans and Matt Lucas whoop it up at the Taboo event at G.A.Y.

did a headstand, spread his legs and shot the contents of an enema over the front row. The crowd was very upset, going on about how disgusting it was. To me it was just what he did: 'It's art, dear, it's art.'

Once after a performance I congratulated him and he said: 'Oh, Mr Boy George, thank you. I really value your opinion.' As he pranced off, I wondered: 'Was that genuine sarcasm?'

Leigh was never particularly horrible to me. He would trot around the clubs with a plastic pig dressed in matching costume, and say: 'I see every living creature as a potential client.' Mostly he seemed to be nasty to Japanese people, and liked kicking them a lot. I remember once, at a John Galliano show, he kept kicking these Japanese buyers who were trying to take his picture. I said: 'Why are you doing that?' and he responded: 'They like it! They like being kicked!'

Leigh was not only a brilliant fashion designer, he was also a canny art director and master of disguise. When he played the role of a prostitute in the video for my 1991 song 'Generations of Love', directed by Baillie Walsh, he became the part. I know he could have been an outstanding actor if he'd so desired. Leigh hadn't even begun to tap into his creative potential at the time of his death. That's why he has to be remembered.

A journalist from the *Guardian* once asked me if Leigh could seriously be called art. I said that if a pile of bricks could be called art, then Leigh most definitely could.

At the time of the aforementioned Amsterdam trip, I introduced my friend Dragana to Leigh at Heathrow airport. He charmed her in his usual manner by taking the mickey out of her name: 'Oohh, George and the dragon.' Afterwards Drags told me: 'That boy is really ill.' She said he was *san paku,* a Japanese term which means looking up to heaven. The white of the eye is markedly notice-able underneath the iris, and it can mean that the person is not taking care of themselves, gravely ill, or even on the verge of death. *San paku* can be clearly detected in photographs and footage of Princess Diana in the months before she died. I thought it was a bit odd, but she was vehement: 'I promise you, that man is not long for this world.'

The last time I saw Leigh was with his band Minty at Madame Jo-Jos, where he did his act of 'giving birth' to his wife Nicola, wearing his grotesque body suit. It was hilariously offensive.

On New Year's Eve 1994 John Maybury called and told me Leigh was in hospital but hadn't wanted to see anybody apart from Fat Sue and Nicola. The next morning I heard he was gone.

How perfect that he went on a visual high. Leigh ordered his close friends to tell the world that he wasn't in hospital but gone to farm pigs in Bolivia or on holiday to Papua New Guinea.

His dying request was that he be buried alongside his mother in Australia. That request was fulfilled after a struggle with the Australian authorities to allow an 'infected' body to be brought in to the country. This was made possible with the assistance of Lucian Freud, whose portraits of Leigh now hang in major collections and museums around the world.

Later, when I drew upon Leigh as one of the influences for my alter ego The Twin, one bitchy queen who knew Leigh well told me: 'Why do you care? You were a much bigger star than he was.' The idiot didn't get it at all.

By the late nineties Leigh was in danger of being almost forgotten, which I thought was really shitty. A lot of the imagery for the T-shirts and promotional material for *Taboo* is based on things I put together around the time of his death. I came up with them as a sort of tribute to him, because his influence was very much in the air, and *Taboo* has made it even more evident.

When I heard Leigh had died, I cried, just like I cried when my teenage idol Marc Bolan hit that tree. The world had lost another couture icon, another mirror ball, which is why I wrote 'Satan's Butterfly Ball' on *Cheapness and Beauty*:

> Goodbye butterfly
> Goodbye Satan's child
> Ah look at you you've got no shame
> Enemas, blood, cocaine
> Caviar and piss
> Disco monster terrorist
> Hanging in the Tate with Turner and Van Gogh.

20

Ode To Attention Seekers

I was worried that the real-life people in *Taboo* would be upset about our portrayal of them: not just Philip and Marilyn but also people like Princess Julia, Fat Sue, Rachel Auburn. But all of them loved it. Sue left me the most emotional answerphone message, crying and saying she thought it was fantastic. Most of the original Taboo crowd – Rachel, Rifat Ozbek, John Maybury and Baillie Walsh – were also very supportive. Baillie said: 'Fuck what anyone says, you fucking did it and it's genius.' I was really touched to hear that, although I also received a few stupid comments, including: 'Leigh was taller.' Cheers. And David Furnish came one night and sent a bunch of notes to me backstage, which really made me chuckle.

I think Philip liked it because a lot of his relatives came along and enjoyed it so much. It's like he's been canonised, which I think he deserves to be. He has the mind of Sigmund Freud, the personality of Pippi Longstocking and, to quote himself, 'the face of a retarded brat'.

Philip has never changed, he's like a force of nature. He's still Philip, always will be, claiming that my problem is that I want to be a woman, and that's why I have a grudge against all women. What a pile of shit! Apart from anything else, he's conveniently ignoring the fact that most of my friends are, and always have been, female.

Philip has a habit of upsetting everybody, mainly because he doesn't think in the same way as the rest of humanity. And that is why I love him. You can argue with Philip for hours, and although he won't necessarily make sense of the subject, he's incredibly entertaining. He is prone to bitch about everyone and his personal comments about me – which are many and twisted – are always reported back to me. It's not as if there aren't plenty of things I can say back. Philip can't stand being called 'old' and he's not too fond of being called 'ugly' but he often brings it on himself.

I've often called Philip ugly but I've never actually thought that. He has the most striking features, hence the line from the song 'Ode to Attention Seekers': 'I've one of those faces you'll never forget.' His eyes are very pretty and whimsical and when he's animated they dance with mischief. I often find Philip's humour and bitchiness refreshing. Sometimes he can be too final about people, but when he says someone's a cunt, he's rarely far off.

Even if I haven't spoken to him for months, I know what to expect when the phone call comes. Invariably he'll say: 'Hold on, what gossip have I got for you?' And, as ever, I'm all ears.

Vassos, our transvestite hooker chum, tortures Philip. He will ring up and put on a sexy voice: 'Uh, uh, uh, uh . . . UGLY!!' Or: 'Philip, you'd better get back into the water, you're drying up, you nasty reptile.'

Marilyn went to see the show in London three times, but the first couple of occasions were disastrous. They were preceded by endless phone calls; it felt like I was communicating with Anneka Rice on mushrooms. Both times he didn't manage to see it all the way through. The first time I organised his tickets, he sat in the audience for ten minutes sneering loudly: 'Who's that supposed to be then?' before storming out. The second time he turned up with one of our old cronies Dencil about five minutes before the end, which resulted in a huge row between us.

When he finally arrived on time it was no less of a drama. My assistant Paul Farrell came backstage and announced: 'Marilyn needs £70.' When I asked why, Paul said: 'He needs to park his car and buy a Chinese meal.' I gave him the money.

He saw the show and wept uncontrollably, telling me it was brilliant. Of course, in interviews it was a different story. But then that's Marilyn for you. He is a victim of his moods and always will be.

Marilyn still lives with his mother in Borehamwood; she must be a saint. He calls from time to time and there'll be a nice message, followed by a really hideous message, then back to nice, then some more horrible ones. Sometimes he disappears for six months and I'll get a text message asking: 'Why aren't you calling me?!' Then it'll be: 'I fucking hate you, you're a cunt, how spiritual are you?'

When we lived in New York in the eighties our thing was to be as horrible as we could to each other. He used to call me Dawn Pigport and I called him Melonhead: 'Your head's too big for your body, you ugly bitch!' People just couldn't take it. I remember Andy Warhol saying: 'You guys are so mean to each other.' I told him: 'We love each other, we're just English.'

I do love Marilyn. He will always be part of my life because we are sisters under the skin. He has a very self-destructive nature but I know how wounded he is, and that makes me love him all the more. All deserted children have an unbearable cross to shoulder, and there are so many of us out there. Marilyn became really upset with me when I called him a damaged child in an interview. Let's face facts! Most of us are damaged children. And what balanced kid dresses up as Marilyn Monroe at the age of fifteen?

Underneath all the bullshit Marilyn is actually a very sweet person, but not many people get to see that. His great line is: 'There are three truths: mine, George's and the truth.'

Marilyn has a habit of calling Philip and slagging me off. Once when I was there I got Philip to put him on speakerphone and sat there listening to him bitching about me. This contrasts with a lot of the personal calls he makes to me; he can be so sweet and logical. It's easy to forget that Marilyn has a brain and he can be surprisingly wise. All the cattiness is insecurity and that is why I have always stayed friendly with him. In general I'm not as sensitive to Marilyn's bitching as other people's. I always think: 'Oh here she goes again.'

A ticket was bought for him for the opening night of *Taboo* in New York. And *quelle surprise*, he didn't make the flight. Less of a surprise was that he blamed me. When I refused to have the production company pay for another ticket I received another batch of nasty text messages and when the New York production closed his eleven text messages sat very badly with me. To quote one: 'Well done. *Taboo*'s closing. Now you know what it's like to be a failure.' Had I responded I would have said: 'You're only a failure if you never try.' I haven't spoken to him since. It goes without saying I didn't receive a congratulatory text from him when we were nominated for four Tony awards.

Philip has said some unbelievably cruel things to Marilyn. He once told him: 'I wish you would just overdose and leave me in peace.' Marilyn would have to sacrifice a child before I said anything so hideous, but Philip will never apologise for saying such things.

I look at Marilyn and I see a lot of hurt and even if I go through periods of despising him, it never lasts.

As for Steve Strange, I was always falling in and out of favour with him in the eighties. He would decide I was de rigueur if I had a good haircut or was working a particularly good look, which he would inevitably steal. And he tells these stories about me giving him an anti-drugs lecture at one of his New Year's Eve parties. In fact it was the opposite. I was doing drugs with him and Ronnie Wood and thinking: 'This is so bizarre. I'm doing drugs with one of the Rolling Stones.'

Steve came along to see *Taboo* and although he's portrayed in a very tongue-in-cheek way, he said the only problem he had was that his character had too strong a Welsh accent. He didn't seem to mind the fact that his character's wardrobe included the snake-skin jacket I acquired from him in the eighties after he utilised my credit card. He claimed that it cost him £15,000 way back when.

Though I'm friendlier with Steve's mother, an adorable woman with a fantastic beehive – I actually joked with her: 'How did you spawn such a monster?' – my relationship with Steve these days has improved tenfold. We speak on the phone from time to time and I find him a much softer person. He often says of me:

'George is less bitchy these days.' I still have my moments but I guess the same can be said of all of us.

21

Neanderthal Lloyd Webber

As the story of *Taboo* developed, I set to work on the music. I already had some suitable songs, such as 'Petrified' and 'Stranger in this World'. The latter was written a couple of years earlier with John Themis and Richie Stevens. It's about my relationship with my mother when I was leaving home:

> You always knew, didn't you, Mother?
> You always knew, as mothers always do.
> You always knew, didn't you, Mother,
> That I was a stranger in this world?

Another song, 'Genocide Peroxide', was from *Cheapness and Beauty* and summed up Marilyn's character to a T:

> Your father's rage and a cocktail dress,
> With a bulletproof heart,
> Why is your life such a mess,
> If you're so damned smart?

I had written, 'Il Adore' several years before for Stevie Hughes, my friend and a brilliant make-up artist who died from an Aids-related illness in 1992, as did another friend Tranny Paul a couple of years later. That was a terrible time, especially for his mother. When people went to see Tranny in hospital they just couldn't relate what he looked like – an alien to be frank – to the incredible person he had been. But 'Il Adore' is about everybody who has gone that way and in the show it is fittingly sung by Big Sue – as we renamed her – as Leigh dies in hospital:

> Here in this cold white room,
> Tied up to these machines,
> It's hard to imagine him as he used to be.
> Laughing screaming tumbling queen,
> Like the most amazing light show you've ever seen,
> Whirling, swirling, never blue,
> How could you go and die?
> What a lonely thing to do.

The rest of the songs were written with Kevan Frost. It was stimulating to be coming from a different perspective. Most of my writing is personal. Having to write songs about other people was a challenge. Even if someone is deceased you have to be sensitive, and even more so if they're living.

I wanted the songs to be self-contained. The finest example is 'Ich Bin Kunst', which sums up Leigh without going into the whole story of how he came over to London and worked in Burger King. That was originally in the script but it became cumbersome to include every last detail.

The idea for 'Ich Bin Kunst' came from a trip to Zurich in the midst of preparations for *Taboo*. I was staying with my friend the singer Eve Gallagher, and one day while we were driving around the city I spotted a grand old building, which Eve told me was the Kunstpalast. I joked: 'Is that where all the cunts live?' She rolled her eyes: 'Kunst means "art"!'

The idea clicked right away for a song for Leigh. After a brief language lesson from the multilingual Eve, I came up with the title, which means 'I Am Art'. It opens with the taunting line:

> Ich bin Kunst
> Can't you see?
> Look at you
> Look at me.

The song encapsulates his journey from Australia and the madness he wreaked on London nightlife:

> My father said 'Don't panic:
> It's a phase.'
> 'Phase one,' I said and snipped and sewed for days.
> I dreamed of London town,
> Art and fashion was my thing
> I arrived and took a job . . . in Burger King.

I drove myself to distraction trying to write a song for Philip Sallon's character, because it had to be comical but not shallow. Then, when I was in the US for a couple of weeks on a solo tour with John Themis, we wrote the bones for 'Ode to Attention Seekers':

> I'm known in all the wrong places
> I'm one of those faces you'll never forget
> And those who may not adore me
> Could never ignore me
> I'm placing a bet.

Once I got the basic melody and premise it just came together. 'Ode to Attention Seekers' has a proper music-hall quality, a bit ragtime and Busby Berkeley-style with a twist of *Oliver!*. When I got back I tried singing it to Philip but he was always distracted. However, he was impressed by the beautiful voices celebrating his legend when he heard it at the workshop we set up in a basement dance studio in Old Street, where Chris and Mark knocked the actors into shape as they came on board.

I suggested bald comedian Matt Lucas to play Leigh, and we were lucky enough to get him. I saw him one night in the Departure Lounge at Heaven and asked him whether he would consider it. Matt said: 'Yeah, phone my agent.' And that was that.

We held the workshop five months after I was first approached by Chris, which is very fast work for the theatre business. And it was so much fun. I was excited to be doing something different

and enjoyed developing the songs, which Philip was really complimentary about, enthusing: 'They're the best thing about it.'

However, Philip could be a nightmare during the workshop
sessions, constantly on the phone to everyone, offering to help
out but actually driving everyone nuts. One day he showed up
with a notepad and pen and sat making notes and grimacing in
front of Mark the scriptwriter. Then he pulled faces at the actors
while they tried to work and moaned that the guy playing him
was 'a hairdresser from Croydon'. Actually, Paul, who played Philip
in the workshop, was the only non-professional actor and was
superb. Philip just couldn't get it into his head that the workshop
was a way of ironing out plot and script problems, so none of it
was permanent. Everyone hated Philip so I had to drag him into
the kitchen and tell him to stop misbehaving, to which he
responded: 'I can't help it if the writer's got no sense of humour.'

But it was Philip who spotted Euan Morton's potential during
one workshop, saying to me: 'That's who should be playing you.
That boy is you. I remember you when you were nineteen. He
looks like you and he's all the things you were at that age. He's
also the best actor and the best singer.' At the time Euan was
playing Trojan, but when the character was dropped from the
script we suggested to Euan that he play me. He didn't seem
interested, though that was probably because Philip had nagged
him constantly.

Eventually Euan was persuaded, which was brilliant because
he is very special. Euan kept asking me for reference material
but I wanted him to keep a bit of himself in the role, so didn't
pressurise him or get too precious about his portrayal. I didn't
want it to be *Stars Up Your Arse*.

When I first saw him in all the drag it was a spooky experience – there were many visual similarities even though he is much
shorter, thinner and more masculine-looking than me. Philip kept
saying he was too camp but I didn't agree. Euan added the essential predatory edge to the role, which was true to life. When I
really came to know Euan, the differences between us became
clear. He is young and has that mix of confidence and indifference, underlined by the desire to be a huge star. Of course, he

will often say 'I don't give a flying fuck' in his broad Scottish accent, but I don't take it seriously. Actors are a strange lot and you never know when they are being real or lost in some character. I came up with the term 'refugees from reality' for them as a result of my forays into the theatrical world.

Later, after the show had opened and I started my first run in the role of Leigh, I was preparing in the dressing room and witnessed Euan ranting at Emma, the sound girl. As he was doing this he was stepping into the Star of David smock dress I wore when Culture Club first broke through, and I had terrible flash-backs. It was like seeing myself.

Euan does Boy George so much better than I ever did. In fact, when he started I couldn't bear to watch him and snuck out for a cigarette every time he was onstage. That also happened when I watched the scenes where Marilyn and I are out of it on drugs. I found them very emotional and would use them as an opportunity for more nicotine consumption.

Whenever I saw Euan unhappy or suffering doubt about himself, I wanted to shake him and say: 'In twenty years' time you will look back and realise that this is such a precious moment.' At the height of my own career I tended to make things more difficult than they needed to be. If I was going through it now I'd squeeze every last drop of joy out of it.

In the role of the ambitious photographer, Luke Evans was perfect. From the moment I saw him audition I said: 'That's Billy.' Luke has the most seductive eyes and a voice to die for, and on top of his other legendary attributes, he has a lot of confidence but is also sensitive and insecure. He really owned the role.

We decided to use only a couple of Culture Club hits in *Taboo*, and even then just as reference points because everyone felt the new songs were strong enough on their own. After three weeks of workshops the story was still a little shaky, but Chris decided to hold a reading for a select audience in the summer of 2001.

I was so nervous. Brian May from Queen and Frank Skinner came along and Brian was quite emotional – I guess a lot of the show related to Freddie as well – and stood up at the end, forcing a standing ovation, which was mad. I loved Queen at school and never imagined I would be showcasing my work in front of their guitarist. I was so overcome myself I had to leave before the last song! As for the look of *Taboo*, it was great to involve Mike Nicholls on the costume design. Initially he wasn't sure whether he could do it, because he'd never been involved in theatre before. When Chris told him how many outfits he had to make, he went green. But he knew the scene and collaborated on the costumes with great people who had worked for Leigh, like David Cabaret and Mr Pearl. Mike's very like me. He knows that there are things you do for money and then there are things you do because they offer you creativity. And often those you don't do for money are the projects you enjoy most. I like that about him; we have a cool understanding. As he always jokes: 'We're punks. Fuck 'em!'

There was a spellbinding moment during rehearsals when Matt Lucas performed 'Ich Bin Kunst', with Leigh behind glass in the Anthony d'Offay art gallery scene. Matt was wearing Leigh's green marabou tutu with latex drips on his head and lovely big boobs sticking out of a satin green fitted jacket. I found myself getting quite emotional, turning to Mike and screaming: 'Fucking genius, you turned it out!'

Christine Bateman, who handled the hair and make-up design of the show, was similarly perfect. She's not only a genius make-up artist but, like Mike, she knows the whole world of Taboo because she was a part of it. Christine is third in line to the Bowery throne, being the sister of Leigh's wife Nicola.

You could rarely meet two sisters more delightfully deranged than Christine and Nicola. One night in a taxi Nicola was telling anyone that would listen how Christine's PMT ruled her life as a child: 'God, she made everyone's life hell.' Then Nicola thought she saw flocks of seagulls flying around in the night sky. 'They're bloody stars,' pointed out Christine.

As we pulled up outside Brighton's Pelirocco Hotel, where we had gone to see if we could consume more alcohol, the cab driver said: 'I've been driving for twenty years and I've never met a more interesting bunch of people. Thank you for making my evening.'

I never really got to know Nicola when she was married to Leigh, beyond exchanging pleasantries in the discos. This was usually no more than a knowing nod, because Nicola often wore bizarre face masks or had jewellery covering her mouth. The most spectacular outfit I recall was an umbrella-like isolation tank made of clear plastic and flashing fairy lights which she wore on her head. I later discovered that Nicola designed these outfits purely to avoid conversation.

There was a lot of bitching about their marriage. Some queens felt it was a mockery and that Leigh was a traitor to the cause. But then Leigh was a traitor to every cause! When they married Leigh claimed it was an 'art ceremony', although I think Leigh liked the security of marriage and having someone to care for him. I guess it counterbalanced his cottaging escapades.

The downside of Nicola's artistic vow of silence was that people were left to make up their own minds about her. So many had the wrong impression that she was stuck up, a bitch or just plain pretentious.

Not that I begrudge these qualities in anybody.

It was only during the run of *Taboo* that I got to know her better and discovered that she was none of those things, although mad as a sack of spanners.

As the whole shebang started to head towards the West End, we looked everywhere for a decent site for the show, and not only traditional theatres but places like Café de Paris and even some shops. But when we saw the Venue off Leicester Square, just round the corner from where the real Taboo had been held, we knew it was right.

Tim Pritchard designed the set, which allowed the audience to be incorporated into the show with a bar where drinks could be bought and seating which made people feel as though they were almost part of the action. My assistant Paul – who was a plasterer in a previous incarnation – actually helped to build the whole thing and even install the toilets.

There were some fights over the sleazy language in certain scenes. Producer Adam Kenwright insisted: 'I'm not producing a show with "cunts" in it.' It was too easy to respond to a statement like that, but you can imagine what I was thinking. I did have some battles. The producers wanted to turn the show into a fashion parade, which is not what Blitz and Taboo were about – they were more about DIY and adapting Oxfam clothes on a budget. There were constant arguments because Mark Davies isn't a pussycat and neither am I; there was one meeting which ended up with him asking Adam Kenwright outside!

However, we understood that we were putting on a show to entertain different types of people, and that it was more important to bring Leigh to public attention than to be too shocking. When it opened we were slated for having a boy-meets-girl thread, but it's hard to win whatever you do. The Pet Shop Boys' musical *Closer to Heaven* was knocked for being 'too gay' while it seemed we received the same treatment for being 'too straight'.

Life back in the New Romantic days was never exclusively gay and most of the boys we chased had girlfriends. Sexuality was less defined and everyone claimed to be bisexual, so the show was a reflection of my world, which is still nothing to do with gay or straight. I don't befriend anyone based on what they do in bed. I don't give out a questionnaire, you know.

It was very emotional when we started our week of previews in January 2002. The first big night was in aid of the Freddie Mercury Trust – Brian May had been a supporter since coming to the workshop performance.

On opening night, 14 January 2002, I was full of fear and so emotional I had to go and get a drink during the drug-taking scenes. The reception was great even though the theatre business was in a very bad way at that time after 11 September; tourism was down, and the reaction to us starting then was: 'Are you mad?' But I was so excited about it I went almost every night for the first three weeks and enjoyed being a part of the company.

It's true that the show took time to pick up speed. For many months I think the term for it was 'a fragile hit' but we held on by the skin of our teeth. The reviews were either oozing with praise or downright nasty.

When the *Daily Telegraph* music critic Neil McCormick congratulated me on my songwriting and compared it to Andrew Lloyd Webber's in his review of the show, I cried for at least an hour and my poor make-up girl Sarah Gregory just couldn't get my mascara to stay on as I was trying to get ready to do a TV appearance. She kept on saying: 'What's the matter? Why has this affected you so much?' I told her: 'You don't understand. All these people like Oasis and George Michael are lauded as great song-writers while I'm just a joke in a hat. This means so much to me.'

I met Neil later, on a DJ trip to Shanghai, and told him: 'Normally when I speak to journalists I want to punch them, but I can't thank you enough for what you wrote. It made me feel like my work was worthwhile.'

In the *Guardian* Lyn Gardner wrote that Euan is 'far prettier' than I ever was in my day – without displaying a picture of herself, of course. But the biggest problem I had was the *Evening Standard* critic Nicholas de Jongh, who described the show as 'aimless'.

He depicted *Taboo* as a sell-out, claiming it followed the tradi-tional boy-meets-girl storyline, proving that some homosexuals exist in an entirely different universe. *Taboo* is more boy-meets-boygirl-meets-girl. In those days everyone was fucking everyone else: girls–boys, boys–girls, girls–girls, boys–boys and, in partic-ular, Leigh. He shagged Rachel, he shagged Princess Julia, and he shagged every single person he ever met in a toilet. He once said that he only made two exceptions, because they were so gross he couldn't bear it.

We made changes to the basic storyline after a few weeks to make it more ambiguous, so that there was a battle about who will have Billy, my character or the fag hag. Both I and Mark Davies (who's straight) always felt that the original storyline was not risky enough, and inserted back into the script what I wanted from day one, fighting everyone else to get it that way.

What infuriated me even more was the way de Jongh then praised the Madness musical *Our House*, calling it 'truly original' when all the songs were old and the storyline was the purest boy-meets-girl. And it was really annoying that every week of the fifteen-month run in the *Evening Standard* listings the review of *Taboo* carried de Jongh's original comments. Let's hope when de Jongh gets to Hell they're out of Merlot.

When Janet Street-Porter came to see *Taboo* she was dancing and smiling along, but then wrote a bitchy piece in the *Independent* which went on about how she discovered the Venue herself back when it was the Notre Dame Hall. She also said the real Taboo was much more depraved than we depicted it. Janet's a bright lady and must realise how hard it was to put the show on in the first place. She only had to look at how scathing the press were about *Closer to Heaven*, which garnered some deeply homophobic comments in papers like the *Daily Mail*. It's a joke: the media can't bear it if you are too gay and they mock you if you skirt around it.

You're damned if you don't, and damned if you don't.

Matt Lucas was an excellent Leigh and even though we didn't become the best of friends I respect his talent, though he was quite fussy and a bit oversensitive. Actually, I don't really know why we stopped talking but we did have a blow-out over an episode when I was smoking in the dressing room and behaving like a drunken lout. He was being very Dame Judi and I said: 'Stop being a bloody queen.'

The next day he walked past me in the bar and said: 'Afternoon, Rock 'n' Roll George.'

I snapped back: 'At least my one-liners are original, baldie.'

When we came to make the *Taboo* cast album Matt was upset that I re-recorded his vocals to 'I'll Have You All', a song about having sex in toilets which he had sung very limply. I asked him to re-record the vocals himself but he wouldn't, so I did. I was about to take over from him in the role of Leigh and I felt I performed it with more conviction, but he sent me a nine-page email rant.

Things got very Bette and Joan after that and he refused to look at me, which is just as well because I didn't fancy being turned to stone. Matt sang two tracks on the record, and they were my songs anyway, so I still don't really understand what he was going on about.

Philip was always saying: 'That Matt Lucas is a social climber,' which is classic coming from Philip, who was hobnobbing with Gareth Gates and Chris Eubank at the time. I think Matt takes himself a bit too seriously but the rift was just that, not an epic drama. It all seemed a bit pointless actually.

Following Matt into Leigh's tutu was daunting because he is a natural comedian but I was determined to play it my own way and had picked up a lot of valuable tricks from watching his performance. It was never part of the plan for me to appear in the show. Chris had said: 'It would be great if you were in it,' but I'd never acted before and just didn't think it was possible. He kept on at me and after a few weeks I started acting classes with a friend of mine, Kay James. It was liberating. After all these years I'm good at remembering lyrics and found that I could remember lines too. But I was still very wary and felt out of my depth. Here I was with a bunch of people who had been to drama school and some were looking at this pop star in their midst as if to say: 'What makes you think you can act?'

In the show Philip was played by Paul 'Hilda' Baker, and how! Paul is not only a master of the stage but also a master of rattling emotional sabres. As Philip he held the show together, winding in and out of scenes, pulling one-liners out of the bag and managing to terrify and titillate the audience. He revelled in the power he commanded onstage, and was one of my biggest detractors when I took on the role of Leigh for the first time. Paul found it hard not to smirk if I fluffed a scene, but I worked hard and in time managed to get him on my side.

We went out one night and got pissed and Paul asked me what I thought of him. I told him that I thought he was such an asset to the show and was a brilliant actor but that he was a bitch because he takes pleasure in other people fucking up. I work quite well when confronted with animosity. If somebody tells me I can't do something that makes me all the more determined even if I fall on my face.

Part of my job had been to teach the others about projection, using things like back-phrasing, a jazzy way of singing against the beat which I guess I'd learned from people like Bowie. I don't think they'd had musical direction like that before, because it was less dramatic and theatrical. I'd tell the cast members: 'Sing like you'd sing a favourite song by Joni Mitchell. Don't just show us how many notes you can do.' That's the problem with people who go to drama schools – they end up with that West End whingey tone to their voices. I think they enjoyed having a chance to find out what you can achieve emotionally through vocals.

Nevertheless, my first night was scary. I sat in the polka-dot loo where Leigh's character makes his first appearance onstage and looked up to heaven: 'If you're watching, Leigh, don't put me off, you jealous bitch!'

There was a bit of a hoo-ha among the company members about what I would be like, and I later found out that Gail Mackinnon, who played Big Sue, had to say to them: 'Hold on a minute. Give the guy a chance. He hasn't done anything yet.' I think the actors in general thought I was going to come in and pull a diva routine, but I left that to Paul Baker. Also, the men's dressing room was far too small for Hollywood egos and I accepted that I was out of my depth, making a conscious decision to keep my head down and watch, listen and learn.

After my first stint of a couple of weeks in Leigh's role, Julian Clary took over and was brilliant. Of course Julian played Leigh as if he was possessed by the spirit of Julian Clary, but then Julian – like Matt – is a master of his craft. When he's not in character he is a very serious and reflective person and a lovely bloke to boot.

I've always been a fan of Julian's, having been to see him in his early days as the Joan Collins Fan Club. I would describe his humour as sardonic *Carry On* and enjoy his deadpan delivery. My favourite ever line of his is: 'I'm sorry to tell you this but Postman Pat is a cunt. I've worked with him and he's a hideous man.'

After Julian, Leigh's role was taken by Mark Little. Mark's very nice but he played Leigh like a straight man playing a homosexual, and that is one of the traps we wanted to avoid. Marilyn, for example, wasn't camp, he was very much a bloke. If the characters were played strictly as 'homosexuals' it became one-dimensional.

I took over the role of Leigh full-time for the final six months in London and thoroughly enjoyed myself. Playing Leigh was a fantastic experience. I had an excuse to wear more make-up than usual, wore such beyond costumes and also got my tits out!

As a singer, if you make a mistake while recording, you go back and redo it. Performing in a show every night, if you make a mistake you learn not to do it again. I learned a lot about comedy and pacing and also learned a lot about myself and what I'm capable of. At first I was very shy but once I got used to it, I really relaxed. If anyone had told me I would one day be sitting in a cramped dressing room surrounded by fit young actors with my tits out and wearing green Lycra tights, I would have gagged!

22

Stranger In This World

Taboo taught me that theatre is absolutely nothing like the experience of being in a band playing a show every night. There are tensions between the performers in the theatre which even we in Culture Club couldn't compete with! But when I took over the role of Leigh I loved being a part of it all, collecting my union rate payslip every week.

When you're sharing a dressing room with ten or twelve other men and a series of quick costume changes you tend to get less precious about letting things hang out, though I'd never have been as brave as Euan Morton, who was fond of whopping out his member at will. It was substantial enough to withstand any unnecessary embarrassment.

So I really did become part of the team and there were so many nice and talented people: Drew Jaymson, who played Steve Strange, is such a sweet person and has a stunning voice. He's very unconfident about it, even though he sings like Stevie Wonder. We keep in touch, and, given his unnatural obsession with Nana Mouskouri, I often receive text messages from Nana.

Gail Mackinnon became a good mate and was always up for practical jokes. If someone is leaving the cast, there is a theatrical tradition that you fuck things up during the matinée. At the end of my first run as Leigh I was doing his deathbed scene when Gail said her line: 'I've cancelled the milk, what about the cats?' I said: 'I'm vegan. What are you going on about *Cats* for? You know I hate Andrew Lloyd Webber.' Gail started to lose it, so I said: 'See, you're insane. You should be in this bed,' and pulled the covers back to reveal that I was wearing a yashmak with DYKE written on it. Then I said: 'I'm not dying. I'm going out dancing,' and walked offstage. And then she had to sing the heartbreaking 'Il Adore'.

Sometimes the impractical jokes got out of hand. Gary Amers, who played Marilyn for a while, once came on sweeping the stage as an old tramp, while Jackie Clunes, who was playing the mother, was attempting to sing another heart-rending ballad. Mostly audiences went with it, and loved it. There were a couple of letters of complaint but fuck 'em if they can't take a joke.

Gary was a total comedian, always taking the piss out of everyone and such an incredible mimic it's uncanny. One night the much berated Alana Phillips, daughter of choreographer Arlene, stood on a safety pin in the dressing room and Gary did this brilliant impression: 'Oh, Mummy, I've got a nail in my footie! Is anybody looking?' Gary would also 'do' Michele Hooper, who played Janey the journalist and was daft as all get-out. He'd stick on one of the girls' wigs, cross his eyes and snap into a stream of Alexis-on-crack banter. And, when he channelled Marilyn, Gary would say: 'Oh, that Boy George – what I can't tell you about him would make me a fortune!'

David Burt, who played the dual roles of Billy's Dad and Petal, was the ultimate seasoned actor, and went mad at me because my messing with Gail on that occasion fucked up his entrance. David would always say: 'Twenty-five years in the business,' whenever anything went wrong.

Declan Bennett, who took over from Luke as Billy, is gorgeous and a great singer-songwriter. I got Declan to support me when I played my recent shows at Ronnie Scott's, and he has modelled for my photography a few times. Any excuse to get him in a pair of sequinned underpants.

Stephen Ashfield, who took over from Euan, became another Scottish Boy George and a gem. Stephen was much quieter and more reserved than his farting, belching predecessor.

Robbie was an all-round good egg and union head Nathan could be a drama queen but was actually quite sweet. Meanwhile, John Partridge played a towering Marilyn and was butch and bitch in the same breath. He's a fantastic actor and handsome out of drag with an amazing body. During his first dress rehearsal his wig was a bit skew-whiff, which Paul Baker found quite amusing. Afterwards in the dressing room John took one of his stilettos off and said to Paul: 'Listen, you motherfucker. You see this? The next time you laugh at me I'll put it through your head.' Paul didn't do it again.

There were always things like that happening backstage. Once I sat and watched Euan take Paul Baker's make-up sponge, stick it up his bottom and rub it around his goolies and then put it back.

I won't forget the company stage manager Mark Pawsey with his clipped vowels and stick-on Mohican that looked like a dyed rat, and Dougie the mumbling stage manager. He's been in theatre for years and was nice enough to tell my assistant Paul that I had proved all the doubters in the company wrong. I think they were surprised that I could keep things going onstage and ad lib off the cuff, but I got that from years of being heckled as a musician.

Then there was Daisy the wardrobe lady. 'What did your last slave die of, you cheeky mare? If you put the clothes back on the hanger they might survive this run! I don't care who you were!' Meanwhile, dishy and sadly straight Dan Carter was the unrequited subject of the lust triangle Julian Clary and I sought to set up.

The girls – Lucy Newton and Lucy Harris, Jodie, Lorna, Tamsin and Zee Asha – were great though some of them loathed their costumes, especially the open-backed baby dolls worn over nasty men's Y-fronts, which caused a lot of grief. Actually, the show was very centred around the boys, who became the male peacocks.

Well, girls get to wear the best frocks most of the time . . .

We had a great set of actresses playing Billy's mother Josie: first of all Gemma Craven, and then ex-New Seeker Lyn Paul, Mari Wilson and Jackie Clunes. We used to joke that the mother role was cursed, because some of them became very twisted when they played that role. Once, when Mike Nicholls gave Gemma Craven her costume, she hissed: 'I wouldn't give these to my worst enemy.' Luckily Mike is a sick queen and thought it very John Waters.

I chose Phil Nicholls to take over the part of Philip from Paul Baker after seeing him doing his comedy routine, but I think he was under the impression I didn't rate him. Actually, I thought he was excellent, although he was at the centre of one of our biggest dramas when he upset Parry, the proprietor of the Venue. Occasionally Parry, who is also known as the Earl of Leicester Square, was prone to let off steam.

One night Phil was making jokes about the war in Iraq, asking Americans in the audience: 'Are you enjoying the war? I think it's great because it teaches Americans where other countries are.'

Parry marched into the dressing room afterwards and asked Phil not to make those sort of jokes. Phil really lost it. In fairness, it is the job of production to give 'notes', the theatre term for criticism, not the proprietor. A shouting match ensued and Parry said he wanted Phil banned from the theatre, which was a bit impractical given that his role was one of the main parts of *Taboo*. I don't think they actually healed the rift, but it did eventually simmer down.

Parry and his partner Kim Whitehorn – a slinky black diva who once punched John Galliano – were very much part of the family. Parry usually had an issue with our producers, and now and then it would cause tornadoes in the theatre. But I always had a good relationship with him because I know his bark is just a bark. Kim could switch from flirty to fierce in a flash but she kept things in order. After all, they had their front-of-house staff to keep in check. A couple of them were even found humping on Paul Baker's pink fun-fur coat one evening. Christine Bateman happened to breeze in on them, but waltzed on out. Very little would disturb our Christine.

Some people became complacent because it was just another job to them and they knew they would be moving on, and there were a couple of shit-stirrers in the company, just like there are everywhere. Once, just before showtime, I'd had enough of all the whingeing in the dressing room about the show closing, the extra matinées and abiding by union rules. I snapped: 'Don't you realise this is my show? Hearing you talk about it like this is really hideous. You know what? Fuck you all. You never invite me to your union meetings and then you sit around moaning all the time. That's it. I've had it, I'm off!'

It took Parry to persuade me to stay, saying: 'George, there's a packed house out there waiting to see you.'

We delayed the start by ten minutes and when I got onstage I admit I really fucked around. There was a scene in the toilet where a girl is really mean to Leigh and unscripted I said: 'I think people who are born beautiful have an obligation to be nice to those of us who are ugly. You're really nasty and you've got a boyfriend too.' She was dumbfounded, and then I came out of the toilet and announced: 'Mirror, mirror on the wall, I'd like to fuck you all – and I'll pay!' It was great fun to play around with the script and ad lib, though I'm sure this added to the view among some of the other actors that it was most unprofessional.

Taboo ended its run at the Venue on a high point. We were nominated for four Olivier Awards: Euan, Paul Baker, Mike and Christine. Paul was the only one who left the ceremonies with an award, while the Madness musical *Our House* swept the board, including the main Hilton Award for Best New Musical. Sitting in the Hilton in full drag that night I thought: 'Of course they're not going to give awards to a show about a bunch of homosexual freaks!'

But someone has to lose and in the grand scheme of things, it's all bullshit. *Our House* still closed a few months later despite the award, and we would have closed even if we had won it.

I must admit I wasn't entirely happy with the way our producers promoted *Taboo* at the Venue. Or rather, didn't promote *Taboo*. For most of the run, I was the mobile promotional budget, running from TV show to press interview plugging away.

I appeared in every paper and magazine and on every available programme, from Frank Skinner and Richard & Judy to *The Kumars at No. 42*. The fact that 'Out of Fashion', from *Taboo*, came out as a single with Judge Jules's band Hi-Gate gave me yet more opportunities and I even went on *The Salon*. What was I thinking?

Despite my promotional activities and the Olivier nominations, there was a weirdness surrounding our final run in London. We had Euan back in the cast, and with his nomination and Paul's award, there was a real opportunity to promote the hell out of it.

At that time no closing date had been set for *Taboo*. The producers had promised they would repromote the show, but nothing happened. Hardly surprising really; we'd had inklings of that earlier, such as when Julian Clary joined the cast. One poster advertising the fact was put up, and that was inside the theatre. Very helpful! Julian also suffered from some other organisational mishaps; on the day of his first dress rehearsal there wasn't even a director there for him, which was pretty embarrassing.

So, if the fact that I was in the media for virtually a whole year had been backed up by some promotion, maybe *Taboo* wouldn't have been allowed to run itself into the ground at the Venue. Lots of promises were made about poster campaigns, but it was all crap.

I kept going back into the show to boost ticket sales, but whatever I think of the way it was managed, I loved every minute of it. That's why it was so depressing when we received news of the closure. The production company AKA kindly stuck an unsigned letter on the noticeboard to clarify the closure date. It was a cold gesture to say the very least.

Not long after that decision was made, I was accidentally included on an email cc list that announced AKA were proud to announce a new client, *Our House*, with Madness singer Suggsy joining his own musical for a five-week spell. For me that was the final kick in the teeth because we lost to them so heavily at the Oliviers. Apparently AKA could get their arse in gear to promote *Our House* but not *Taboo*. Emily from AKA came to the theatre and gave me a card to say she was sorry about the way I had found out but I told her that she had nothing to apologise for. Producer Adam Kenwright had, however, and when he came to see me he said: 'It's just business.'

You can use that excuse for so many actions. It would be like

me allowing 'Karma Chameleon' in an advertising campaign for
Burger King. If I were different I'd accept the £140,000 – or
whatever it is – that is on offer. 'It's just business' would be my
excuse too.

I paid £120,000 of my own money for the *Taboo* DVD, which
includes a backstage documentary and interviews with the people
who are portrayed in the show. It's great; very funny with everyone
contradicting each other and Philip being an absolute bitch: 'Steve
Strange used to look good before time ravaged him!'

The last few weeks at the Venue were just incredible, filled with
so much warmth. A lot of the people who had come early on
returned to see it and you got this feeling that there was a select
crowd who had got it, singing along with every song.

On the last night all my family was there – though we had to
pay for their tickets – and we had a fantastic time, playing tricks
onstage with each other and deliberately delivering different lines.
Although I was very tired by the end, I was also upset because it
had been such a great experience, particularly the last run. It has
been very inspiring being part of *Taboo*, like being given an opportunity to have a holiday in another reality.

Philip has always said to me that actors are strange creatures
because they spend so much time being other people. I felt that
I had really learned to act, to lighten certain scenes with comedy.
I didn't really have any guidance because when I started the
direction was very limited, so my coach Kay was there every night
working on me and helping me out in terms of light and shade.
I can see now why big actors return to the theatre because it is
much more immediate. I'm not about to go into straight acting
(as if!). I've been offered loads of film roles down the years, but
they are always *Transvestite Lands on the Moon*. If I did act in a
film it would have to be a very different role from who I'm
perceived to be. Sometimes I think I'd like to play a thug, giving
it some south-east London.

One day during the run of the show I went down to Brighton
to see Nicola Bateman. Late in the evening I was sitting in her
loft surrounded by Leigh's wardrobe. She has kept everything;
Leigh's life is there. Remembering certain outfits from clubs and

parties made me feel melancholy. He would give names to the outfits like: Mincing Nellie or Princess Michael of Cunt.

Leigh was a real one-off.

Who knows what he would have thought of the whole circus that *Taboo* became? Fat Sue Tilley told me: 'He would have loved every second. But he'd have wanted to play himself.'

23

Safe In The City

One grey Saturday afternoon a few months into the London run of *Taboo*, when I had taken over as Leigh Bowery from Matt Lucas, we were literally playing to three old ladies and a poinsettia! Some of those matinées were pointless to say the least. Communication between cast members on such days was made up of much eye-rolling and heavy sighing.

One of those ladies in the audience – not the poinsettia – happened to be American comedienne Rosie O'Donnell. She was actually in town to see her friend Madonna in another theatrical production and had been told to check out our show.

When anyone of note was in the house there was always a buzz backstage. For example, the day Pete Burns arrived, he was in full spooky drag with jangling bells on his ankles and you could hear them in the dressing room. All manner of celebrities local and international came along, and this always made the cast work harder.

When we were told that Rosie was in the house, at least I knew who she was; most people didn't recognise her name. I said: 'She's that mate of Madonna's,' which was always a worry for me.

After that matinée, I had planned to stay in my Leigh costume and hit the London streets to do some filming with Mike Nicholls for the DVD of the show, and also to have a record of *Taboo*.

I received a message saying that Rosie wanted to meet me. She'd been in the bar chatting to cast members and had no idea that the apparition onstage was my good self. She had watched the entire show wishing there was more of Euan Morton and wondering why the Leigh character was there in the first place. A lot of people had thought the same thing since Leigh wasn't a household name. One of the cast said: 'Oh, that's Boy George.'

'You're shitting me!' was her reply. So after I'd had my make-up retouched I appeared wearing that huge chequerboard bustle dress and the headdress of rubber spikes which had so failed to impress the other members of Culture Club.

Rosie told me she loved the show and we posed for photographs together before I ran off to upset the tourists in Leicester Square. Her parting comment was: 'I want to take this thing to Broadway.' Using my best Leigh voice I said: 'Be my guest.' I honestly thought Rosie was joshing and I'd never see her again.

The amusing thing about my forays into the streets as Leigh was that builders would always shout: 'All right, George!' I guess they knew I was the only lunatic who would adopt such a look. Generally, Londoners would pretend I wasn't there, while confused tourists would approach me and ask: 'What are you?'

That day Michael Jackson's blacked-out limo was parked bang outside the Venue surrounded by hordes of Jacko's wackos. I ran into the midst of them, and started banging on the car window, screaming: 'Michael! I'm your most hugest fan!'

The next day a full-page story appeared in the press with the headline: LET ME SHOW YOU HOW TO GET YOUR FACE COMPLETELY WHITE, claiming Jacko was cowering inside the limo.

I forgot about Rosie, thinking that the offer she had made was nice and assumed it was one of those grandiose American gestures. But to my surprise she appeared again a month or so later with a group of business associates and sat in on the show five times. It soon became clear she was very serious, especially when she sent me a CD-Rom where she had cut dozens of visuals of Leigh to the show's song 'Il Adore'. It was so bloody beautiful and moving I cried. Rosie must have gone back to New York and yelled: 'Everything on Leigh Bowery NOW!' The CD was frighteningly comprehensive. Along with it she sent a book of collages she had made. I thought: She actually gets it.

To be fair, I didn't know too much about Rosie other than she was a larger-than-life character. She took me for dinner at the Ivy and of course the subject of her superstar friend was raised. She seemed to understand Madonna and have a pretty real relationship with her. I didn't shy away from telling her what I thought about Her Royal Madgeness and, in that American way, she told me: 'You guys would get on great.'

We've had more than two decades to do so, and it hasn't happened yet.

Rosie brought theatrical producer Dan Macdonald on board and announced she would be putting $10 million of her own money into the show, but there were still quite a few months before the contracts were signed and we could safely say we would be going to Broadway.

Always one to shoot from the lip, she was hysterical when talking about her wrangles with the London producers AKA. In fact, I've rarely met anyone with such a hurricane of a personality or the ability to silence Philip Sallon. Rosie has a habit of constantly mentioning money and Philip claims that when they first met she said to him: 'You know I'm worth a hundred million dollars.' Philip said: 'I thought that was an odd thing to say to someone you hardly know,' before adding: 'She's a hard-nosed bitch for sure.' That seemed to be a funny thing to say about somebody he'd just met.

In a way, Philip's policy is always scorched earth; basically everyone is accused of being 'false', 'insincere', 'a social climber' or 'an upstart'. For example, when he first met our director Chris Renshaw, he told him: 'You look really theatrical. You'll probably be found dead backstage with a glass of wine in your hand.'

With hindsight, Rosie offering the sun, moon, stars and Tony Awards to AKA contributed to their loss of interest in the London production. They must have thought: we're quids in here, let's cut our losses and salivate over the bigger picture. I guess they fell for Rosie's seductive offer. After all, it was full of promise. I was later to discover that her promises often have one broken heel.

After the show closed at the Venue there was a lot of humming and hahing as we prepared to organise the transfer to the Plymouth Theatre on Broadway. In fact, there was a period of two weeks when it didn't look as though it was going to happen at all. A union issue arose over Kevan Frost playing in the band. He co-wrote most of the songs with me, and I felt it was his right to be there. Kevan had also made the cast album of *Taboo* for a tin of beans. He spent a lot of time making sure it wasn't just a routine crap cast album.

Early on a couple of important creative decisions were made without my involvement, which really upset me. Rosie, without consulting me, hired her friend Bobby Pearce to supervise and design the costumes, but there was no way Mike Nicholls was going to be usurped after working so bloody hard, again on a shoestring, for more than a year in London. *Taboo* had been Mike's first theatrical production and his work had been constantly praised in reviews. His nomination for an Olivier Award should have been good enough for Rosie. I know now that Rosie was dead set on having her own team work on the Broadway production. I had words with her manager Bernie Young, who told me: 'There are rules on Broadway. Union stuff to deal with. It's not about Bobby taking Mike's job, he's there to help him, make things easier.' Bernie is as smooth as Rosie is explosive. I know that this issue wasn't about offering assistance to Mike, but more about Rosie's need to control every aspect of *Taboo* USA.

In her first ever email to me, she promised to 'protect my art' and said: 'I don't want to change very much, maybe some of the girls' costumes. Small changes, tweaks and improvements to the story.'

So Bobby – whose drag name is Beverly Hills – arrived one Saturday in London and we met in the bar next to the theatre. It was clear Bobby had been thrown in the deep end and it was not entirely his fault. He was edgy at that meeting. I suspect Rosie had promised him the job and thought that she could talk me round. I made it clear that if Mike wasn't involved it would be a deal-breaker. It was later decided Bobby and Mike should have joint billing on costume design. It was ridiculous, since Mike had

Left: Euan Morton in New York: a voice so flawless and full of feeling.

Above: Euan without the slap.

Below left: With my friend, personal assistant and driver Paul Farrell.

Below: Nicola Bowery revives one of her landmark Taboo outfits for the opening of the London exhibition of Fergus Greer's photographs of Leigh in summer 2002.

Top left: Tits out in my Broadway dressing room.

Middle: Beaming with my dresser Alessandro.

Bottom left: Posing for the press with Rosie O'Donnell.

Bottom right: Rehearsing the urinal scene at the Plymouth Theatre.

Top: In front of a portrait of Leigh's band Raw Sewage.

Left: Live at Ronnie Scott's, summer 2003.

Below: Sisters and seamstresses Chesca and Becca Grover of C33X.

Above: "We're punks - fuck 'em!"
With Mike Nicholls, 2002.

Right: My portrait of the self-created vision that is Amanda LePore.

Above: One of the Trinity Drew Elliott, or Drewpsie as he is known.

Right: Alex, one of my favourite models when taking Rude photographs.

Below: Christine Bateman. Havoc, harmony and all manner of creations. Her ideas have ideas.

Top left: Aimee Phillips in a Rude hat. As inventive with her repartee as she is with her ever-changing wardrobe.

Above: My absolute favourites, the urbaned-up Shangri-Las, Avenue D.

Bottom left: Miss Guy. Toilet Boy with a look "like Pamela Anderson on MDMA".

Top right: Self portrait.
Middle right: Michael Cavadias aka Lily
Of The Valley: Drag queen, political activist
and Donald Duck impersonator.

Bottom right: The Broadway apartment
before we turned it into our sweatshop-
cum-squat.

A MIND FULL OF CHAOS
LUST DRAMA
AND LOVE

From my gaydar profile. Available for barmitzvahs and weddings.

already done all the work. I knew that Mike was really affronted. We talked long and hard and he decided that nothing was going to stop him going to Broadway.

While everyone was raving about what a fantastic opportunity this presented, I was always rolling my eyes and saying: 'It will end in tears.' I also had to battle to get Christine on board. Most Broadway shows don't employ make-up artists. Apart from theatrical megastars, most actors do their own, so by Broadway rules, Christine would have been employed just to design the make-up and then let the cast get on with it. Under those circumstances I believe *Taboo* couldn't have run smoothly without her. The show is as much about make-up as it is about freaks, gender confusion and social alienation.

My suspicions about the American team reached new heights, and it took a few terse emails to make them realise I would not agree to every decision they made. I also demanded to be consulted on everything; despite being assured that it would never happen again, it happened. Again. And again. And again . . .

To show a united front, I flew Mike and Christine over for a week during the auditions, not only to thank them for all their hard work but also because I was worried they were going to be excluded. I had to show Rosie and the other producers that without them there would be no me.

I told them that even if Christine didn't do all the cast make-up she was definitely going to do mine, so they had better sort a visa for her. I can see how Rosie was thinking: 'I'm putting $10 million into this – I'll fucking decide who does what!' We had a bit of a conflab over one particular issue after a meeting where she said to me: 'You can't just say no,' and I said: 'Fine. But neither can you.'

Whenever she talked about how much money she ploughed into *Taboo* I thought: 'Well, no one asked you to. You didn't have to get involved.'

During the auditions Rosie seemed genuinely interested in my opinions, saying the right things and making Mike and Christine welcome. That trip was productive and Rosie started to win my trust again, being amusing at times. The casting director told her he was having trouble finding an actress to play Big Sue. 'Don't tell me we can't find a fat woman in New York who can act and sing,' she bellowed.

I also went to some other Broadway productions to see how they handled set design and costumes. I thought *Hairspray* was brilliant and a great night out; a good old-fashioned musical. *Hairspray* the movie was a send-up of fifties kitsch, warped by John Waters in his inimitable way. The musical simply appropriated the film designs whereas *Taboo* needed more than a set of direct eighties references. It's all too easy to get it wrong. Look at the way Madonna came up with her punk look for the 'Ray of Light' tour. No self-respecting punk would have been seen in that dodgy high street kilt.

In the halcyon days of exhibitionism, plenty of people were ostracised with a sneer for omitting the tiniest detail. At clubs like Billy's and Blitz there were lots of fashion faux partisans who didn't even make it past the door.

Like Blitz, Taboo the club was a tiny sanctuary of style aberration. And much like Blitz, the characters who inhabited Taboo went out of their way to defy the conventions of fashion. The term 'spooky drag' was defined there and then. Some very attractive people did their utmost to appear like car crashes; viciously chopped nylon wigs and lipstick applied from the Robert Smith School of Beauty. For instance, Mr Pearl, who had an eighteen-inch waist tightly trussed into one of his legendary handmade fine bone corsets, ran a hairdressing service with fashion designer Dean (or Deana) Bright in a basement in All Saints Road called Salon Severity. The American reference points for that scene were the watered-down Michael Alig club kids who frequented New York's Limelight in the early nineties. Those kids had some great looks, though they were mostly Leigh-inspired and always slightly wide of the mark.

I originally thought Rosie was talking about adding extra pizzazz and sparkle to what we already had. That didn't seem too great a compromise but it was frustrating that Rosie insisted on using an established costume house, which meant that everything cost a fortune. Leigh's ostrich feather costume was the most expensive outfit in the London production at £700. In New York it was close to $35,000 and, on top of that, was hideously uncomfortable. Certainly some of the New York designs were exquisitely made, but Leigh bought his fabrics in Brick Lane and the beadwork was done by Nicola or whoever else he could rope in.

Mike suggested we take David Cabaret to the US, who had worked alongside him (and Leigh) in London. The idea was to have a small cheap workspace where the costumes could have been created for far less. We felt it was important to involve people who were there in the first place and knew all the little design quirks that made Leigh's creations so particular. Again I was told this would be against union rules, a line I heard ad infinitum and which I also discovered to be yet another control mechanism. Ridiculous amounts of money were wasted on costumes which appeared onstage for a blink. A fun-fur coat worn by Philip's character was a staggering $10,000. The idea of Philip spending $10,000 on anything buggers belief! The kimono worn by Euan Morton during the brief seduction scene came to $30,000, and was sent off to India to be hand-jewelled. The legendary bedraggled kimono on which this was based cost nothing – I stole it from a shop in Kensington! At the time I would have loved nothing more than to have paraded around in the New York creation, and when Euan swanned into my dressing room to show it off, my reaction was: 'As if.'

Meanwhile, we were being told that there was no budget for this or that. Well, no wonder; the cost of everything – Leigh's sequinned crash helmet, the Mohican of spectacles, even the shoes – were astronomical.

Both Mike and I dreamed that when we got to New York we could take what we already had and explore the outer limits of gorgeousness. Sadly, it all went a bit Liza with a Z. In particular, the scene set in Taboo became a huge bone of contention for Mike. He would send sketches to Bobby only to have them returned with crosses through them, courtesy of Rosie. The only comment she made was that it should look like the masquerade scene in *Phantom of the Opera*.

In London, Mike showed me Bobby's suggestions and I laughed

hysterically. My Ali Baba look, which I first premiered on the train from Blackheath to Charing Cross, was pure panto. They had outfits for Philip which made him look like Buttons, and even suggested a T-shirt with the word 'Queen' emblazoned in rhinestones. Why state the obvious? Meanwhile, Big Sue looked like Widow Twankey, or a serving wench in a medieval-themed steakhouse. The most offensive was a billowing mustard-yellow frock accompanied by an oversized green bow for the hair. Christine, not one of Sue's greatest admirers, snipped: 'Good. I want her to look ridiculous.' Always being quite fond of Sue myself, I would have preferred the costumes to have been exact. Leigh's creations for Sue were barking enough and he gave them fancy names such as Ruby and Rusty.

Via Bobby, our costume objections were communicated to Rosie, who was apparently none too pleased. Mike was in New York for costume preparation and arrived at Rosie's offices to find Bobby deathly pale and in a cold sweat talking on a walkie-talkie – all Rosie's important staff members were issued with them so that she had access to them at all times. As Bobby manically leafed through the book of numbered costume designs, she could be heard hollering: 'OK, what's wrong with twenty-seven??!! What about thirty-five??!!' On seeing Mike, Bobby implored: 'Help me!'

Mike took the walkie-talkie and as Rosie continued her rant, said: 'I can hear you.' She continued at top volume until a meeting was arranged to discuss our concerns.

We sat with the book of designs and tried to explain why certain things were wrong. Rosie told us that the production process was underway, adding: 'Let them be made. If you hate them you can chuck paint on them or do whatever the fuck you want.'

The meeting reached the height of ridiculousness during a debate about a costume for Marilyn's character, which Mike wanted to be a pink sequinned suit. Rosie said: 'We can't have Marilyn pulling focus,' suggesting that the audience would be distracted from the main characters. She then took a sequinned swatch and threw it at Mike: 'You got your sequins! All right!!'

Rosie kept saying: 'There are rules on Broadway.' To which Mike calmly replied: 'Aren't we supposed to be challenging them?'

In a later exchange, filmed by Rosie's documentary crew – who were a permanent presence – she prodded Mike in the chest, saying: 'I've compromised, now you've gotta compromise!'

There was an awful lot of 'move that building' behaviour from Rosie. She demanded quick results at every turn and, to be fair, made some very insightful and intelligent contributions. Unfortunately, such input was all too often overshadowed by sheer whim.

During the auditions I attended for the main call-backs Rosie was spot on in all her choices. I felt the final line-up was perfect. She had her eye on established Broadway star Raul Esparza for Philip's character, and went out of her way to convince him. At first he was reticent and actually turned down her offer. Although her private response was 'Fuck him', she used all her powers to get him on board. She flew Raul to London to shadow Philip and one night at Heaven he even managed to emulate Philip's weird munchkin dance and mimicked his voice brilliantly. Raul had already played Riff Raff in *The Rocky Horror Show* and the MC of *Cabaret* on Broadway, so he had the right training.

Some of the actors who auditioned for the roles in New York were overly literal. The gay actors stuck out like a pert bottom. In London it wasn't always obvious, as in the case of Luke Evans, who played Billy. It was important that this ambiguity wasn't lost in New York.

Thankfully we ended up with a perfect cast, with no obviously dodgy English accents and excellent vocal performances.

As for the adaptation of Mark Davies's script, I think Charles Busch was the wrong choice. He has created some fine work, such as *The Vampire Lesbians of Sodom* which ran off-Broadway for years, but when I received his first draft I sat for hours rewriting parts to make the language correct.

The arc of the new story was more simplistic; the role of Leigh had been given more depth and the new character of Nicola had been introduced as a further sexual twist. However, there was a lot of dialogue which would never have come out of Leigh's, Philip's or my own mouth. One draft had me saying, at the age of seventeen: 'What's the point of being fabulous unless every person in every city in every country of the world knows who

you are?' At that age my world never extended beyond the param-
eters of London's West End.

I read some of Busch's writing to Philip, who said: 'Too pretentious. The same problem with the London script: everyone is
bitchy and shallow, constantly spitting out one-liners. You need
that, but you also need heart and soul, or no one will care about
the characters. It's one thing for Leigh to be pretentious, because
that's what he was. When I met you, you were vulnerable. You
were bitchy too, but that wasn't all you were.'

Philip also pointed out that Americans are generally more
concerned with dynamics. That's why they make great block-
busters. Everything is overblown but sometimes they underestimate character, a crucial element of *Taboo*.

Busch paid lip-service to my comments, and added a fair
amount of my suggestions, but I don't think he liked me having
any involvement. His attitude often implied this, which again I
think is very American. Charles is a proven successful scriptwriter and he thought he knew better, though I did tell him:
'Unfortunately this is a real-life story and it's my life.' In an early
scene in the show, Philip and I were sat in a cafeteria and the
banter again buggered belief, with Philip sounding off like a sage,
saying: 'Have you ever heard of Jean Cocteau? "Emphasise everything people condemn you for, because it is who you truly are."'

Don't get me wrong, Philip is a sage of sorts, and prone to
unleash his immense knowledge of history, fashion and art. He
once accompanied me to the Houses of Parliament where I was
giving my tuppence on the age of consent. As we walked through
the Grand Hall (Philip sporting a crown of shaving-foam spikes)
we stopped to ask a copper to direct us to the meeting room.
The policeman's jaw dropped to the floor when Philip started to
point out which parts of the building had been reconstructed
after bomb damage. That encounter was interesting to watch,
because the cop went from 'What have we got here?'
to genuine interest in a matter of seconds.

We're all guilty of making assumptions about people based on
their appearance. From the gay perspective, one would assume
Charles Busch would have more of an insight than your average

Joe. But he inhabits a dreamlike state of Hollywood kitsch and camp where leading ladies in beaded gowns and elbow-length gloves dispense brittle asides like: 'There's a name for people like you, and it's not used in polite society . . . outside of a kennel.'

Us Blitz kids may have aspired to Hollywood glamour but we did so in our typically British flea-bitten style. Less Hollywood, more *Hollyoaks*.

This was one of many flaws in the script and the production; it was too literal. Rosie assumed that a cross-dressing homosexual writer would be a gift to me from the gay gods. The reality is that the only things we have in common are the desire for members of the same sex and a penchant for drag.

Some dreadful lines remained in the final script, despite my best efforts. At one point, my character says to Marilyn: 'What can I say, girl? The best is yet to come. Life's a bowl of cherries. I did it my way.' During one performance Euan changed it to: 'Life's a bowl of cherries. Una Paloma Blanca.'

If I complained about a line in rehearsals, Charles would say: 'Please try it as it is, we'll look at it later.' In frustration I would tell Rosie: 'I'm not saying it.' Of course, Charles rarely argued with her. 'It's out!' she would say, and that would be the end of it.

Rosie took the Steve Strange character out of the American script, which was a problem for me, like removing support from a wall and wondering why it falls down. Steve's character set up the whole club element in the British version of *Taboo* and the sense of us all competing against each other.

More alarming was the threat to remove the Marilyn character altogether, since he refused to sign the contract. I had to put my foot down. There was no way I wanted to lose Marilyn from *Taboo*. I rang him and, after much reasoning – I pointed out that the show would be ruined without him – he agreed to sign.

I also wanted to make sure we didn't treat the American audience as though they were complete retards. New York is a very hip place, people are clued up and know what's going on, so there was no need to say: 'Oh look, there's Boy George standing by a London phone box and, by Jove, he's drinking a cup of English breakfast tea during the New Romantic period!'

I understood that certain elements wouldn't translate in America and accepted that I wasn't always right and gave in when I genuinely believed that those changes served the show rather than the facts. However, in rehearsals the bedroom scene between my character and the Jon Moss facsimile Marcus was unconvincing because there was no sexual charge. In the space of a few minutes you were meant to believe that a hitherto heterosexual becomes smitten by a gay geisha. It was Rosie who stood up and said: 'Who's going to believe that? They've gotta kiss!'

That was a brave move, but elsewhere Rosie panicked unnecessarily. She wouldn't let any of the larger female cast members wear the sort of clothes Leigh would put big girls in. This is the man, after all, who would send Bucket Jill out to the disco with a plastic pail on her head, a star painted over one eye and nothing else hiding her, shall we say, Rubenesque proportions.

Another female cast member was ordered not to wear a Vivienne Westwood-style tie with a playing card of a naked man on it. I knew that the London version, which was very bawdy and confrontational, wouldn't have worked in the US. However, there was far too much caution about the sexual elements of the show and this contradictory attitude seemed to reflect Rosie's overall nature. Just like my father, when you expect her to fly off the handle, she doesn't, and likewise, when you anticipate a cool reaction, she can be incredibly conventional. It's easy to make big verbal or financial gestures but it's much more of a challenge truly to reveal your vulnerability. But that's very American. There is much emphasis in the US on being able to express yourself, and freedom of speech is, after all, written into the American Constitution. Quite often that actually means: You're free to agree with us. I'm not saying that the British are more evolved in this area, but *Taboo* on Broadway really brought to the surface our vital cultural differences.

And the contradictions kept on coming. During the press junkets Rosie adopted an almost apologetic tone, constantly comparing *Taboo* to *Pippin* or *Annie*, and portraying it as 'a family show'. I'm sorry, but where in *Annie* do you see a character suffocating inside a latex body suit with a club foot?

Whenever I turned up for TV interviews in full Leigh drag, there would be a ridiculous fuss. Once Christine was even approached by Rosie's manager and asked if she would tone down my make-up. Christine told me straight away and for my next TV interview I appeared in super-grotesque style.

When I talked to Rosie about this she said: 'I understand. You're like me. When someone tells me not to do something, I say: Fuck 'em. It makes me want to do it more.'

Like me, she has a similar contempt for authority but yet she can be so authoritarian. Don't you often end up being the thing you rebel against?

I failed to realise at the outset that Rosie was the puppeteer supreme. Even a cockroach didn't crawl across a dressing-room floor without her say-so. I understand that in such ventures one person has to hold the reins, and financially, as we were often reminded, Rosie had put her money almost where her mouth was. At the same time it seemed pointless to have amassed such a plethora of creative minds and constantly cut off their balls.

There were many times when I could have let rip at Rosie, but I could see what a vulnerable human being she is. During the zitsprobe – when the entire score, music and songs are performed for the first time in rehearsals – she was so overcome with emotion she wept openly. At such moments I could make sense of what it is I like about her. I know the story and the songs spoke to the most important part of her, and she truly loved *Taboo*.

I thought *Taboo* on Broadway was a brilliant night out. The production values were breathtaking, especially my 'Ich Bin Kunst' scene, which ended with me surrounded by several incarnations of Leigh.

Leigh's death scene culminated in front of a huge gauze curtain on to which were projected heart-rending images of his life, from boyhood in Australia to his camp reign in eighties London. It was the same footage Rosie had originally sent me on CD-Rom which had so moved me.

In America, *Taboo* started in a derelict space which had once been the glamorous nightclub Taboo. Big Sue – played by Liz McCartney, who was pregnant when the show opened – encounters Philip. They reminisce about the old days, lamenting that everything is so dull now. Before bursting into the opening number, Philip says: 'We were different, we were special, we were loved.'

Leigh's wife Nicola was introduced as a winsome character being rejected from the queue of Philip's club Planets. Big Sue adopts her and promises to introduce her to Leigh, who the soon-to-be Mrs Bowery secretly worships. As the story unfolds, Nicola is revealed to be much more scheming than she is in real life. When she came to the big opening night, she said: 'I'd much rather be the scheming minx than the doormat Sue describes in her book!'

Much truer was the idea of two women battling for the attentions of a sexually predatory gay man whose attitude to his own sexuality was just as contradictory as his morality and fashion sense. Leigh absolutely created divisions between certain friends, a true Aquarian. He kept them separate but also at war, spreading fantastically malicious gossip from one to the other.

The first time I saw the thirty-foot billboard of Leigh towering over Times Square in front of a businessman pissing in a urinal I was so proud. As I looked up I thought Leigh would be so tickled, all the while pretending not to give a hoot.

Often when things were going haywire I'd imagine Leigh cackling on a cloud, phone at his ear: 'Well, exactly, Rosie. I don't know why you put up with that hideous creature Boy George.' And then switching swiftly to: 'Absolutely, George. I agree. She's got it entirely wrong.'

24

Wake Up New York

Before I left for New York my therapist Jamie asked me whether I was excited. I told him that I wasn't. He said: 'You're lying to protect yourself from disappointment. Because of your position in the public eye you have to manage a lot more of that than most of us.'

I decided to take my friend and assistant Paul Farrell to New York because I knew I'd need someone practical around to offer a degree of sanity amid all the threatening madness.

I met Paul for the first time in the mid-nineties, after returning from a promotional trip to France with Sue Bignall, a New Zealander who was working part-time in the Virgin press office. I arrived back at Hampstead to discover that my house was slowly turning into a swimming pool; the salt tank had burst and water was coming out of the light fittings and down the stairs. I screamed, at a total loss at what to do. For some reason, probably because she had been the last person I'd seen, I decided to call Sue instead of relying on my builder family.

'Don't panic,' she said, 'I know just the man.' Paul and his partner Ray arrived shortly afterwards and spent a couple of hours fiddling around on my roof. I couldn't believe how quickly they had turned up and with how little fuss the job was executed. I took their number in case any other biblical misfortune should rain upon my Gothic pile.

As it turned out there was constantly work to be done, given the age of the house. So I started to see a lot more of Paul and Ray.

Some months later I decided to refurbish my kitchen and gave them the job, which took for ever, mainly because Paul and I spent so much time chatting over endless cups of tea. We developed a great friendship and I got so used to his company I decided I'd have to employ him. When *Taboo* opened in London, Paul and Ray were employed to build the toilets and dressing rooms, and, in a sense, Paul became as much of a fixture of the show as the green marabou tutu.

You could never accuse Paul and me of having an ordinary employer/employee relationship. First and foremost he's my friend and, as cantankerous as he can sometimes be, there's very little he wouldn't do for me (oh, and by the way, he has a lovely girl-friend called Annie, in case your mind has raced into overdrive). I suspect people imagine that all my friends are weirdos and vagabonds, and in comparison Paul can safely be described as a regular chap, though I would hesitate to use the word normal when describing him.

He has very strongly held opinions and is never afraid – or prevented – from voicing them. On meeting supermodel Linda Evangelista, whom he found more than a little snooty, he uttered the classic: 'Who are you?' She was most upset and as I trounced down the red carpet into the Metropolitan Museum of Art with her, she hissed: 'Your assistant was really rude! He asked me who I was!' I assured her: 'He knows exactly who you are. He's just being rude because you're beautiful.'

My all-time favourite Paul comment occurred when I took him to a London hotel to meet my friend Paul Starr, who was in town making up Renée Zellwegger for press and promotion for one of her films. All of a sudden Renée bounded into the room and flopped on to the bed. Within seconds Mr Farrell and Renée were engaged in a debate after he announced: 'All you women are bitches.' Of course, having pretended to be completely indifferent to her, Paul was straight on the phone telling his brother: 'Guess who I've just met? Renée Zellwegger. And I called her a bitch!'

When I spoke to Paul Starr the following day, he was halfway across the Atlantic. Renée had woken from a power snooze and worriedly proclaimed: 'I have to convince that guy Paul that not all women are bitches.' Paul Starr assured her: 'That really isn't necessary.'

In August 2003, the pack of four – Paul, Christine, Mike and myself – took up residence in Manhattan. For the first couple of weeks I really felt like I was on holiday, but that illusion was soon quashed along with several others!

Before I left London I had a three-day electricity blackout, parallel with the one which paralysed New York City around the same time. I was preparing to leave for eight months and in typical fashion had left packing until the last breath. Trying to stow Philip Treacy fedoras and my favourite apparel by candle-light as ten LEB brutes fiddled with my circuitry was as aggra-vating as it was pleasing. When I rang the electricity board the next day, having already made about five hundred calls, they claimed there had been absolutely no report of the power cut. I screamed: 'Look, love, I am homosexual, you know. I do know when I've had teams of electricians bounding through my house!' Eventually, after two days, they finally dragged a prehistoric gener-ator and erected it outside my gate. It was a joyous moment to re-enter the light.

After the fortnight's furlough in New York we were straight into rehearsals and administered with day planners. I remember thinking: 'There goes the disco.' Of course, I managed to squeeze in a bit of 'here I am' at the Bowery Bar, Plaid, the Coral Room, the Park, the Cock, Opaline, Crobar, the Marquis, Boy's Room, to name but a few. Running up and down three flights of stairs and scrubbing off the latex drips for my death scene was the last thing on my mind.

Silly me, I really had no idea how much work was involved in a Broadway production. Eight shows a week, including matinées on Saturday and Sunday. Monday was our official day off, and coincided with the most boring night in New York. At the rehearsal studios on 42nd Street, with Jackie Mason preparing for his new show downstairs, we occupied an entire floor, with coaching commanded by Candy (surname definitely not Darling) in one room, dancers in another and actors in a third.

Working from noon until 6 p.m. every day, I was constantly nipping off for a cigarette, which had to be smoked out on the street under New York's draconian anti-tobacco laws.

At least 42nd Street was rich with legends, lunatics and theatrical queens.

Christine mentioned openly in the lift to Mike and me that she was in dire need of a sanitary towel. Some camp chap said: 'Honey, get yourself to the first floor where all the dancing girls are. They'll be chucking them at you like Carrie in the locker room!'

Another day, heading for a fag break, Paul and I encountered actor Kevin Kline in the elevator. Paul told him: '*A Fish Called Wanda* killed me.' Kline responded: 'Are you OK now?'

That sharp New York humour is constant relief from the angsty hustle-bustle of the city.

While our gargantuan downtown loft was being made ready, Mike, Christine and I were put up at a hotel by Central Park. The afternoon we moved in I was involved in a press junket, so Mike and Christine took up residence ahead of me. As the day's interviews came to an end, I received a worried phone call from Mike, who told me Christine had demanded her room be painted a different colour. I thought: 'How Michael Jackson of her.' Knowing her tendency to be a bit of a madam I imagined her screaming at our wispy Japanese landlady Waco: 'Sorry, but I don't do canary yellow.' The truth was that Waco had made the mistake of asking Christine if she liked the colour of her boudoir and she had snapped: 'Not particularly,' probably coupled with one of her highly informative cod sneers.

At the time I was being shadowed by Rosie's personal documentary team, a constant presence throughout the *Taboo* experience, headed by the formidable Jennifer Lebeau, and dragged them along with me to the loft. I arrived to find the apartment door wide open and gasped at the size of the place – a huge industrial space with exposed pipes and eighteenth-century French flourishes: candelabra lights, big fat columns and ornate furnishings.

Waco was hovering in the hallway while electronica blared from the stereo in Mike's room. Christine was sitting on the wooden floor sorting through her make-up kit and looked bemused when I shouted, slightly acting up for the cameras: 'What's going on, Wacko Jacko?'

I peeped into her room and couldn't help but notice a shirtless young Colombian busily covering the bright yellow walls with a coat of cream. It seemed Philippe, the in-house DIY man, had taken an immediate shine to Christine and as soon as he heard she didn't like the colour was straight up that ladder.

Of course, the story of Christine's demands had been typically dressed up by Mike, who was busily arranging his own room to the strains of Fad Gadget's 'Back to Nature'.

My room was at the end with its own en suite bathroom, walk-in wardrobe and a jacuzzi. I remember thinking that Rosie had excelled herself. Mike and I felt like seventeen-year-old punks all over again. It was as if we had lucked out and found the most luxurious squat in town. The splendour of the apartment and the thrill of being in New York only made the situation more surreal.

My first day in rehearsal was like my first day at school. I felt as though I was being treated with a mix of reverence and fear, and that these seasoned theatrical types were contemplating a diva routine. I assume there had been some discussion about how I should be handled. The last sense of me in America was at the height of Culture Club when my reputation always preceded me. Back then I was difficult for all the clichéd reasons; yes, the pressure of fame, but more than anything my discomfort at being treated like some fragile eccentric child.

My manager Tony had a habit of saying: 'Don't tell Georgie,' as if springing things on me at the last minute would make them go smoothly. I have always preferred to know the facts, the truth. If a venue's half empty it's not half full, at least in rock 'n' roll terms, if not Buddhist.

Stars in America expect to be treated as such, and the public seems to demand you behave like one too. If you're recognised in the street or in a store, they expect grandiose behaviour and don't like it at all if you shy away from attention. On certain days

I can rarely go ten yards in New York without somebody shouting: 'Hey, Boy George!' Sometimes I say: 'Thanks for telling me. Ten out of ten for observation.' Heaven forbid that you should venture forth without security or an entourage because certain people feel that they have the right to be overly tactile. This is more the case when I'm in full regalia, but even then I'd prefer to say myself: 'Look, I'm having a night off,' rather than having them pushed out of the way by some big lug.

At times I have resorted to out-and-out frankness, such as 'Fuck off', especially when people walk up with those damn picture-phones and shove them in my face. Sorry, those days of being all-singing and all-smiling are long gone. I don't have a series of stock celebrity responses. At the end of the day it's about how people approach me. Like any other human, it depends on my mood. Sometimes I can chat happily for hours to a complete stranger if they have something to say for themselves.

My favourite experience was in Dallas. I was seated in a sectioned-off area in a club with some friends. Suddenly I heard this booming camp voice: 'Boy George chile! I bin standing here for twenty minutes! And all I want is a picture with your pretty ass!' I looked up to see a towering black drag queen with a Supremes beehive and an understated cocktail dress. I could see quite clearly she wasn't going to take no for an answer. I found it hilarious and said: 'Come on down, sister.' True to her word she snapped and dashed. As she walked away she screamed – proving that a direct and succinct approach is always best: 'I live for you, chile, and just you remember that.'

It's often people's misconceptions which inform invasive and awkward behaviour. Whoever you are, entering into a situation where you're mixing with complete strangers is always strained at first. This is amplified when you're seen as not only a star but a premier-league bitch. As one Madonna fan put it in *AXM* maga-zine: 'Madonna does so many spiritual things and writes books for children. All Boy George ever seems to give us is bitterness.' Being observant and bitter are two very different things, but most people don't realise that.

So with more Louis Vuitton baggage than Joan Collins could

possibly cope with, I entered rehearsals at 42nd Street. The cast and crew were clearly checking their behaviour towards me and this made some of the production staff come across as strict and cold. My terrible timekeeping is legendary and there was a lot of emphasis on being punctual.

Producer Lori Said was most certainly my favourite force of energy among the executive throng. She'd been brought in by Rosie because she is well connected with the East Village scene and is friendly with people like Charlie Atlas and had known Leigh. I'd met Lori many times over the years before we worked together on *Taboo*. Even when she disagreed with Rosie's decisions and behaviour, Lori was forced to juggle her loyalties. She loved Rosie and would protect her with her life, but at the same time she was cool and sensitive enough to understand the complexities the rest of us faced.

One day quite early on I really had it out with Rosie. The cast performed a selection of songs for the press and she had asked me to be there from the start to present a united front. I arrived in time for the one-to-one interviews yet I could see Rosie was fuming. It's true, we had taken our time getting ready while having our usual morning debate over several cups of coffee under a cloud of Marlboro Lights. Rosie summoned me afterwards and in a hurt tone said: 'I can't believe you turned up late. Do you know how disrespectful that is to everyone working on this project?'

I apologised and pointed out that I had actually fulfilled my commitment. I'm not some eager theatrical starlet, a Sparkle Tina Sparkle type who limbers up before breakfast and does scales in the shower.

Rosie stared at me. 'I accept that you're sorry. It will never happen again.'

I felt as though I was being reprimanded by my secondary school headmaster and told her: 'Look, I'm not your fucking child. Don't talk to me like that,' and stormed off.

To my further fury I later heard that she had cornered Paul Farrell and bawled him out in front of her camera crew.

She asked: 'Tell me what your job is!'

Paul replied: 'I look after George.'

She snapped: 'Which means getting him here on time, right? And if you can't even do that we'll have to find someone who can.'

I don't think I've ever seen Paul so upset. Still, he kept calm because he wanted to be respectful to my relationship with Rosie. I told him: 'You should have told her to fuck right off. She has no right to talk to you like that.'

Her manager Bernie attempted to smooth things out. I raged about the broken promises and misinformation, telling him: 'How would you like it if I said to you: "It will never happen again" every time you make an important decision without informing me?' The following morning Rosie called and apologised.

Rosie wasn't always at rehearsals, but when she did show, an extra tension was added. Some of this was the actors, including myself, wanting to impress her, and she could be very encouraging. She'd rise to her feet, full of pride, and tell us: 'You guys are doing an awesome job.'

Mark Dendy, our choreographer, suffered the most over Rosie's reservations about some of the dance routines. She had a particular gripe about the opening number, 'Ode to Attention Seekers'. So many changes were made I imagine the dancers felt as though they were trapped for ever in the movie *The Red Shoes*.

I didn't take to Mark at first, until he unleashed his wicked humour on me. Mark is verbally and physically very expressive, as you'd expect from a dancer, and when he was given notes – especially ones he disagreed with – he was quite happy to inform anyone within earshot.

Rosie hired Mark because he is downtown and edgy, and then tried to force him to become what she called 'more Broadway'; one afternoon she even stood up and busted a few moves to illustrate what she was looking for. However, the two of them finally had a heated exchange and Mark's card was numbered.

By the time we moved to the Plymouth Theatre another choreographer, Jeff Calhoun, had been brought in under the guise of assisting Mark. Jeff was a director as well, and dragging him into the picture at such a late stage indicated that Rosie was also unhappy with Chris Renshaw's direction. Rosie thought Chris was limp and would say to me: 'He's got no balls!' I disagreed. Chris had done a perfectly good job in London and it's not his style to engage in unnecessary confrontation. He can be extremely forthright but he's no slugger. I got the sense that Rosie would have liked Chris to square up to her. Chris never did. A couple of times he was reduced to tears and bringing in Jeff was another slap round the face.

It's not done for a producer to be around during what's known as 'teching' – the laborious process of working out set movements, lighting and placement of actors. Even in a good atmosphere, this is the kind of 'hurry up and wait' situation which would drive a saint to spite. With Rosie as a constant presence, there was an added layer of stop-start.

The classic example was the day Rosie started shouting directions to Raul Esparza. Again, this just isn't done in the theatre. 'Notes' are supposed to come to the actor via the director or the writer, but Rosie would have none of that and stuck her oar in whenever she felt like it.

This day she'd already passed a note to Chris Renshaw saying that she wanted Raul off the stage during a certain sequence. Chris decided to look at the bigger picture and work the entire scene through rather than become bogged down in nit-picking. When Raul didn't make the exit Rosie demanded, she yelled: 'Hey, I don't like that! Get him off the stage!' Raul shouted back: 'I've fucking had enough,' and stormed off. The problem was that he was dressed in a particularly preposterous costume of Philip's (which didn't eventually make it into the show): a crown, an ermine-lined robe, hose, Elizabethan knickerbockers and little buckled shoes. He looked comical as he flounced out. The lesson learned is: if you're going to make a dramatic exit, always check what you're wearing first.

Rosie declared that she 'didn't give a shit' if he ever returned and if he wasn't back by 8 p.m. it was over for him. For me it was a huge deal, because Raul was brilliant and his performance glued the show together. How were we going to find a replacement with less than three weeks to first previews? There was already sniping in the press about how badly things were going.

Thankfully tempers cooled. Raul returned, telling me: 'I'm only here because of your beautiful score.' I was proud of him for returning and also for having the guts to express the tension we were all feeling.

The worst wrangling was over the end of Act One, which didn't make any sense. Originally there was a cleaned-up version of the famous performance where Leigh 'gives birth' to Nicola. That was replaced by a scene where I performed in a puffball mask, singing and berating the cast and the audience. The scene had no structure and like everybody else, I was lost.

I was grateful when Rosie screamed: 'Get rid of the puffballs!' However, apart from telling us that she hated the scene, she couldn't offer a single concrete suggestion, telling me: 'Just go up there and go crazy like Leigh would!'

One day, after trying to make it work for hours, I decided to call Rosie and see if I could fathom what she was after. She'd been in court, embroiled in a hugely publicised court case over her magazine, and was clearly a little frazzled. We spoke for twenty minutes and still she could offer no solution. So a decision was made to return to a glittering rather than gruesome birth scene.

On top of this, Rosie's concerns over the opening number were sending Raul and the ensemble into a well of gloom. To me there had never been anything wrong with it, the idea of starting with Big Sue encountering Philip in a desolate Taboo always worked.

One day just two weeks before opening night I was feeling particularly emotional because of all the chopping and changing and the volatile atmosphere throughout rehearsals and during the previews. Scrub that: I felt like I was about to have a nervous breakdown. All I could hear over the tannoy in my dressing room was the intro changing again and again, with those opening lines gnawing at my cranium: 'I'm known in all the wrong places . . .'

I was summoned to a late-night meeting at a nearby hotel which was supposed to be with Rosie, Bernie and production manager Charlotte Wilcox. I was taken aback to find Rosie not present. Apparently she had fallen asleep after a massage. Lucky her!

Bernie and Charlotte calmly told me Rosie had lost faith in Chris Renshaw and wanted to replace him with Chris Atkins, a US director who had worked on *The Rocky Horror Show*. It emerged that they had snuck Atkins into some of the previews and asked his advice on what they thought was wrong. There had already been a write-up in the *Post* about Jeff Calhoun's presence and rumours about Chris Atkins being brought in. I told Bernie and Charlotte: 'Why don't we dig up Shakespeare and Cole Porter while we're at it? At some point we have to believe in what we're doing and I think we have a great show. Plus, how can Chris be expected to do his job properly when Rosie constantly gets in his way?' During one rehearsal Rosie had gone so far as to attack Chris in front of the entire cast and crew with the gem: 'With all due respect, I don't give a flying fuck what anyone thinks!' I had a choice: to let rip or walk away. I knew if I said what I really felt it would have been ugly. I felt a bit like the kid at school who stands back and watches someone get beaten up. Raul spoke up again, asking: 'How can I do my job if the director isn't allowed to direct?' Rosie told Raul: 'Trust me. I am your mother.'

Imparting this information to Bernie and Charlotte made no difference. It was obvious Rosie had ordered them to make the chop, and it was their job to convince me.

I was calm but adamant that I wouldn't stab Chris in the back.

Bernie and Charlotte agreed that there were script problems but felt that replacing Chris was the best move, even when I pointed out that *Taboo* was his idea in the first place. He came to me in London with the original idea and saw it through all the way to Broadway. I said: 'Isn't all this a little late? Rosie has worked with Chris for over a year and now she's decided he's no good?' I warned them that replacing Chris would bring morale among the cast and crew crashing to the ground, adding: 'If you do this now it's going to fucking ruin everything. I know Rosie's worried that she's going to be slagged off by the critics. But guess what? She's going to be slagged off whether Chris goes or not. Rosie may be used to walking around telling people to move that building or "lose that hat!" but it isn't going to happen to Chris with my help.'

I also pointed out that we were slated in London when the show opened there because people missed the point, but we still ran for well over a year. However, Bernie and Charlotte asked me to think about it overnight. I told them that my answer would be the same in the morning and returned to the loft to talk it through with Mike and Christine. Mike had had his differences with Chris, but our conversation confirmed that I couldn't be responsible for the destruction of Chris's career; being fired from this project would be the end for him. Morally it couldn't be justified.

As we talked I became angrier and angrier about Rosie not being present at the meeting. So I wrote her an email, pointing out where I thought the problems lay. I also said that if she kept stopping people from carrying out their jobs, she was never going to be happy.

I ended the email by stating that if Chris was going then I would have to leave as well. After pressing the 'send' button I did go through a phase of 'Oh fucking hell, what have I done?' I hadn't played that card before, but it felt necessary.

I phoned Chris and told him what was going on and that if he wanted to walk that would be OK. But I did stress I'd put my neck on the line for him and that he shouldn't go without thinking it through.

After the next night's preview Bernie and Charlotte came to see me in my dressing room and said: 'Everything's back to normal. Chris is directing the show and won't be replaced.'

On reflection I believe this was the moment when Rosie decided to pull the show. Within two days a huge article appeared in the *Post* suggesting that, among the many problems we were supposed to be facing, Rosie was 'rolling over like a pussycat to the diva demands of Boy George'.

For me, the problems with the show during previews were nothing to do with the direction, the set, costumes, music or acting. There is no doubt in my mind that Charles Busch's script was the problem. It's true, under pressure he produced excellent material; however, at certain points the script didn't make any sense, particularly when it came to Nicola and Leigh's relationship. I never felt it was sufficiently explained why a rampant cottage queen fell in love with, and married, a woman.

Whatever the script or behind the scenes shenanigans, from our very first preview night we received standing ovations. And there were no drawing pins on any of the seats, even if there were plenty of pricks in the press.

Throughout the three weeks of previews, I was happy to be finally performing the show. After all, there were plenty of aspects of the London production that niggled me, but my attitude has always been: whether you're playing to fifty people in a leather bar in Arkansas or a packed theatre on Broadway, just get on with it and remember you're lucky not to be stacking shelves in Tesco's.

25

Off Broadway

After all the drama, cloak-and-daggering, gossip-tree-shaking and pointing of fingers that had gone before, opening night on Broadway was a mince through the park.

Raul Esparza's stomp-out had prompted yet another verbal dart from the *Post*. Like most of the stories about the show, Michael Reidel's piece contained too much fact for it not to have come from a source within the company. Reidel literally swooned over Raul, with a bizarre reference to the temperamental star allegedly swanning around backstage in his underwear. I don't know why he didn't just come out and say: 'Raul Esparza has got a big cock!'

I never saw Raul parading his privates. After this story, however, it was hard to avert your eyes from that area, and of course Raul played it up with aplomb. It also prompted some off-script commentary. Raul tried to throw me during a scene: 'Oh Leigh, they must have widened the doors tonight to let you in!' I eyed his package du plenty, and said: 'Is that really all yours?' The silence from the audience was deafening and Raul was worried that he had hurt my feelings. I went to his dressing room and said: 'Keep it up. It was pure Philip and Leigh.'

Once we had an audience, I imagine the entire cast felt as I did, pure relief at finally performing the show with no fear of imperious commands such as: 'I don't like it! Lose the Boy George character!'

A major frustration were the many union rules; one in particular dictates that a script has to be sealed on the final night of previews. For me this was one of the most unhealthy aspects of doing *Taboo* on Broadway. It was even suggested that actors could be fined for changing lines, a warning I flagrantly ignored. Surely the luxury of live theatre is being able to rework a line if it fails to get a reaction?

Often, during the London run, pure anarchy prevailed where the script was concerned and, true, it sometimes got out of hand. Having flexibility generally worked better in London, because of the intimate set-up at the Venue. Being in the round allowed us intimate physical and comical flexibility. I often found myself face to face with some cod housewife, and that wonderful opportunity to ad lib could make a scene jump out of its puce-green tights. One such time, I sneered at some doom-faced woman with a dodgy seventies feather-cut and an unhealthy amount of Dusty Springfield eyeliner: 'You were fantastic in *Rock Follies!*'

The proscenium arch of the Plymouth Theatre prevented such intimate exchanges but, at the same time, afforded other production gorgeousness.

On opening night, just before I went onstage, I scribbled a couple of lines on the back of a good-luck card: 'You really have to watch your back, / When even the smile is an act.'

I wasn't totally jitter-free as I emerged from the toilet cubicle in the first scene. All you can think is: 'What if I forget a line?' If you're lucky enough to be working with fast-reacting actors they can pull you out of the abyss. I guess having been through opening night in London I already knew that the success of the show was in the lap – not of the gods – but of the critics, who assume godlike powers nonetheless.

That night I remember thinking: 'If people only knew how much heartache goes into providing just a couple of hours of entertainment . . .'

All the negativity surrounding the show had most certainly taken its toll, but in the throes of pulling on your tutu and

hurriedly reshaping your lips a wonderful and mischievous cama-
raderie takes hold, and you share an experience with your fellow
performers that is an entirely different show within itself.

There were several moments when I was convinced I wouldn't
make my cues, because of the complicated costumes I had to
hurry in and out of. I lucked out having Alessandro as my dresser
because he is a chain-smoking neurotic Sicilian housewife trapped
in a gay man's body, and has a similar disrespect to myself for the
dos and don'ts. I loved his hands-to-heaven gesticulating and
ranting: 'Dese faakin' petty union ass-kissers! They make me so
crazy!' One of his regulars was: 'Don't trust anybody in thees
faakin' place! They have many faces!'

From day one the management repeatedly pinned 'No Smoking'
signs on my dressing-room door, so Alessandro and I hung out
the window when the complaints got too much.

The pregnant Liz McCartney was housed in a dressing room
three floors above me, and claimed she could smell our tobacco
fumes, which, more often than not, left her fuming. There'd be a
thud on the door followed by the yell: 'Are you guys smoking in
there?!' Being highly hormonal probably didn't help matters, but
I appreciated Liz's directness. If she was angry about something
it came across with the same power as her thunderous renditions
of the songs. I absolutely loved hearing her sing 'Talk Amongst
Yourselves', because she's the only person I've ever heard do it
justice.

Attending the opening night were the usual hotchpotch of
high-profile American celebrities like Kathleen Turner, Barbara
Walters, Elaine Stritch, Chita Rivera and Gene Simmons mingling
with freaks about town like Amanda LePore, Richie Rich and
Kenny Ken.

I could hear people laughing in the right spots and the energy
level felt strong. Sometimes there were inappropriate yet understandable titters when Nicola and Leigh performed 'Love is a
Question Mark'. Even though my costume was toned down and
in keeping with Leigh's disturbing daywear, it was hard to convince
myself – let alone the audience – that I was being truly heartfelt
while dressed in a grey schoolgirl's pleated skirt over woolly white

socks and a grey blazer trimmed with diamanté which was danger-
ously Michael Jackson.

From the moment I stepped forward from the sewing machine
I caught smirks and elbows being prodded into ribs. So I took
to writing fake phone numbers on my knees and slogans like 'Of
course I'm gay', just to let them know I was in on the joke.

Before opening night we received a visit from her Royal
Madgeness. Rosie's good friend Madonna slunk to her seat as the
lights went down, but the hulking bodyguards gave the game
away. Afterwards I was told that she had been moved by the show,
which was ironic. In London we were issued with a cease-and-
desist order from her publishers when we sent up 'Vogue' in the
middle of 'Everything Taboo':

Ginger Rogers, Fred Astaire, that Madonna dyes her hair,
They had style, they had grace, didn't sit on Sean Penn's face.
Strike Madonna!

As Kenny Everett would say, it was all done in the best possible
taste. We were then told we could sing the original lyrics, which
wasn't helpful in a scene steeped in sarcasm.

The pesky Michael Reidel, who is actually a theatre gossip
columnist at the *Post*, not a theatre critic, was still baiting us in
print. He wrote an open letter to Rosie, beseeching her to delay
the opening because the production was so muddled and akin to
'a train-wreck' in his view.

Much the same as in London, the reviews were mixed, so no
real surprise there. Many of them were complimentary about my
score; one even said it was the best they had heard in twenty years.

As always the most important observation came from Alessandro,
who said: 'The backstage crew are singing along to your songs.
Bloody big butch straight men mouthing along to "Gimme a
Freak!". Trus' me, eet never 'appens. Eet's an omen.'

Despite Alessandro's optimism, I felt that we had been buried
before we'd been birthed. Reidel's constant sniping had created a
wave of negativity that became gospel.

After one performance a paper claimed there had been two

hundred people in the theatre when actually we were packed to the rafters. I remember asking: 'Surely that's not legal?' So I wrote a letter to Reidel, something I regretted immediately afterwards. In it I said, among other things: 'People keep saying that theatre is a precious art form which needs to be saved. And yet those closest to it seem to be doing their damnedest to destroy it.' To his credit he printed my letter almost word for word, but still couldn't resist a bit of Kentucky Fried psychology.

At the opening-night party a journalist enquired: 'Hey, how do you feel about Michael Reidel?'

I said: 'Oscar Wilde was put in prison for buggery and Reidel does that to the English language on a daily basis.'

Rosie's people barred him from attending the bash, but he slipped in and approached me.

'You don't know who I am, do you?' he asked.

I felt like saying: 'Yes I do. You're the last breath of human kindness.' Instead I replied: 'You're Michael Reidel.'

Nervously, he said: 'You know I was banned from this party?'

'Not by me,' I said.

At the party Reidel also said: 'You know, you've written a brilliant score.'

I asked: 'Why did you say it was just OK in your review if you thought it was brilliant? The two things are very different.'

He muttered something about it all being 'showbiz nonsense' and I told him: 'Not for the people up there onstage working their bollocks off.'

Then I left to dance to Nag Nag Nag's Jonny Slut's warped and wonderful DJ set and drank enough to traumatise my liver.

Soon after in the *Post* Reidel invited me to engage in a 'battle of the wits' on his TV show on a local cable channel. In my opinion he had nothing witty or interesting to contribute, though I decided to take him up on his offer and not give him what he expected: defensive, bitchy, gay rhetoric. Instead I quizzed him about his criteria as a writer and talked about what it was like for people on the receiving end. Again I mentioned his comment about the score being brilliant, to which he glibly replied: 'Oh, that was just opening-night schmooze.'

In my Irish heart my instinct was to punch his lights out. I remained calm, because it was obvious he was out of his depth and actually had the sort of personality that belongs behind a pen.

In truth, it's folly to think that Reidel was solely responsible for *Taboo*'s short shelf-life on Broadway. It's impossible to know what was going on behind the scenes. As in London, I was not always privy to the managerial machinations. I was reassured by an email I received from Rosie a couple of weeks into the run which said: 'Fuck 'em, we stay open till June.' I took her at her word, with the knowledge that the $10 million she had sunk into the production was a mere sea slug in her ocean of wealth.

When it came to the reviews, it was interesting, as always, to hear heterosexuals comment on a world as alien as theirs often is to us. Silly middle-aged fools offering their spin on the dark seedy club scene of the eighties, into which they themselves never ventured.

The bitchy exchanges they found so tiresome are true to life, designed by outcasts as a defence mechanism. If you shut people out by calling them faggots and queers, they have to find a language to fight back and say: 'Fuck you.' Let's face it, 'Fuck you' sounds so much better coming out of a pair of pouting glittery lips.

Often the songs were misread. Even noted gay writer Michael Musto, who was invited to the very first press call at rehearsals, commented: 'If you are a freak, you never say you're a freak.' He was referring to 'Ode to Attention Seekers', where Philip's character sings quite clearly:

> Gimme a freak,
> Any day of the week,
> I'm comfortable with those you call demented.

Even more disappointing was Musto's barb about 'Stranger in this World' being a song about craving fame. I raged: 'How could any gay man listen to that song and not fucking hear it, let alone ignore Euan Morton's heaven-sent voice?'

In another piece Musto made a snide comment about 'Il Adore' which, I hear, he called 'over-sentimental', an emotion impossible to avoid in a song about close friends dying of Aids. This is the man who I applauded for his criticism of Madonna's support for Eminem, in which he said: 'Instead of saying he has a right to his opinion, she should be saying: "Leave my gay brothers and sisters alone".'

The songs in *Taboo* are some of the most direct I have ever written and were part of the narrative. Take the line 'I can never get this shit from round my eyes' from 'Pretty Lies', any woman or drag queen can understand where that is coming from.

A lot of people felt there was a homophobic tinge to much of what was written about *Taboo*. My friend Johnny Dynell, who – along with his wife Chi-Chi Valente – has been hosting clubs and DJing in New York for years and even helped organise the opening-night spectacle, told me: '*Taboo* has become a political issue in New York for a lot of gays. There's stuff all over the Internet. The sisters are really worked up and pledging to support the show.'

The main agenda, it seemed, was a relentless attack on Rosie, who had gone from being America's favourite chat-show host to public enemy number one in less time than it takes a *Pop Idol* contestant to lose their record deal. Mike and I would sit in the loft and read such testaments to literature as the *National Enquirer* and *Star* magazine. Having experienced the wrath of Rosie at first-hand, Mike found it hard not to believe reports claiming that among her other antics, she had once threatened to throw an employee from an eleventh-floor window. Mike said: 'It's all very John Waters. I can't think why he hasn't snapped her up,' adding with dramatic sarcasm: 'I can't believe any of this could possibly be true!' The John Waters element to Rosie's character appealed very much to our twisted sense of humour. If Rosie's wardrobe had consisted of a one-armed leopard-skin Lycra dress combined with a butchered Mohican (as sported by Divine in *Female Trouble*) her outbursts would have been seen as completely reasonable, even camp, brought on by the pressures of intense glamour. The problem with such diva-like behaviour is that it's always much more enjoyable when witnessed at a distance or fixed in legend. That's why we revel in the feuding which went on between the likes of Joan

Crawford and Bette Davis. Queens in particular are always lamenting that those golden days of tongue sorcery are long gone. A hard-nosed woman who exudes glamour, especially in an Edith Head couture gown, tarantula eyelashes, overpainted glossy pursed lips and a perfectly plucked cocked brow, can get away with the most outrageous behaviour.

Rosie's appearance sneers at glamour. She once commented to my manager Tony: 'I like to stay big enough so that I'm unattractive to men and small enough to fit into Gap clothing.'

It's all about assimilating on one level while ready to give the 'fuck-you' finger at any moment.

I believe one of Rosie's most provocative acts was to adopt a lifestyle, modelled on, yet unacceptable to, Middle America. A lot of gay people think that if they live like 'normal folks' this will eventually result in acceptance. Rosie adopted her children while in a publicly acknowledged lesbian relationship, then her partner Kelly gave birth by insemination to a child of their own. This enraged her public, who had barely got used to her coming out. Of course, this is her right, and one which I support wholeheartedly. The underlying message, whether deliberate or not, is that 'fuck-you' finger to ridiculously guarded wholesome family values.

I guess like many of us, including myself, Rosie is a thunderous ball of contradictions. My biggest regret is that I never got to spend any quality time with her. Had I been her host in my city, I would have opened myself up to her. The difference between us is that she presents herself as 'one of the people' yet she is incredibly shy and reclusive. Perhaps this is why she puts on such a big show when she has an audience. On the one hand you have a person who dresses to avoid standing out and is terribly self-effacing, saying openly to the press: 'I've been at the all-you-can-eat buffet for longer than I can remember.' This is then contradicted by a force-of-nature energy; Rosie will often apologise and accelerate into a rage in the same breath. It's safe to say that everyone – apart from the British gang – was intimidated by her.

I certainly did my turn as Attila the Hun-cum-Shirley Temple in the eighties. I don't think I was ever quite as ebullient as Rosie, though.

Rosie was at her most likeable when you got her on her own or with Kelly. She could be so unbelievably grounded, insightful and all the things I believe she truly is. If it sounds as though I have any deep-rooted dislike of Rosie, it's only because talking about someone so complex and contradictory is like trying to blend oil and water.

Even at the worst moments I would say: 'She brought my fucking show to Broadway.' In tears, she once said to me: 'For years I've been the boss of everything. I'm just trying to learn how to live in this world.' OK, the cynic might sniff and suggest such self-revelation is a luxury given to those who can afford it. I myself have learned (not entirely) that people are less willing to wipe away a rich man or woman's tears.

In America far more value is placed upon what you own, and success and wealth are seen as a cure-all panacea. You could say that in America money equals power while in Britain money equals popularity. In all instances, as Quentin Crisp once said to me: 'Popularity breeds contempt.'

I believe that when Rosie took on this project, it was more about the heart than the wallet. The problem was that eventually huge pressure was put on her to pull the show. When she sent me that 'Fuck 'em, we stay open' email, she meant it. Explaining Rosie would be like explaining my own father; a man who has great qualities that are often overshadowed by irrational rage and the need to control everything (I could almost be talking about myself here!). If it's true, as most therapists claim, that anger is something we use to protect ourselves when we feel vulnerable, then Rosie and my father are both very angry and very vulnerable.

During the court hearings over her magazine, the publishers claimed that when she came to London and met me she turned all avant-garde and edgy, which wasn't the image they wanted for their publication. Even funnier, they said she had got herself a Helen Terry wedge haircut! As I told the *New York Times*, I'm not so shallow a person that I would only befriend someone sporting the right hairstyle.

This was spawned from a phone conversation between us one

night after I had rolled out of a hardcore house club after a DJ session in the north of England.

'Where the hell are you?' Rosie said. When I explained, she laughed. 'Jesus, how glamorous.'

'Where are you?' I slurred.

'Outside Target. I've just been buying school supplies for the kids.'

'How suburban!' I joked.

Rosie reworked the story in the US press, claiming that I had said to her:'I couldn't possibly work with you, you're too suburban.'

She's obviously never been to Eltham.

26

Billowing Breasts & Latex Drips

Euan, Raul and I were all housed in dressing rooms on the third floor. Mine was slightly larger, to accommodate Leigh's billowing costumes (and, perhaps in some of the cast's eyes, my ego as well!).

Euan is a complex character, and being so close to him meant that I soaked up his gritty yet flamboyant humour along with the extremities of his personality. Like myself with Alessandro, Euan would often use his dresser Pip as an emotional dartboard. Dressers on Broadway are a bit akin to hairdressers to cranky old actresses in Hollywood. They get all the dish, and all the darts as well. Often they would arrive hours before they were meant to, and did extra work late into the night simply because they love theatre, despite lousy pay and aggravation from all sides.

I'm sure there was plenty of eye-rolling between Pip, Alessandro and Raul's adorable dresser Ray as they brushed costumes in the cramped corridors. Alessandro's eagerness to please and his fault-less efficiency could be as annoying as it was a blessing. It took him a while to work out when to leave me alone and when to steam into action and gossip. We are both Geminis and quickly developed telepathy and empathy. Once he uttered after a ratty night: 'OK, it's over. Now we smoke a cigarette and judge the cunts.'

Alessandro had lost his life partner just nine months before

Taboo opened, and was never afraid to reveal his feelings. I really felt for him, especially having to watch Leigh's death scene every night, and deeply admired his stoicism. He even said about 'Il Adore' one night: 'I thank you from my heart for this music.'

Euan's talent accelerated even more on Broadway and this was rightly recognised by the media and New York's theatrical stalwarts. Often I would rush downstairs half dressed to watch him sing 'Stranger in this World' – he was never less than perfect.

As an actor (or actress) Jeffrey Carlson, who played Marilyn, was flawless. Even during rehearsals he painstakingly wore high heels and for me he was a brilliant Marilyn. When I first heard him speak I said: 'He sounds like Keith Richards and looks like Grace Kelly.' Jeffrey was the only cast member never to miss a performance and I wasn't surprised when he was nominated for the NY critics' Desktop Drama Awards for best supporting actor. His onstage chemistry with Euan was uncannily like my own with Marilyn, and just like Maz, one facial expression could – and often did – bring the house down. I will always think of him as the unsung hero of *Taboo* in New York, and chuckle when I recall the clicking of those heels as he flew downstairs to make his entrance.

There were three or four parts of the New York production that I treasure: Raul singing 'Petrified', Liz McCartney performing 'Talk Amongst Yourselves' and Euan singing anything. Watching actors perform my songs – in both the London and New York productions – gave me the first opportunity in my career to judge my work objectively and appreciate what I am capable of. In fact, there were times when I thought: 'Maybe I should just write for other people and give up trying to be a performer.' I'm sure there are plenty who would agree. Frankly, I don't think I could ever become a songs-for-sale merchant. I have been asked to write for artists I have no respect for, and have always said no. I'd rather work with someone with no money or record deal who has integrity.

Even though the songs in *Taboo* were sung by others, they express my emotions, and there is nothing more satisfying than hearing a heartfelt interpretation of my work.

Years ago I wrote and produced 'Black Angel' for Brit soul diva Mica Paris. Working with such a soaring voice — which could reach notes I can only dream of — was a thrilling experience. I also wrote a song for Soul II Soul's Caron Wheeler. In a perfect world I would only write for black voices, or those whiteys who can pull it off!

From what I was told by *Taboo*'s dressers and production crew we were an unusually harmonious cast (apart from the odd smiling Judas or Judy Garland). The world of theatre is notorious for mass outbreaks of venom between actors. When things got tetchy I would think: 'This is bad enough. Imagine how murky it could really get.'

A few actors would regularly visit the production office to voice mild complaints, my smoking and ad libbing being the main subjects.

After emerging from the toilet one night I ran my eyes over Sarah Uriarte Berry (dressed in Nicola's multi-tiered glittering swimming-cap creation), and boomed: 'Esther Williams on crack. You do look splendiferous.' It got the biggest laugh yet, and completely threw Sarah, who was none too pleased. This led to the inevitable moan about my liberty-taking.

Similarly, in the same scene, I replaced a line delivered to Liz McCartney, who was trying to persuade Leigh to employ her fictitious friend David as a design assistant. I pursed: 'I love it when you get all forceful.' To which Liz bellowed: 'JUST DO IT!!'

After complaining, both of them reluctantly went along with my continuing ad libs, though a notice was pinned up by the management stating that the line-changing was getting out of hand. I ignored it.

Raul was a ready accomplice, and this caused a huge rift between him and Liz. In my view, if a scene was meant to be funny and not getting the right reaction, it was our duty to make it work.

During 'Ich Bin Kunst' I was alone onstage and it was my only opportunity to try out new lines. One night before I went on I had a row with a tech backstage who informed me he was a

Republican. I used the confrontation to full advantage. Every night as I emerged inside my perspex box, the gasps and titters ran through the stalls. I suspect no Broadway audience has ever seen such a look and the tighter my corset got, the more my breasts billowed. I'd start by singing the song perched on a chaise longue, then stand and slowly slide open the perspex door. This particular night I walked forward, raised my arm like Eva Peron and said straight-faced: 'My fellow Republicans . . .' This worked a treat and became a staple. When I appeared side stage, the tech winked: 'You son of a bitch, that was awesome!'

After that he fed me some other great lines courtesy of his even more Republican father, which I adapted and used: 'You Americans are very uptight about the sexual thing. You've got a president called Bush, a vice-president called Dick. Make your bloody minds up.'

When things were running smoothly, joy abounded and even some of the clearly homophobic backstage hands would openly flirt and make jokes about my tits. I never felt more confident or fearless. It was a testament to Leigh's genius that he had conjured up a look that transcended all sexual boundaries and rendered everybody but myself speechless.

Once, I *was* rendered speechless when, unannounced, Euan and Cary Shields – who played Marcus – appeared at my dressing-room door seeking a smoking haven. Euan was in my classic dreadlocks and Star of David ensemble, and Cary was dressed in a Union Jack T-shirt and tight black jeans. They looked *exactly* like Jon and I. At the time I was half naked, with a chalky white base on my face. Not a pretty sight. I screamed at Euan: 'Don't haunt me at a time like this!'

Every night their onstage kiss got longer and longer, so maybe history was being recycled?

It was clear from the start that the American management, including Rosie, were worried that the English contingent were going to prove troublesome. When they gave up trying to halt my smoking, there was a petty debate about my wearing home the custom-made underwear they had provided. When I got wind of this I skipped past the office in my black tutu singing: 'I don't really care about your motherfucking underwear . . .' I had no intention of keeping the unflattering Lycra butt-scrunchers and, magnanimously, they let the issue drop.

As it turned out the Brits caused the least drama and Rosie once said: 'You know, Kelly told me: "You were worried about the Brits but look how brilliant they have been."'

In particular, Kevan should have been given a medal. Not only had he co-written most of the score, he also played live nightly in the house band and constantly helped the other musicians to get the feel right. Like Mike Nicholls, Kevan was provided with an American counterpart, John McDaniel and, like Mike, was forced to share billing. In John's case I do feel that he was essential because he contributed clever arrangements. And, aside from a few early teething problems between us, I found him polite and a joy to work with. Some of the actors moaned about his alleged rudeness but I never saw that side of him, and singer-actors can be hugely oversensitive.

I feel Kevan was treated with utter disrespect by Rosie and he was the only Brit who didn't receive a per diem and had to pay for his own flat out of his weekly wage. I took this up with Bernie Young who said there was no more money in the budget to support the extra costs for Kevan. I told Bernie: 'It's disgusting. Without him there'd be no score and on top of that he has written four extra songs with me during rehearsals to accommodate changes.'

Later, Bernie approached me to ask if I minded if Kevan's name was put forward for a Tony nomination. I replied: 'Why are you asking me? Of course he should.' Sadly that never happened. My name, and my name alone, appeared on the nomination for best music and lyrics, which was a terrible embarrassment to me.

Around this time the whispers about the run of *Taboo* coming to an end were becoming louder and more commonplace. I spoke with both my manager Tony and Rosie, and was told that we would run for another six months, whatever the loss.

Once the show was up and running we saw less and less of Rosie, who had been so wounded by some of the more important scathing reviews in the *New York Times* and, of course – no surprise here – the *Post*.

Over Christmas Rosie retreated to Miami with her family. The cast were given only two days off over the holiday – Christmas Eve and Christmas Day – and returned for two-show marathons on Boxing Day and most of the following week.

On Christmas Day I drove to Connecticut with my friends Amanda, Paul Starr and Maria Smith to spend the day with Amanda's family at her sister Samantha's house. It was the most surreal Christmas I've ever experienced, and immense fun. I called my mum on Christmas morning and she said: 'How's Cincinatti?' I laughed: 'I'm in Connecticut, you silly sod. You've just heard the word Cincinatti in some old song.'

I was sad to be away from my family, but the madness of sharing Christmas with my adopted family the Goseins made up for it. Samantha and her husband John live with their four kids in a beautiful, converted barn with one glass wall overlooking a misty lake surrounded by a forest. It was like being in a movie.

Paul was looking after Menudo, a tiny pampered dog owned by one of our other eccentric acquaintances, Christine XX. Paul had been forced to transport the dog in a Louis Vuitton handbag and warned under threat of death to ensure its safe return. Menudo is named after the Mexican boy band which once featured a teenage Ricky Martin, with whom Christine is unnaturally obsessed.

Amanda's other sister Tracy and her husband Nick brought their bruiser dog from New York and shortly after dinner there was a fierce canine scrap between Tracy's dog and one of Samantha's four hounds. Paul nervously clutched Menudo as the two dogs fought it out underneath the dining table. Samantha's dog was badly wounded and I ran into the loo to escape. When I reappeared one of Samantha's handsome young friends was standing there dressed like an ER cast member in a green surgeon's get-up complete with stethoscope. I asked innocently if he intended to operate on the dog there and then but it turned out he was off to do the nightshift at the local A&E.

Both Paul and I were sure he had donned the garb as a total pose – surely you're not supposed to wear that stuff outside of a sanitised surgical environment? It was a hot look nonetheless and

Paul and I kept cracking queeny jokes like 'Help, help, I think I've twisted my ankle' and 'Someone give me mouth to mouth.'

It seemed I'd been given time off from one lunatic production only to be plunged straight into another.

Things calmed down in the evening when Samantha's brother-in-law arrived to play the piano. We all sat around singing jazz songs and stuffing more food down our gullets. Later, as we were packing the car to leave for New York, our gracious host John asked: 'I hope you've had a good time.' I said: 'It's been adorable,' which of course it had been. Rather like having the O'Dowd family Christmas experience transported to a far more luxurious location.

I'd been pre-warned of the hectic schedule that would kick in after the holidays, and made the decision to enjoy it no matter how hard that might be.

Liz McCartney had gone off to have her baby and Sarah, who played Nicola, had chosen the perfect moment to take a break, avoiding that hellish stint of daily double shows. The upside was that I got to work with their understudies: Brooke Elliott, who took over from Liz, and Denise Summerford and Jen Mrozik, who in turn played Nicola. Some of the cast gave Brooke the cold shoulder, apparently routine when a major role is taken by an understudy. I found this particularly upsetting, because anyone who acts knows how tough it is to be thrown into a role and in *Taboo* in New York the understudies were given little chance for preparation. Brooke was understandably nervous at first but she got better and better. I liked her; sometimes she'd give me a sly wink onstage which showed her good humour in the face of adversity.

My favourite cast member was Lisa Gajda, one of the ensemble. She constantly talked about sex and was a consummate non-moaner. I also had a soft spot for Dioni Collins, a small voluptuous black girl who, like me, wasn't a typical dancer but we always had fun bumping and grinding during 'Everything Taboo'. Alex Quiroga was the company's suave-ette, while Gregory Treco was a glittering mulatto Nijinsky. My own understudy Bob Gaynor was politeness himself, square-jawed, handsome and very fetching in his doctor's uniform.

Oh, and let's not forget Curtis Holbrook, who was a member of the ensemble and has a cute butt you could park a bike (or a tongue) in.

27

Taboo Boo Hoo

No matter how prepared you think you are, or how in place your powers of indifference, facing the end (which I have done many times) is never easy. The rumours of our impending closure had become an unconfirmed fact by the start of the new year.

The basement – which housed wardrobe, wigs, make-up, band lockers and miscellaneous subterranean creatures who turned the cogs and wheels of the production – was the centre of stitching and bitching. If a costume started to fray, fell apart or dug into the ribs of some sensitive thespian, this is where it was put right.

At times, I imagine, the eye-rolling and sighing down there made the dressers on our floor seem totally stress-less. Of course they never were (sometimes being at the beck and call of one principal can be like working for several people at once). Down in the bowels of the Plymouth, each character, regardless of which department they ruled or served, was of a type, or a hysteria-type. Like the actors and actresses who donned the more extreme apparel of the show, they had to work with swiftness while remaining graceful under pressure.

Often I would drop down to pick up Christine for lunch or to drag her home. One of my good friend Tasty Tim's best friends (or sistas) Steven, aka Perfidia, had been employed for his inside knowledge of the intricacies of wig-dom. Steven is a quiet but colourful character who would occasionally spit out a gem. He gave all the wigs names, as well as the costumes in this dressing-up cavern of life. Wardrobe mistress Wanda Gregory had the most formidable energy. Mike and I affectionately named her Wanda the Witch because Christine was often far too enamoured by her stories and predictions.

Wanda had been wafting up smoke signals for a number of weeks. But even she was surprised when the news of the closure finally broke.

I had been in constant contact with my manager Tony, who kept telling me ticket sales were on the up for February – a notoriously bad month for theatre – and that he had heard nothing to suggest the rumours were true. A couple of weeks later, in the middle of January, two hours before I was leaving for that night's performance, I received a phone call from Rosie. She sounded sad: 'I didn't want to do this but I'm calling to tell you we close *Taboo* in three weeks.' She followed this bombshell with what sounded to me like a lot of positive jumble: 'This doesn't mean the end . . . we can open again . . . it was an overnight decision.' I was so numb I couldn't hear what she was saying, but I remember mumbling: 'If that's what you need to do . . .'

The reality hit when I put the phone down. As I sat there holding my head in my hands, Paul asked: 'What's wrong?'

I burst into tears. 'She's fucking closing the show,' I told him. Paul immediately put in a call to Bernie, who told him Rosie was in pieces and on her way to Miami.

New York was snowbound and as cold as a rent boy's heart. The image of Rosie soaking up the sun at her gargantuan villa while we had to shiver in New York and face the music only added to the upset.

Even worse, I was told that Charlotte Wilcox would be bringing the bad news to the rest of the cast, a job I felt Rosie was responsible for, as did everyone in the company. Had Rosie done so, I believe there would have been less bad feeling towards her from the cast, because of all the promises and assurances she had made. We were the public face of the show and had to bear the brunt of the news.

I lost it.

Totally.

Her email which said 'Fuck 'em, we stay open until June' was saved on my desktop and I clicked it open and raged: 'Right – I'm not going in! I'm not doing the show tonight! Why couldn't they have told me this morning or tomorrow?! I'm supposed to perform feeling like this?!'

Paul rang company manager Peter Wolf and told him I was taking the night off. I rang Kevan and told him to do the same.

Kevan and I had already started working on our song 'Panic' and I decided I wanted to finish it while emotions were at their rawest. Kev was as devastated as me, and duly called in sick.

Suddenly there was mass panic – it looked like I was leading a mutiny among the British contingent. In fact, on hearing that I was taking the night off, Christine started manically packing her make-up case because she knew she'd have to work with my understudy Bob Gaynor, who had never performed in the role and would have to be placed in a bald cap because he refused to shave his head. Before she had even left the apartment, Paul received a frantic call from Bernie Young saying: 'If Christine doesn't turn up at the show, I'll sue her sorry ass!' The language out of Christine's mouth succeeding that phone call is far too psychedelic for public consumption. As much of a madam as she can be, when the chips are down she's a pure roll-up-your-sleeves gal.

Christine knew that my taking that night's show off would mean chaos and possible cancellation without her presence, and the very idea that she would let the cast and her own team down brought out a side of her I hadn't seen before. On arriving at the Plymouth she got on with the extra-complicated job at hand and waited until mid-show to march into the production office and announce: 'Get that fucking Bernie Young on the phone! Now!'

Apparently the conversation went as follows:

Christine: 'I'd like to see you sue my sorry ass when your fucking company hasn't even got it together for me to sign a contract! Don't ever accuse me of shirking my responsibilities because this show is far more important to me than it is to you!'

Bernie denied ever saying such a thing. Within minutes executive producer Lori Said arrived with a gift for her. In fact, Lori, being the peacemaker and sweetheart that she is, probably took it upon herself to make the gesture. In true dyke fashion she came to the dressing-room door bearing a bottle of beer and some flowers in a brown paper bag. Lori was openly distraught at the news of the closure and later I'd often catch her weeping.

The day after the news broke Mike and I went to a studio uptown where I recorded a duet with my friend Antony, who has this extraordinary group Antony and the Johnsons. His music is peculiarly beautiful, often centred around a simple piano figure and washes of strings. Antony sings like a white Nina Simone with added operatic tones.

He had written a simple melody with the lyrics: 'You are my sister and I love you, / May all of your dreams come true.' It was perfect timing to be singing with Antony at such a brittle moment, and the simplicity of the words seemed to make the universe right.

Later, he played it to Lou Reed, who described my vocal as 'pure emotion'. He was right there, and working with Antony helped me snap out of my psychotic rage.

When we left the studio I said to Mike: 'Moments like that make you realise why you do what you do.'

I returned to the theatre that night determined to see the job through. Knowing we were closing added an extra *joie de vivre*, and the last thing I wanted to hear was how sorry people were. I knew if I connected with their sadness I would be useless. To compensate I turned the whole thing into a black joke, especially onstage.

The night I didn't show up, hordes of people had asked for their money back and the atmosphere was so grim Raul quipped, in true Philip fashion: 'Oh calm down, the show's much better without him anyway!'

On my return, the tension in the audience was electric. As I emerged from the toilet the roars went on for so long I fought back the tears and shouted: 'Enough!' The reaction was so warm I decided, from that point, I would make the reality and the sadness of the situation work in the show's favour. During 'Ich

Bin Kunst', I joked: 'Don't think of it as the show closing, think of it as Rosie's purse shutting!' Then I added: 'That Rosie, she's a bit of a dyke-chotomy.' I was ticked off by the production office but I told them: 'It's not like the audience aren't in on the joke. They know we're closing.'

After the announcement the show took on a whole new life and energy and people who had been planning to come started flooding in. Our attendances had never been low, ever. There were a few nights when half the balcony was empty, but there were many other Broadway shows playing to near empty houses at the time.

Often what was being conveyed in the press and in whispers outside the theatre simply did not reflect the truth. Everyone had differing opinions on why it hadn't worked. In time the missing facts may well be revealed. Rosie herself told a camera crew on the red carpet at the Tony Awards: 'It's all my fault. I shouldn't have pulled the money so early.' Certainly this confirms Wanda's speculations that the show should have been allowed to grow and find its audience.

My theory?

Rosie absolutely intended to see our run through until June as promised. Having been battered so publicly during her magazine case, then having to suffer the slings and arrows of the Broadway jackals, she was unimaginably wounded. I know that Rosie felt deeply let down by the Broadway community and as I've already said she had done so much to help them. Plus, this was her first serious media mauling. I, of all people, know what that is like. During my drug crisis, the attacks on me by the media made me similarly retreat. If there's one difference, I didn't have quite as many responsibilities to shoulder.

What Rosie should have done was face the cast and crew as near as possible to the decision. I had an acute understanding of her vulnerability from the minute I met her. The rest of the company only knew her ebullient persona, and she had suddenly switched from being the guiding force to an uncontactable figure in the shadows.

What I should have done is picked up the phone and spoken

to her at the point when I could see the cast turning on her. I know Euan kept in close contact with Kelly and Rosie, and both had given him their word that they would look after him. They maintained the rent on his apartment and looked for sponsors to support him staying in the States.

An article appeared in gossip queen Liz Smith's column. For once it was a positive piece alluding to the fact that *Taboo* had been reinvigorated and was now 'unmissable'. Smith quoted some of my Rosie comments. She could tell they weren't coming from a place of animosity. And they weren't. Trust me. If I hated Rosie I wouldn't have been on that stage for love, money or fear of lawsuits.

Bernie called: 'You must desist from making further comments about Rosie onstage. She is deeply upset and if you continue we will pull the show now.'

I burst into tears. 'She's upset? Then why am I talking to you?'

Bernie's call was followed by one from Tony Gordon: 'George, what's going on? I've had Rosie on the line in tears.'

I was still crying myself, and again yelled: 'Then tell her to fucking call me!'

Seconds later her voice appeared on my mobile. I was off at first, saying: 'I really don't think I can deal with this right now.'

She broke down. 'My whole world's falling apart here, so hear me out. I understand you're not attacking me, but people don't see that. I want us to finish this with our heads held high.'

I don't think Rosie ever realised that the best way to win me over is with open dialogue, and the absence of this had been the major problem all along. Hearing her cry, and at her most vulnerable, affected me deeply. I couldn't be angry, vindictive or vengeful. I said to her: 'Rosie, this is all you've ever needed to do.'

I should point out that, even during such an emotional exchange, she couldn't help but mention she had sunk $10 million into the show. It was inappropriate, but at least added a comical edge.

She said: 'I'll buy the fucking apartment for ya.'

Had I been a cheaper queen I would have said yes. I also had a vision of Kelly jabbing her with a soup ladle as she made the offer, which I knew was a gesture made in haste.

Rosie told me she would continue paying for our apartment until the end of June. I was relieved because I certainly didn't want to leave New York as though my tail was between my legs.

The final weekend of *Taboo* was full of emotional mayhem. After the Saturday-night performance, Mike and I went to Crobar to dress a bunch of gorgeous go-go boys in my Rude clothing, a collection I'd been working on throughout the run of the show.

Johnny Dynell and Chi-Chi Valente were throwing a party and we sat backstage watching the boys dress. While the boys took turns dancing Mike filmed their pert butts squeezing into my Rude underwear and we chatted with the go-go boys taking a breather. Also very much there was Goddess Diana, a fabulous transsexual goth drummer who told Mike: 'Hey. I have a great ass too. Wanna see it?' As she revealed it she told me I was her inspiration for becoming the only transsexual drummer in New York. I love the way New York freaks are so particular about their *raison d'être*.

As Diana continued to tell her tale of escaping from the corn-fields of someplace or other my mobile rang. It was amazing that I heard it in such a loud club, and when I picked up I camped: 'House of Horror.'

Christine's panic-stricken voice barked back at me: 'I've had a terrible accident. It's OK. I'm not going to die. I'm covered in glass though and I'm bleeding badly.' I put the phone down and told Mike, whose face drained of all colour. Along with our friend Hans we raced from Crobar and tried to hail a cab amid Bridge & Tunnel mayhem.

Mike asked a young guy if he would give up his taxi, saying: 'I think my friend's really badly hurt at our apartment. We have to get back there now.'

The guy replied: 'Hey, that's not my problem.'

It was one of those nights when you really hate humanity.

We decided to dash some of the way on foot to constant catcalls of 'Hey, Boy George!' My lack of response was greeted with 'Hey, we're your fans! Don't be so stuck-up!' So, the next time you see Gwyneth Paltrow rushing headlong and ignoring your request for an autograph – or a picture snapped on your mobile – don't assume she's being rude. Chris might be at home choking on a tofu burger.

As for me, I had visions of Christine with a huge shard of glass in her neck and was terrified as we entered the loft. Mike and I screamed out her name and heard whimpering from the kitchen, where she was standing naked with her bleeding hands under the cold tap and cut glass all over her legs and feet. Our immediate response was to call 911 but Christine said: 'No, I don't want any dramatics.' As if the situation wasn't drama enough.

It transpired that Christine had been in the shower and turned on the steamer. As she swung round a jet of boiling hot steam blasted her hand. Grabbing the shower rail shattered the glass door, which rained down all over her.

I felt so ill at the sight of the blood and her condition and insisted: 'Get an ambulance, I'll pay for it.'

Still she resisted and even asked if one of us would vacuum the tiny pieces of glass from her body.

Instead, Hans helped to carefully pick the splinters from her and then Christine promptly demanded a cup of coffee and a Mars bar. Once she got those, and only after she had done her make-up, did she go off to A&E with Mike and Hans. I tried to sleep but it was pointless. This was the last thing any of us needed as we faced the final two shows of *Taboo*.

Having barely slept, Christine – bandaged and painkillered to the hilt – and I trudged off to the Plymouth. I couldn't believe she had insisted on coming to work, but she felt it was such an important day, and a near-death encounter wasn't going to stop her.

Our usual dressing-room torture routine had to be scaled down. In fact, I'd go as far to say I was nice to Madam. I told everyone that she had nearly died, but they couldn't take it in, because there she was, getting on with it.

Euan was paralytic that afternoon, and I said to Christine: 'How is he going to get through the show?' The son of a bitch did, note- and script-perfect.

There was a lot of sobbing in the theatre and yet a kind of come-together Beatles vibe.

The matinée was unbelievable, full of good humour and even

Liz chucked in a few ad libs, and added the most fantastic rock phrasing to the song 'Sexual Confusion'.

I really played around with the audience in my first scene, changing the words to 'I'll Have You All': 'I've had lawyers, doctors, judges . . . and . . . him,' pointing at some unfortunate chap. As I exited back into the toilet, I turned to the audience and, in my best Joan Crawford tone, snarled: 'DON'T YOU JUDGE ME . . .'

The audience had become part of the show and, in fact, at the previous evening's performance, as I was camping it up in 'Ich Bin Kunst', I couldn't control my laughter and somebody from the balcony snapped a picture. Striking a pose, I said: 'Break the fucking rules. What are they going to do? Fire me?' Cameras were wrenched from handbags and back pockets as flashes exploded all over the theatre. For literally ten minutes, ushers frantically and unsuccessfully tried to halt the magical moment. I left the stage in tears, feeling a well-loved old dame du boards.

On the final day I didn't leave the theatre. Between performances I ate lunch with Christine, Perfidia and Mike, but didn't take visits from anybody else.

That last performance was packed with all those who loved and had supported the show, rather like in London. Sometimes the singing along and quoting of lines drowned us out, which Raul used to best effect: 'Shut up, dear, this is my moment!'

In 'Ich Bin Kunst', I had my final chance to say thank you to the cast and to all the New Yorkers who had wrongly been accused of not supporting us. So many people had sent messages from the UK saying: 'Sorry the yanks don't get it.' Yet I always defended them, because I felt that in New York those that got it absolutely got it, while those who didn't see it didn't deserve to.

I thanked Rosie from the stage for having faith in my work and the balls to bring the show to New York. I also thanked the cast but, as always with these things, I missed out someone: actress Jen Cody sharply poked me in the ribs.

Everyone in the theatre that night – in the audience and onstage – had tears in their eyes. Rosie and Kelly were openly bereft. Again, for me, Rosie's honest and public display of emotion made all the hoo-ha seem exactly what it was. The parallel between Rosie and my dad will always exist. I love her, just as I love him. Let's face it, you always know where you stand with a lunatic. I, of all people, am well placed to make this statement.

A few weeks passed and I rang Rosie. She, Kelly, Paul Farrell and I went out for a Chinese. We had a great time. As we left Rosie whispered in my ear: 'You've got me for life, my friend.'

Just as well perhaps, because sometimes it takes a lifetime to work some people out.

28

An Englishman In New York

No sooner had the show ended than I was bombarded with calls pressing me to return to work offers in London.

As ever, bids for Culture Club tours in South America, Vegas and Outer Mongolia were lucrative. I'm not opposed to spells of nostalgia yet knew I needed to concentrate on the here and now.

I was the most emotionally exhausted I had ever been in my entire career. I asked my manager, my DJ agents, everyone, to back off and let me think about what I wanted to do next. I did a lot of soul-searching and pondered on the fact that for the best part of fifteen years my career had been non-directional. Work has been coming my way in a random and unfocused fashion and I felt I needed a plan. The problem with having managers and agents is that they rely on you for their livelihoods, and while I am always conscious of that, I knew I had to stop, take stock and start thinking about myself.

I'd been developing my Rude clothing line and also my photographic skills. Like most things these started accidentally.

Through playing Leigh I was once again bitten by the drag bug. My appearance had been somewhat understated, for me at least, for some time. Four years in a loose-fitted suit and a Philip Treacy fedora was frankly long enough, hence my quip-in-a-hat label.

Taboo's popularity in London coincided with the rise of clubs like Nag Nag Nag and Kashpoint and again there was an eighties nostalgia stench permeating the air. Every time there is an eighties revival – which happened with alarming regularity during the late nineties and the early noughties – I was wheeled out (and often paid) to say my piece. To be honest I hate mindless nostalgia. As Morrissey said, you should respect the past but not wallow in it. Perhaps, for many, that's all I'd ever done!

Most people have no idea that I've DJed for a decade and a half, dragging my twelve-inch box all over the world, let alone that I've recorded several solo albums, had a cable TV chat show, a radio talk show and dance slots on KISS and Galaxy.

Going to Nag Nag Nag was like visiting Blitz back in the day. Who would have thought that kids who weren't around in 1979 would be going mental to electro in the twenty-first century? You can be really cynical and say: 'I've seen it all before,' but why is it OK to reference the Beatles and the Rolling Stones for eternity and not people who influenced you as a teenager, like Gary Numan and David Bowie? These are artists who are just as relevant. There is a new wave of kids who realise that they have been manipulated by record companies. My hope is that this scene is the beginning of young people immersing themselves in interesting musical ideas again.

Nag Nag Nag became a Wednesday-night fixture and a freak of my standing wasn't going to let a bunch of fashion-school upstarts grab all the attention. Mike, Christine and I had such fun reapplying the make-up after *Taboo* performances to head to Jonny Slut's electro cesspit.

It was as if life had come full circle: Jonny had walked into my shop the Foundry in the early eighties and asked: 'Got any jobs?' I told him I barely had one myself but gave him the number of our designer Sue Clowes who he ended up working for. Jonny had also been in the pre-goth band the Specimen with Ollie, who was a friend of mine and Mike's. Mike also DJed at the Batcave, where the Specimen were the house band. Hope you're keeping up.

Aside from Ollie, who has relocated to foreign parts – Thailand, the last I heard – all those old but relentless freaks were rearing their heads again. Some still had hair, while others used their stripped crania as yet another make-up opportunity. The likes of Princess Julia, Tasty Tim, Wayne Shires, Fat Tony and Rod Lay were all DJing or putting on nights again. *Taboo* was surfing the Zeitgeist and let's face it Leigh had always been ahead of his peers.

I'd been making clothes for myself for a while and then started putting pieces together for friends. Mike and Christine became my personal muses as I heat-pressed images of naked men and slogans on to charity-shop shirts and suits. I turned my Hampstead living room into a sweatshop and employed out-of-work friends such as Becca and Chesca Grover, the two sisters from the band C33X, to stitch, sequin and bead. Becca and Chesca I now count among my dearest and most trusted friends.

At that point there was no rhyme or reason beyond pots of colourful sequins and a wooden floor sparkling with glitterdust.

Mike was constantly asked where he got his shirts, which was amusing since he had previously designed stuff for me. Both he and Christine had also worked at the high end of couture for the likes of Mr Mugler and Christian Lacroix under the haughty glare of Mr Pearl.

Mike, who did a film degree, came on board to shoot all The Twin live shows and videos with his partner Nigel Nuts. It was great not to have to pander to MTV limitations, or sexual or cultural ones for that matter.

My performances as The Twin bastardised some of Leigh's images, chucking in enough Bowie references to rattle some people. I'd receive letters from fans saying: 'Why do you paint your face black? It's hideous. When are you going to sing some sweet songs?' There were debates raging on my many websites questioning my sanity. It felt like a mild revolution. As I said earlier, I'd removed myself from the usual avenues of pop promotion because of the Radio One ban, and because I knew songs like 'Elektro Hetero', with its lyric 'Roderick you weren't joking, / You really had me choking . . .' wouldn't have even made the Z-list.

I wasn't being mindlessly provocative, just tapping into the darker sides of my persona.

I decided to create a range of clothing that related to my frustrations about pop music, gay assimilation and the lie that the world has become more tolerant. The electro scene was just like the Blitz scene: a cultural pinhead feeding off itself. The fact that credible dance-music journalists were dissing it made it all the more alluring to me.

My clothing is of the moment. The name Rude arose from a comment somebody made about Mike's shirt, which was a scan of the front of a gay porn video: a man on his knees servicing another.

'That's a bit rude,' this person said.

Perfect.

29

Who Am I Today?

In a bizarre sense, being Leigh liberated me. You can't inhabit those clothes without inhabiting that distorted and mischievous spirit.

At the height of my career in the eighties the only parts of flesh I shared with the world were my face, neck and hands. This was partly because I felt I should always look how other people expected me to. My relationship with Jon, however complex and turbulent, was one of the few in my life in which I was never, ever made to feel unattractive. Jon could be cruel, as could I, yet I always felt that he found me attractive.

In the past I've called myself the Liz Taylor of Pop because people have often said I have her eyes, and there have been plenty of times when I had her hips. I've never been a classic beauty. This does not mean that I think I'm hideously unattractive or God's gift either.

In a way it's better to be born average and work on yourself. I have friends who are drop-dead gorgeous and constantly looking in the mirror for lines. I don't do that at forty-three, and certainly didn't when I was twenty-five. What may appear as vanity to some is just making good from what I have. When I discovered the magic that could be created by make-up and how the right lighting can create illusions of perfection, it changed my life.

Mind you, if you were to apply the same make-up I wear to any other face it would never look identical. We all have our own quirks and qualities. No amount of eyeliner could give Maggie Thatcher, Kate (or Jon) Moss my appearance, even in the unlikely event of them wanting to look like me.

Beauty like success is only revered in its finest hour. We can all – ugly or otherwise – create different types of success, but if you put all your stock in the vanity vault, a crash will inevitably follow. I imagine Kate will be far more devastated than me when time takes its toll.

We're in the grip of a panic of perfection; in my case you can't grieve over what came from the cosmetics counters of Selfridges and Harvey Nicks in the first place.

Unfortunately we live in a culture which has warped ideas about beauty and always demands perfection from public figures. So what if my public figure is imperfect? My mind is a super-model. It's not as though I would ever contemplate going out in a tight white T-shirt and lamé batty-riders. I'm still a prisoner of my physicality, but far less so since baring my breasts on Broadway.

I've already talked about the nightmare experience of sharing the Venue's cramped dressing room with a bevy of beautiful, svelte boys. On Broadway Leigh's character had more depth and this brought forth some important personal realisations. One of the greatest quotes of Leigh's in the show is his line: 'The agenda isn't ugliness, or beauty. That's all your ideas.' I'm not suggesting for a second that I was possessed by his spirit although some fools thought otherwise.

I saw a photo of a handbag in *The Face* designed by artist and gay journalist Donald Urquhart which had the slogan 'Boy George is not Leigh Bowery'. How insightful. In fact, Donald saw it as his cause célèbre to point out to me the absolutely bleeding obvious, and this was someone who had met Leigh twice and rolled around on my bed in the video for 'Ich Bin Kunst'.

Before *The Face* folded (boo-hoo) it ran an article accusing me of robbing Leigh's grave for credibility. I've never had credibility or sought it out. I have no inkling who dishes it out in the first place and no desire to meet them. I have my suspicions they are the chief buyers for achingly chic boutique Voyage. Cool takes too much time and energy. Any drag queen worth her slap can get ready, if need be, in twenty minutes flat. A terminally hip type will spend four hours deciding how to wear a plain white T-shirt with his Levi's.

In a funny way, I am scuzziness personified. I often treat my own wardrobe – which is purchased mainly from Marks & Spencer's and charity shops – with the same disregard as Leigh would a piece that had been painstakingly beaded for two weeks.

Acting made me realise that everything we do is an act of sorts. No matter how sincere you think you're being, you can't control how people read your moves and moods.

For the first part of the run I would often come offstage feeling utterly empty despite laughter and applause and I couldn't work out why I was so unhappy. One evening after such a show I had one of my not untypical wide-ranging debates with Christine which often ran from who was top of that day's shit-list, through her obsession with palaeantology to why I was stalking a particular boy (Ken, Ken, and Ken!). That afternoon she had already informed me she was the more evolved of us because I had admitted to being a gay chauvinist pig. We'd been talking about sex, and in particular open relationships. I confessed that although I hated being the jealous person that I am, if my partner suggested an open relationship I would respond thus:

'You want an open relationship? Open the door and fuck off!'

Christine told me: 'You've got the sensibilities of a caveman; knock 'em on the head and drag 'em by the hair into the bedroom.'

All day I tortured her: 'Excuse me, more evolved being, would you pass the eyeliner?'

This was much like the time she told Mike she intended to become a nurse after *Taboo* ended, and was furious when Mike told me of this plan. Mike chuckled: 'I told Christine it was a very unwise move considering she is the least altruistic person I've ever known.'

I started calling her Nurse Ratched: 'Oh, Nurse Ratched, my bedpan needs changing.'

'Oh shut up, I'm trying to apply individual lashes.'

Or even more to my amusement: 'Nurse Ratched, what the hell has happened to the patient?'

'Well, that machine kept making a hideous beeping noise, so I ripped the plug out. I think he's just sleeping.'

During our evening conversation it became clear that she just might have the evolutionary edge. I talked about my post-performance comedowns. Her observations were illuminating: 'Look at the situation. You're playing Leigh Bowery, who never gave a fuck about the audience except for six of his closest friends. On top of this you're watching a younger version of yourself receiving the love and warmth which you've come to expect for more than twenty years.' It was true. Most of the audience didn't know who the hell Leigh was.

Christine had touched on something significant. The reason I felt so down was that I was trying to get the audience to love somebody who was completely contrary and borderline unlovable.

The next night I emerged from that toilet in unapologetic fashion, and I felt invigorated. I came offstage almost punching the air, thinking of that Quentin Crisp quote: 'London has not seen a performance like that since Sybil Thorndike the Third!'

My entire life and career has been a bit of a free-for-all and my humour has always been quick yet defensive. Exploring spirituality and the many ups and downs of my career had helped me achieve a certain amount of balance. My therapist Jamie pointed out years ago that being Boy George was playing a role anyway. I guess I needed the experience of playing someone else – and who better than the extraordinary and complex Leigh Bowery? – to crack the shell. I'm not talking about the script, half of which was outer-planetary crafted, nor the routine or structure of performing. For me *Taboo* became an emotional exorcism, not the first, but perhaps the most enlightening.

The difference between me and everybody else in the show was that it was my life up there. For more than a year I'd been telling journalists it wasn't strange playing somebody I knew opposite somebody playing me.

Of course it was weird! It was fucking weird!

I had been in that famous river in Egypt: Denial.

The media tried to paint a Dorian Gray portrait, with myself as the ageing image in the attic.

I always got the sense that the line of questioning was steeped in insincere concern, which I encounter constantly from the media. Let's face it, they love nothing more than a bitter, grieving has-been.

Pity is a very arrogant assumption and dying as Leigh on a nightly basis over two years made me realise why he didn't want to pass away in the full glare of it. And more importantly, why I have no desire to live with it either.

At a recent live gig a female journalist rushed backstage and splurted: 'You were just as good as when you were –'

I ended the sentence for her: 'You mean, famous.' She wasn't being mean, simply buying into the idea that once you've attained the level of fame I have, your every living breath is centred around its propagation.

I don't want to be Madonna, I really don't. I realise saying it in print will only make you think: 'She protesteth too much.' If I am indeed deluding myself, then I've wasted thousands on therapy!

Actually I don't even think Esther wants to be Madonna any more. She's working it out at the Can't Copa Kabbalah.

30

Silicone & Lobsters

While in New York I hooked up with some old friends and a whole new breed of star-spangly debutantes.

The older breed are made up of the likes of Lily of the Valley (aka Michael Cavadias), Richie Rich, Lady Bunny, Johnny Dynell and Chi-Chi Valente and Kenny Ken.

I first met Lily when he was a full-on drag queen collecting glasses at the nightclub Jackie 60. He's a great thinker and, unlike most drag queens, has a raging political conscience and for hours will happily discuss the electoral caucuses and Bush's diminishing ratings. In 2004 Lily set up a benefit for John Kerry in a venue opposite the Republican Convention. In between his political activities he DJs, does a fine impersonation of Donald Duck and fronted a band called Bullet for a while. Last year we recorded the duet 'Be Nice', in which he acts as my quasi-therapist as I hatch plans to take revenge on yet another straight boy.

Lily DJs for club promoter and social-lite Eric Conrad who runs the nights Beige, Plaid and a Sunday soirée at the Maritime Hotel. Trying to describe Eric is pointless, because he's summed up best by his own one-liners. He was once asked by a journalist: 'Where do you think your customers live?' Eric replied: 'I dunno. On airplanes?'

Two of my other favourite characters in New York are the

comedy duo the Duelling Bankheads, who appear onstage dressed as dishevelled versions of the movie legend Tallulah, bowing to their own canned applause. The Bankheads bastardise pop classics such as 'Why are you gay? / It's time to think about it . . .' and 'Supercalifragilistic, / You've got halitosis . . .'

This set personifies the East Village bohemian rhapsody, but the bitching is always finely crafted. Back home, once you've received a lashing from the likes of Fat Tony you know you've been tangoed. When I first started living back in New York, I found myself frustrated by the lack of decent British back-stabbing. Then I met Miss Guy!

We were having brunch one Sunday, and the merits of another human being were being discussed and Guy said: 'Actually, I think he's kind of an asshole.' I thought: 'Thank God for you!'

Of course, now that we have become real friends, most of the bile is directed at each other, in true Gemini fashion. He calls me Gary Glitter, and I continually ask him when he's going to reform the Electric Chairs.

We first compared eyeliner from a distance at the legendary punk disco haunt Squeezebox. Miss Guy was the DJ and, I guess like me in my early days at Planets, thoroughly enjoyed being up there in the pulsating pulpit. (He once fronted a band called the Toilet Boys, who were pre-Manson and premenstrual, with Guy looking like Pamela Anderson on MDMA.) In between the sniping we've actually managed to write a gorge song together called 'Pretty Boys', the main subject of our conversation beyond MAC's latest glitter range.

Guy is very old school, and exudes what can only be described as adjacent cool, happy to sit back and draw back a brow at the antics of the latest star-spangled fashionistas, such as the Trinity headed by Drew Elliot, or Drewpsie to those close enough to withstand his Truman Capote-esque froideur. Very early on in our friendship I made the mistake of battling with him over columnist Michael Musto (or Michael Mustgo, and even if he doesn't somebody will phone it in for him). Drew sprang to Mustgo's defence, and I foolishly accused him of being 'corporate'. The chill which followed that remark could be felt in Nebraska and I shivered through it for three months.

That's not to say that the rest of the Trinity are any less super-cool or caustic. Mack ('Mackie') Dugan hails from New Zealand and is head of stitch and sew with quirky design house Heatherette while Aimee Phillips lives between phone calls in her capacity as Heatherette (and self-) publicist, along with her relentless attempt to recreate every single one of Cher's looks since the seventies. Aimee has become a very close friend, and I love her dearly. She once said about Christine: 'Her look is making me panic.' She is as inventive with her repartee as she is with her ever-changing wardrobe.

Heatherette is run by ex-lovers Traver Rains and Michael Aligera grown-up club kid Richie Rich. Richie frequented every New York disco in the early nineties, and I knew of him long before we became friendly. It wasn't until I arrived in New York for *Taboo* that we spoke for the first time. I saw him at Beige and said: 'Love the look. It's very Lou Reed *Rock 'n' Roll Animal.*' He was even wearing a Lou-style tiny leather jacket with 'Heatherette' studded in diamanté on the back. At first I thought it was his drag name. There are some pretty unusual ones in New York: Mistress Formica, Lady Bunny, Flawless Sabrina . . .

Richie told me he had started his own fashion company named after Heather, a girl he knew at school in San Francisco who allegedly had one arm (the lip lines between fact and fiction are often overdrawn come closing time at Beige). Traver pitched up in town having been a rodeo star in Montana, and by the time he met Richie was giving horse-riding lessons to the glitterati at New York's famed Chelsea Pier. They fell in love and, though they subsequently broke up, decided to set up shop together. Traver is the only man to this day I've ever met who can carry off cowboy boots with conviction. The song 'Zoo York', which Kevan and I wrote for a Heatherette catwalk show, mentions all of them, and of Traver I sing:

> I'm really liking the way you braid your hair,
> Traver is a cowboy,
> He got sweet derrière.

Heatherette's in-house muse is the self-created vision Amanda LePore. If Lou Reed had written 'Walk on the Wild Side' in 2004, it would be Amanda – not Candy Darling – who plucked her eyebrows and shaved her legs until . . . The first time I saw Amanda was courtesy of photographer David LaChapelle who took her on as his own freak muse in the late nineties.

There are so many stories about how Amanda became the creation she is today. My favourite is that, as a young gender-confused boy-girl, she sewed gowns for a transsexual stripper who paid her in hormones. A then girlfriend hooked her up with a nice boy who had no idea Amanda was, in fact, quite a few stiletto steps away from being a real lady. They fooled around, Amanda always avoided going too far, and then she dropped the bomb-shell. The boy, freaked to capacity, froze her out until he decided to get over it and talk to his own father about the predicament. The father (this is no Waltons scenario) decides to help this androgynous waif and paid for the chop. The young Amanda moved into the family home and became a prisoner; partly because the boy she then wed (are you gagging?) became obsessed and the family were terrified the secret might sneak from under the welcome mat.

Her outings were limited to plastic surgery sculpture, medical check-ups and visits to the beauty parlour. By this time Amanda was a suburban housewife-cum-Jeff Koons porcelain Pandora. While panic-stricken hubby worked, his mother kept a steady eye on Amanda and the struggle to be who she always knew she was inside her once distorted male shell was replaced by new constraints. In numerous ways this family deserves some applause for embracing the situation. Can you imagine this going down well in Catford?

Trapped in Jersey City Amanda worked in a bookstore and started to pinch bucks from her husband, who was wealthy from an inheritance windfall. This is where one version of her libera-tion from suburban hell gets gilded. Before meeting Amanda I had heard some hysterical tale of her saving up milk tokens and escaping through a bathroom window into a snow blizzard. Then I was told she offered to fetch a Chinese takeaway and took off to New York City and never looked back.

Who really cares if any of these stories are factual? Any human being who has dedicated so much time and silicone turning herself into an *über*-babe has every right to make us suffer for the truth as she has suffered for her vision of perfection.

Apparently, after leaving hubby she worked as a dominatrix, club hostess and was hired for bar mitzvahs until LaChapelle saw her visual potential and brought her to wider public attention with his Busby Beserkley photography, pop videos and TV commercials. Her face has been used to promote everything from fashion campaigns and Heatherette to Mont Blanc Pens and Sharper Image, a company that sells time-saving gadgets to the rich and lazy.

Since hitting New York she has lived in a tiny room at the city's legendary Hotel 17. After years of existing among her multitude of frocks and wigs in a boxy closet she has upgraded to a marginally larger room but still shares a communal bathroom with the other inhabitants on her landing.

Sometimes Amanda has a definite *Mars Attacks!* quality, and is even prone to dispense style advice to mutts. Heatherette's other – less shapely – mascot is a sausage dog named Thurston, after Thurston Moore of Sonic Youth (who is not a dachshund, by the way). One day the poor dog was thrust into a minuscule pink tutu for a shopping trip, and Traver was painting its claws a fetching shade of green. As the pooch struggled against enforced feminisation, Amanda cooed: 'Thurston, never fear change. The green is a little goth, I know, but I do think it works, and that's the important thing.'

Describing Amanda's own look is a tough one. It hints at Hollywood, if the dull wooden sign were to be covered in pink holographic sequins by Heatherette. At one of their fashion shows Amanda catwalked with a tiny sprig of feathers and gems on her (hardly private) parts.

LePore loves to go butt naked. She is constantly surrounded and fêted by a posse of pretty young gay boys to whom she is a star as worthy of worship as Britney or our Kylie. She has even released a single called 'Champagne', which suggests her life is one big fizz. Not so. She works hard to maintain her look and often pops to Mexico to have ribs broken and fresh silicone injected where she

Straight

has discovered a design flaw. Recently she was flown to Brazil and came back jazzing about her royalty-style treatment: 'They flew me first class and laid on a limousine and I had fans,' she cooed in that soft voice that suggests a dizzy blonde. The 'dizzy' act is in my opinion a clever veil to assure that the many 'straight' boys who queue to suck on her missile breasts are never threatened.

Her one-liners are scarce but gorgeously sly. 'You look slightly underdressed,' I quipped while about to ride to the lobby in a Dallas hotel lift with her. 'I was in a full evening gown but it got caught in the elevator door,' she retorted with a wink as she checked her scatter-cushion lips in a minuscule compact, dressed in flesh-coloured sparkling panties and bra to match.

If it all sounds like a fairy story, it's one that was struggled for and this particular fairy has had many of her bones broken by hammers. Recently in Moscow she and Aimee Phillips were turned away from a gay club – 'only males tonight' – and Amanda and Aimee retreated to the hotel to paint their nails with Amanda announcing: 'They thought I was a woman. I live!'

And when it comes to Moscow 'I live' for the men with all their brutish, cold charm. Maybe it's a father-fixation thing, part of the continuing battle against authority, since there is no city on earth which has such an air of authoritarianism.

In Tokyo and New York there are similarly imposing structures, though they are much more sleek as they rise upwards like exploding champagne bottles celebrating wealth and power. When I look at the Trump Towers I get this disturbing image of a drunk Donald Trump flat on his back in a penguin suit admiring his huge symbolic erection shooting towards the stars.

In Moscow, like most Eastern European cities, the architecture is squat and imposing, sending out the clear message that the state is more important than the individual. Maybe this is why the men compensate by being so aggressive and indifferent? And maybe this is why I find them so sexy.

In a funny way, even an exotic creature like Amanda, who is by her own admission a disproportionate architectural structure, could be placed on a plinth in the middle of Red Square with those swirling minarets as the perfect backdrop. For me she is the finest example of someone who fits in absolutely nowhere, which is why she never looks out of place. Hail the new alien!

Which brings me seamlessly to her encounter with a lobster in the back of a limousine speeding through Moscow.

Heatherette had been invited to Moscow Fashion Week to present their circus-themed collection and, typically, the Russian hosts could provide an elephant but no hangers or Sellotape. After the show the Heatherette crew were on the way to a nightclub, moaning that they hadn't been fed for days. As Richie Rich said: 'A girl can only live on vodka for so long.'

A Russian freak who was acting as their cosmopolitan sherpa told them he knew somewhere to obtain pizza. They handed over their dollars and off he trotted. Forty-five minutes later he finally returned with a tray of tiny hamburgers. As they hungrily consumed them, he pulled something wriggling out of his pocket and chucked it on to the dimly lit limousine floor.

For a few seconds panic reigned, since no one knew what the creature was. It turned out to be a live lobster. Amanda – who is placidity itself and never raises her voice above a whisper – started shrieking: 'Stop this fucking goddam car and let me out now!!'

Aimee said to her: 'Amanda, you're a transsexual wearing nothing but feathers covering your vagina and nipples in the middle of Moscow. You're not going anywhere!'

There was a move to throw the lobster, claws akimbo, out of the car. This was momentarily halted by New York club promoter and social-lite Eric Conrad. He grabbed the lobster and slurred: 'This creature has a soul,' and proceeded to chant 'om' to the unfortunate crustacean, which was probably thinking 'Where's Dali when you need him?' as it finally met its fate hurled through the window.

Around such characters I get the same feeling I had when I was living off my wit long before anyone outside of the hippest discos of London knew who the hell I was.

31

Rude Snaps

Of course, it would take a lot more than a few sparkling creatures to lure me away from the place I love more than anywhere
in the world: my home, London. If you had told me four years
ago that I would be packing up my house for rent and moving
my arse and my Philip Treacy fedoras to New York I would have
replied: 'And then you woke up.'

Having soaked up the sounds of new New York electronica at
Nag Nag Nag, I became a huge fan of the likes of *über*-producer
Larry Tee (the other man behind RuPaul), Tobell Von Cartier (a
psychotic Southern black tranny who makes cracks like: 'Ya'll wan'
sum Black Pussy Surprise? The surprise is there is no pussy!') and
my absolute favourites, the urbaned-up Shangri-Las, Avenue D.
Arriving in Manhattan I was surprised to discover that they were
already over it and all you ever heard in clubs was eighties nostalgia
or Milkshake by Kelis. When I came back for *Taboo*, people like
Larry Tee told me: 'You have woken up New York club life. All
the freaks are creaking out of the woodwork again!'

The once-great thing about New York was that it was always
described as 'a tiny island off the edge of America'. Under Rudy
Giuliani's clean-up clampdown it had become apologetic.

This wasn't helped in the early nineties by the dreadful antics
of disco monster Michael Alig, who not only believed in his

wardrobe but allowed it to consume him. Alig was obsessed by Leigh and was always flying him over, and even offered to rent him a flat. Leigh was far too savvy; a case of: 'I'll decide who uses me and when.'

Alig and his club kids had been all over the media, and the shock of his involvement in the murder of drug dealer Angel Melendez was akin to Leigh appearing on Jonathan Ross and then being discovered to have physically (rather than verbally) decapitated Eartha Kitt.

The public reaction was one of understandable revulsion, and resulted in a dark cloud being cast on flamboyancy. The term 'freak' – hitherto loaded with affection – took on Charles Manson-style connotations. To be a freak was to be evil. For example, during the London run of *Taboo* I would often mince into the crowd and ask: 'Have you ever seen a serial killer dressed like this?' In America the answer had become 'Yes', and I couldn't use it.

By the same token, my notorious Grammys acceptance speech (when I said: 'Thank you, America, you've got style and taste and you know a good drag queen when you see one') signalled the end of my career. In America's eyes, by using the term 'drag queen' I was announcing that I was a sexual deviant. The fact is it was a throwaway quip not unlike 'Sex? I'd rather have a cup of tea', but, like Philip says, Americans tend to turn everything into a blockbuster. Following the 'drag queen' comment there were campus debates and a media furore about what exactly I meant. It was, in a sense, my coming-out speech: in America they never had Danny La Rue or Dick Emery, only Archie Bunker and Bill Cosby. The upside of that comment was that I became the Patron Saint of Cross-Dressers.

However, the Alig affair rendered kamikaze exhibitionism repellent. Imagine how all those legendary New York Look-At-Mes must have felt having put in so many years in front of the mirror for the cause. Those that were already gone were spinning in their graves and those on the waiting list started digging their own plots.

Taboo caught the mood in New York just as it had done in London, revitalised by a mixture of fresh clubbers, drag queens and go-go boys, many of whom were early models for my fledgling fashion and photography adventures. Taking photographs of beautiful boys in states of undress could never be described as painful, and broke up the conformity of theatre (and the theatre of life – not to be confused with the band Theatre of Hate, whose conformity was never broken!).

My photographic career started by immortalising my various looks in the photo booths at Charing Cross and Lewisham stations; I always thought that if you could pull off a look in that brutal glare in front of the nasty orange – or grey if you're lucky – nylon curtains, then it would work anywhere.

When I wasn't haunting those photo booths, my other obsession was Dial-a-Disc, which played snippets of the top ten. If a record sounded exciting down the crackling phone line in Eltham, it had to be bought.

To this day, I often check mixes by telephone, which really irks musician friends like Kinky Roland, whose Vorsprung Durch Technik sensibilities are rattled by my approach. 'You are cra-azy, you can't hear the bass!'

But I can hear if a keyboard or vocal is loud enough, and I do have the respect to wait until the finished track is MP3-ed or i-Disc-ed to me before making my final comments.

Once I listened to a version of 'Generations of Love' – which had been remixed by producer Bruce Forest – on a hotel telephone from Delhi. I kept saying: 'My voice sounds like Mickey Mouse,' and he tried to convince me that it was the phone line affecting my judgement. When I managed to get him to deliver the cassette to me, I was indeed right. Bruce had sped my voice into cartoon rodent hell. I called him: 'There's nothing wrong with my fucking ears, slow the bastard down.'

It won't surprise you to know I've always been an image collector; photo albums, Polaroids, pictures ripped out of magazines, anything that inspires. Once I started making money I began buying various cameras, and took pictures everywhere we went. While Jon was photographing Mount Fuji, with himself standing in front of it, I was photographing him or chasing after old ladies in kimonos.

I've never really been interested in still lifes or landscapes (unless

it's the landscape of human flesh, or a heavily made-up eye). Even
when I painted at school – the only subject I excelled at – I was
constantly reprimanded for drawing portraits of Marc Bolan or
David Bowie rather than Van Gogh's *Sunflowers*. For me it's natural
to photograph other people since I've spent so much of my life
in front of the camera as the subject for legends such as Avedon,
Leibowitz, the complete genius Nick Knight, Uli Webber, and of
course David Bailey, who cracked me up with his line: 'Oy. One
side of your fucking face is more miserable than the other. Sort
it out or crack a bloody smile.' A genuine smile appeared on my
face and after ten rapid clicks he simply said: 'Gotcha. Now piss
off and be miserable somewhere else.' I normally hate smiling in
photographs. His picture is one of the rare ones I love: truth
captured in a flash.

Just before I left for the *Taboo* rehearsals in New York, a
photographer/stylist came to my house to shoot a beautiful Eastern
European model called Ludovic in my clobber. I was very unhappy
with the styling and called the agency and asked whether I could
photograph him myself. They were reluctant, since I'm not a
known photographer, and told me they had much better models.
After sending me reams of portfolios I called them back: 'No, I
want to photograph Ludovic.'

With Christine's assistance we turned him into a Ziggy-esque
preppy prince, and when I sent the photographs to the agency,
his booker rang back screaming: 'He looks fucking beautiful,' and
then asked me to shoot their new calendar. It was a massive
compliment but two days later I was leaving for New York, where,
much to my delight, I discovered an equally plentiful landscape
of masculine beauty.

I try to avoid working with models and overly confident or
muscular gay men. They tend to have a void of vulnerability. If I
see someone in the street or in a nightclub I may approach them
timidly, and they always think I'm a complete pervert. Well, I am.
What's the point in photographing someone I don't have an overbearing attraction to?

Most professional male and female models wouldn't be seen
dead wearing the clothes they parade on the catwalk or in maga-

zines. Backstage at fashion shows they hop into their 501s and CBGBs T-shirts as soon as they can. Fashion is all about selling an illusion of perfection to the imperfect. Homoerotic beauty has been hijacked by the fashion industry for aeons, and simultaneously underplayed by majorly gay designers.

I remember standing in front of a giant billboard of Freddie Ljungberg towering over Times Square. Next to me were three very vocal black women. When I said: 'He's looking at me,' one said: 'He seems to be lookin' at all of we. Maybe 'im can't make up his mind.' I said that the underwear was quite nasty, and one of them joked: 'Yeah, but that ain't what we're checking!' A slogan sprang to mind: 'Clothing is just the wrapping on the sweetie.'

Although my photographs have a homoerotic edge, and often go beyond the knuckle, I prefer shooting partially clothed men because it's the temptation or suggestive element which is truly erotic. It's all about what you can't have (welcome to my world).

What I have found, to my interest, is that straight boys are less uncomfortable about putting on eye make-up, a bra or a skirt, while the gay ones moan: 'It makes me look gay.'

This proves my earlier point about the hijacking of camp by the likes of Beckham. Historically it was always men who were the dandies and peacocks but for decades gay men have done their utmost to avoid looking *gay*.

As I have also said, the price of assimilation has been the loss of individuality, which is frowned upon more than ever. My photography – like the rest of my work and life – is about putting a magnifying glass up to issues such as this.

As a gay man, from the forceps to the stone (sorry, Joni), you are forced to assess your masculinity against the overriding constraints of the time. Unlike those ridiculous *Queer Eye* queens, I am more interested in playing with the boundaries of masculinity – and the important differences – certainly not in propagating the myth that if you dress the same, you think the same: an Armani suit does not make all men equal.

Rosie's gift of the gargantuan loft on Broadway provided enough space and light to double up as a photography studio. One of my first models was the American porn star Johnny Hazzard and I went further with him (shutterly speaking) than any other model. I decided to whip the lie from the underwear and shot and filmed him in fashion pornography style.

I managed to secure Johnny through my drag queen pornographer friend Chi-Chi La Rue. The day I worked with him I was the one shaking. I started him off in full Rude attire and slowly he stripped off completely. His absolute ease about being naked was completely at odds with myself, being an un-naturist. I dress up, not down.

At one point he smirked: 'Shall I get hard?'

I almost choked and mumbled: 'If you like . . .' in a voice which must have sounded like Rita Tushingham in *A Taste of Honey*.

At first the experience was deeply erotic but after twenty minutes it seemed perfectly normal to be snapping away at a perfectly sculpted and confident vision of sexual confidence.

My encounter with Johnny – who is the most polite, well-mannered individual – taught me that some of us become giants when stripped of our armour. In his everyday clothes, Johnny seems quite tiny and jockey-like. Naked, rather like Amanda LePore who tottered around the loft in nothing but a tie, hat and high heels, Johnny seemed liberated and powerful.

I've now become quite an experienced photographer. My favourite model is Alex, a straight boy I met in a club. I've probably taken more shots of him than anyone and every time he's like a different person. You learn a lot about human psychology from the other side of the camera and the most interesting aspect is that I'm not the subject for once.

Part of my reason for photographing men is that I find them utterly irresistible in all their many shapes and forms. It wasn't until I shot a campaign for my friends at Heatherette which included female models Lydia Hearst, Patty's daughter, and an amazing Japanese supermodel called Rila, that I realised I also have an eye for the girls.

It's not that strange. Most fashion designers, stylists and big-name photographers are homosexuals, but that doesn't stop them iconising femininity.

Girls have an innate love of dressing up, boys take a little more convincing, especially if you want to put them in heavy eyeliner and a printed tennis skirt. But on the right man it doesn't look overtly feminine.

If someone hasn't been photographed professionally before, you have to move quickly to put them at ease. Male or female, once you show them a picture of how gorgeous they look, they always relax.

I expected and received the typical derogatory comments from other snappers. Whatever. It's no different from when I started DJing or working in any other area where people feel I haven't earned my dues. So I was particularly gratified when I signed up with New York photo agency PMI who allow me to cherry-pick the type of assignments that suit me.

My latest New York apartment is not only a studio for my photography sessions, it's also a print house, graphics studio, an art space and the place where Christine creates havoc, harmony and all manner of other artefacts. I often rib her: 'Your brains are in your hands.' Of course she has brains elsewhere, but when her fingers start twitching over a bag of beads or a pot of paint, her abilities are endless. She'll argue with me for hours over the difference between a block and a street corner, but give her a pile of dried centipedes' legs and she'll turn out a beyond headdress. Let's just say her ideas have ideas.

On the recording front, as I've said, I haven't had a record deal since 1995. Hopefully, by the time you gnaw your way through this tome, I'll have found a more interesting way to communicate my musical ideas.

For me music, clothing, art, photography, and of course boys, have collided. I guess I use all these elements, partly as a way of keeping myself off the streets, but mainly because I have to create.

STRAWBERRY LOGIC

I think Christine is insane
Or is it

Me?
She just stomped out of her room
For a morning pee
A face of rage
Peach nightie
Savage hair
Coffee?
Tea
She is thinking
Why must you talk to me?
It's not personal
She likes her own company

An hour later
Maybe more
She is painted
Eyes lifted up
A hint of silver glitter
Full lips
Gloss
Checking herself in the mirror
She is satisfied
Ready to communicate

We leave together
She moves at her own pace
I snap
'Hurry up'
She rolls her eyes
In the lift
She ties
Her shoelaces
I smile
Christine is insane
I am thinking
Again

At work I pinch her breast
Occasionally
She will contest
My impatience
I am snappy
A little rude
'Stop showing off'
She says
'Do it now'
I say
Then all camp
I mince away
An explosion of green
Freaky
Sweetly mean
We understand each other
Does she know how much I love her?

I tell her she is beautiful
She doesn't agree
On the street boys shout at me
'Keep hold of her'
Stupid boys
She is oblivious
She is not mine
Or yours
She is her own property
Sometimes she walks ahead of me
Or lags behind
No sense of time

Her logic
Is unique
She tells a story
Embellishing it with white lies
Then laughs
Caught out

She owns up
The truth is elastic
Christine is fantastic
Completely insane
Insecure
Strangely vain
She paints her face again
And becomes indignant and cold
Distant for a while
She never looks old

Christine could be made of bone china
I pick her up
I shake her
Touch her vagina
She slaps my bum
I run
To show off
In heavy lashes
Glittery eyes
'Powder your lips'
She shouts
I love the way
She pouts
Her mouth
Christine
Is intoxicating
Tomorrow
She will keep me waiting
Again

Afterword

When people ask me what turns me on these days I tell them: 'Ideas.' As they say, you can't take your wealth with you. Or your fame. You can certainly leave your mark with ideas though.

Often I can be very impatient when seeing a project through. My impatience with my work is similar to my impatience with myself and other human beings.

For example, why lie in someone's arms and say: 'I'm frightened of hurting you or of being hurt'? Talk about pass me another cliché!

We spend far too much time worrying about how the past is going to affect the future, and far too little time enjoying the moment.

I guess I like things that are tangible: honest human emotion, a well-lit photograph, a finely printed T-shirt, evocative music, beauty and imperfection. Often true beauty resides in imperfection.

Like my mother I have the ability to see through the rogue to the heart of the person, and, like her, this has lead me to more trouble than I need. Sadly, seeing the goodness in someone else often has little effect on their behaviour.

A few years ago something happened which I never thought I would see in my lifetime. My father, after having an affair, divorced my mother and married again. It was shocking because

I had spent so many years listening to him rant on about the importance of 'family loyalty' and how blood was thicker than water.

From as early as I can remember I urged my mother to walk away from what was always a loveless marriage.

I know her biggest regret is that she didn't at an earlier stage. However badly my father treated my mother she believed in the sanctity of marriage so being left for another woman after forty-three years was the ultimate and final insult.

The circumstances surrounding their divorce brought out the very traditional values that he instilled in me. I'm not suggesting they should have stayed together till the bitter end because believe me, it would have been bitter. I feel my father should have divorced my mother before conducting a relationship with someone else. For months he maintained that his new partner was a platonic friend and because of this my mother allowed her to sleep over as a guest in her home. Dad even brought his 'platonic' friend to my home in Hampstead for Mum's sixtieth birthday bash. His friend was visibly hostile to my mother and I cornered my father and asked: 'Are you having an affair?' He flatly denied it but it wasn't long before the truth was out. I paid for my father to take a holiday in Ireland and asked my sister to check the flight details with the travel agent, who innocently blurted: 'That's two flights, right?' and read out the names. It transpired that I had paid for the two of them to travel and also for the country cottage where they would relax for two weeks. I pleaded with Siobhan to keep it from Mum but a few days later she found a holiday brochure along with a confirmation letter and was devastated. I never confronted him about it but, had I bothered, he would have probably accused Mum of driving him to it. Towards the end of their marriage, there never seemed to be a day of peace. Early one morning my father rang my intercom. I was tired and after picking up the receiver I grumbled: 'You've got a bloody key, why are you waking me up?' His stern reply: 'I wasn't sure if you wanted me here.'

If there is any truth in Chaos Theory, I imagine Mum pulled back the duvet at exactly the same time while puffing and rolling

her eyes (possibly uttering something in Gaelic). I marched downstairs to open the door and put the kettle on.

Dad was in a tetchy mood, talking a lot, as he did, but about
nothing in particular. Once tea was made and laid on the table
he started to go on about Siobhan and my mother. As the youngest
my sister lived with their turmoil longer than the rest of us and
had to develop a tough spine to survive it.

If Shivs (as we all affectionately call her) ever saw my father
acting badly towards my mother, like myself, she didn't hold back.
Being a smart girl, she'd long worked out that Dad's biggest
weapon was the fear factor and she would tell him to his face:
'Hit me. I ain't fucking scared of you.'

Dad was always talking about how the family had made him
an outsider and picked Shivs as the main troublemaker: 'She
always sides with your mother. They gang up on me, the two of
them.'

That morning he started pulling them apart: 'Your sister and
your mother, you don't know what they're like because you don't
have to live with them.'

I said: 'If you've only come here to talk badly about them then
I'd prefer it if you left.'

'Right, fuck ya!' he said and marched out of the kitchen and
sat looking hurt on the sofa in the hallway.

There was a five-minute silence until I went out and asked:
'Cup of tea?'

'All right, son.'

We spoke calmly after that, although it was always difficult with
my father to stop a few tidal waves crashing into even the most
civilised conversation. I told him that I wouldn't sit and listen to
my mother badmouthing him, or anyone else for that matter, and
pointed out that they chose to marry and both had plenty of
opportunities to knock it on the head.

'I wish you'd just divorce each other and try and be friends,'
I said. 'You've never got on.'

He would always shake his head at such suggestions, and say:
'It's not that simple, son.'

I recognise that I am a confused composite of my mother and

father. I have Mum's martyr complex, her heart and emotional generosity (and, unfortunately, her wispy hair). I also have my dad's selfishness, jealousy and need for revenge. It's ironic because I put so much effort in my life into becoming the opposite of him. Sometimes the further you run, the closer you get. I have many of my father's better qualities too, his (often misguided) generosity, his charm and ability to talk all four legs, ears and hooves off a donkey. I wish I could say my dad was an entirely reprehensible human being. It's a lot easier if someone is all bad. He wasn't.

Sadly, when we lived as a family, he reserved most of his kindness and fierce loyalty for outsiders, strangers or members of his own family, who often treated him with disrespect. With Mum, there is a feeling that she wasted too many years of her life.

The seeds of their split go back to when I was ill with my addiction. My parents moved in with me in Hampstead for a few months. As I recovered Mum left and Dad stayed on for a while. When he eventually went home, Mum had moved into another bedroom.

I persuaded them to come to the Turning Point therapy seminars I was attending at that time. I don't think Mum felt she got much out of the courses but I feel it made her more assertive.

Dad, on the other hand, became heavily involved and started working as a helper on various courses. This brought out a side of him that was most unexpected. He started learning reiki healing and took massage courses, becoming a bit of a suburban guru.

Being part of the Turning Point crowd allowed him to create a new persona. Still, it didn't stop him being verbally abusive to Mum. I thought it was good that he had found this new path but I'm sure he didn't display his dark side to his new spiritual circle. It was on the Turning Point courses that Dad met the woman who would become his future wife. His insistence that their friendship was platonic was so hypocritical. If Mum had brought a man into her life, platonic or otherwise, he would have gone berserk.

Shortly before the divorce, Mum was hospitalised with acute emphysema. For a while we thought we were going to lose her. It broke my heart to see her so defenceless and weak. For days I lived at the hospital, until the doctors told me to go home for a few hours and get some sleep. I tried, but I couldn't stop fearing the worst. At 3 a.m. one night I took a cab back to the hospital in Woolwich and sat holding her hand till she woke at 7 a.m. Her first words to me were: 'Blimey, what are you doing here?'

Dad visited her just once, and couldn't bring himself to hold her or show affection. After that visit Mum told me: 'My marriage is over.'

Shortly before the divorce I bought my parents' house from the council. Dad had some idea about selling it and splitting the proceeds. I offered to buy him out so that Mum could keep the house and we had a very serious altercation about money.

We never spoke again.

I was in Los Angeles last September when I heard that Dad had passed away while on holiday in Egypt. At first I was numb and then came all the sadness at not having the chance to say goodbye or to resolve the bad feeling between us. I had no relationship with his new family – his partner has children of her own – and I have no desire to. Their relationship wasn't the problem. The way in which they got together brought out all my protective instincts towards my mother. This made straightforward grieving almost impossible and, as I write this, I don't suppose I'll ever know how I really feel.

The loss of my father, who had such a powerful effect on my existence, is hard to express.

'What if?' and 'if only' are redundant.

I loved him and I know he loved me.

With death there is a tendency to romanticise the past, to recreate history as you want it to be. My main concern was for Mum's well-being because I felt she had suffered far more than she deserved.

I hope that Dad was happy and that his new family brought him the contentment he didn't seem to enjoy with us.

There is a part of my nature which is on one hand screaming: 'Love me,' and on the other: 'Screw you.'

I feel strangely comfortable with that duality because it has informed so much of my life and my music. For heaven's sake, my first big hit was called 'Do You Really Want To Hurt Me?'

There is a part of me which wallows in the energy of indifference and simultaneously is utterly appalled by it.

A lot of the men that I have loved, stalked and continue to fall in love with could best be described as emotionally unavailable. It's too simplistic to sum this up with the glib phrase: 'You only want what you can't have.' Still it's irritatingly true! That doesn't stop the endless wrestle to capture the heart of another human being who, more often than not, has no intention of surrendering. For me a lot of sex is merely wrestling in lipgloss.

Perhaps I delude myself in thinking that those who encase their hearts so vigorously are terrified because they actually have so much love to give. There's a part of me which accepts that the standard clichés and therapeutic analysis of this type of desire are wholly true. So what? It will never be resolved, and perhaps that's the beauty of it.

I don't want to sound like I blame Dad for everything that has gone wrong in my life. I just had to accept that he was the one man I could never change. But that's not going to stop me trying with all the others.

This wilfulness is the backbone of much of what I do, hacking away at steel walls of emotion with a bent fork (and yes I get the irony of that).

We often typecast ourselves as much as we are typecast by others. I remember Sandra Bernhardt telling this great story about how she is always cast as the neurotic Jew. 'I am a neurotic Jew,' she said. 'But that's not all I am!' Equally I've cast myself as a melancholy merchant in terms of my songwriting. Just because you tap into the miseries of love and relationships doesn't mean you don't have spells of sunshine. Even at my most bitter there's always a sense of optimism and whatever people think, I do have the ability to laugh at myself while tripping over yet another contradiction in my clay high heels.

I'm not looking for acceptance, tolerance or even permission.

My work is about exploring emotional unavailability and perhaps the person to whom I'm most emotionally unavailable is myself. As I've grown older – I won't say grown up – I realise that much of my life has, and continues to be, entangled in the hope that there is always hope.

I can be terribly disparaging, one of my many well-crafted defence mechanisms. A lot of my behaviour is defensive and this has become habit.

Years and years of therapy have barely scratched the veneer. Sometimes I think the rest of the world should go into therapy to shake off their preconceptions of who they think I am!

No matter what you learn from life, you still have to get on with it. I wish I could force myself into a routine that allowed for deep prana breathing in the morning and a spell of meditation before tea.

Nevertheless, there are T-shirts to create, graphics to design, screens to print, frames to adorn, boys to adore, and, of course, songs to write about them.

All these things reflect – and are part of the process of making sense of – myself, those I have loved for ever and those I fall in love with on an hourly basis.

I'm always being asked: 'Are you happy?'

That's like trying to explain love, God or flying dragons.

> Are you happy?
> Not all the time,
> They'd lock me up for the laughing crime!

Index